ON THE ROAD WITH SAINT AUGUSTINE

ON THE ROAD WITH SAINT AUGUSTINE

A Real-World Spirituality for Restless Hearts

JAMES K. A. SMITH

BrazosPress

a division of Baker Publishing Group
Grand Rapids, Michigan

© 2019 by James K. A. Smith

Published by Brazos Press
a division of Baker Publishing Group
PO Box 6287, Grand Rapids, MI 49516-6287
www.brazospress.com

Printed in the United States of America

Library of Congress Cataloging-in-Publication Data
Names: Smith, James K. A., 1970– author.
Title: On the road with Saint Augustine : a real-world spirituality for restless hearts / James K.A. Smith.
Description: Grand Rapids, Michigan : Brazos Press, a division of Baker Publishing Group, 2019. | Includes bibliographical references and index.
Identifiers: LCCN 2019039590 | ISBN 9781587433894 (cloth)
Subjects: LCSH: Augustine, of Hippo, Saint, 354-430. | Spirituality—Christianity. | Spiritual life—Christianity. | Christian life.
Classification: LCC BR65.A9 S625 2019 | DDC 248—dc23
LC record available at https://lccn.loc.gov/2019039590

ISBN 978-1-58743-446-4 (ITPE)

Interior design by Brian Brunsting

20 21 22 23 24 25 26   8 7 6 5 4 3 2

For Deanna,
my Alypius:
co-pilgrim, faithful friend, kindred soul

"You boys going to get somewhere, or just going?" We didn't understand his question, and it was a damned good question.

—Jack Kerouac, *On the Road*

A heart on the run keeps a hand on the gun
You can't trust anyone.

—Jason Isbell, "Cover Me Up"

Imagine you've been flailing and flailing and expecting to drown and your foot hits bottom.

—Thomas Wolfe, *The Story of a Novel*

Look, you're here, freeing us from our unhappy wandering,
    setting us firmly on your track, comforting us and saying,
"Run the race! *I'll* carry you! *I'll* carry you clear to the end,
and even at the end, *I'll* carry you."

—Augustine, *Confessions*

CONTE

N T S

INTRODUCTION

This is not a biography. This is not a book about Augustine. In a way, it's a book Augustine has written about you. It's a journey with Augustine as a journey into oneself. It's a travelogue of the heart. It's a road trip with a prodigal who's already been where you think you need to go.

But it's also the testimony of someone who has spent time on the road with Augustine. In Jack Kerouac's iconic novel *On the Road*, the narrator Sal Paradise plays chronicler to the antics of the star of the story, Dean Moriarty, who is really the exemplar, the hero, the model. So just call me Sal. I've been on a ride with Augustine. Here's what I've seen; here's what he's shown me (about myself); here's why you might consider coming along.

This is an invitation to journey with an ancient African who will surprise you by the extent to which he knows you. It's not because he's some guru, some Freudian analyst who haughtily sees through you. He only knows you because he's been there, because he has a sense of the solidarity of the human race in our foibles and frustrations and failed pursuits. If he jackhammers his way into the secret corners of our hearts, unearthing our hungers and fears, it's only because it's familiar territory: he's seen it all in his own soul. Augustine isn't a judge; he's more like an AA sponsor. "Nothing you could tell me would surprise me," he would say. "Let me tell you my story." One could say of Augustine what Leslie Jamison notes about Don Gately in *Infinite Jest*: He's "no saint. That's why he made salvation seem possible."[1]

But the reason to consider Augustine as a guide for the journey is not just because he's an incisive psychologist familiar with the antics of the mind in exile, or because he's mapped the joyrides of "liberated" selves. What makes Augustine a guide worth considering is that, unlike Sal's Dean, he knows where home is, where rest can be found, what peace feels like, even if it is sometimes ephemeral and elusive along the way.

I won't pretend there isn't something scandalous about his advice. Augustine will unapologetically suggest that you were made for God—that home is found beyond yourself, that Jesus is the way, that the cross is a raft in the storm-tossed sea we call "the world." But what I hope you'll hear in this is not a solution or an answer, not merely a dogmatic claim or demand. For Augustine, this was a hard-fought epiphany that emerged after trying everything else, after a long time on the road, at the end of his rope. The Christian gospel, for Augustine, wasn't just the answer to an intellectual question (though it was that); it was more like a shelter in a storm, a port for a wayward soul, nourishment for a prodigal who was famished, whose own heart had become, he said, "a famished land."[2] It was, he would later testify, like someone had finally shown him his home country, even though he'd never been there before. It was the Father he'd spent a lifetime looking for, saying to him, "Welcome home."

Augustine is uncanny for us: he is so ancient he is strange, and yet his experiences are so common they feel contemporary. My hope is that this uncanniness might give you a sense of what an authentic Christianity feels like from the inside. The wager here is that an ancient African might make Christianity plausible for you, mired in the anxieties and disappointments of the twenty-first century. That's not necessarily because you've been looking for God, but because you've been trying to find yourself. When you go spelunking in the caves of your soul with Augustine, you might be surprised who you meet down there.

Augustine might make Christianity believable for you even if you've heard it all, been there, done that, and left the stupid Christian T-shirt at home. Here's a Christianity to consider before you stop believing. Augustine might make Christianity plausible *again* for those who've been burned—who suspect that the "Christianity" they've seen is just a cover for power plays and self-interest, or a tired moralism that seems angry all the time, or a version of middle-class comfort too often confused with the so-called American Dream. If the only faith you can imagine is the faith of your parents, Augustine has been down that road. What if it was precisely the strangeness of his ancient struggles that made Augustine perennial, someone with the distance from our own immersion to give us a vantage point for seeing ourselves—and the Christian faith—anew?

IN HER MEMOIR *Hold Still*, photographer Sally Mann quotes one of her father's diary entries: "Do you know how a boatman faces one direction, while rowing in another?"[3] This book you are holding is an invitation to a posture like that: to move forward by looking back, to make progress by considering ancient wisdom. To get in a boat headed for a new future, looking back to Augustine on the North African shore as a landmark to orient us.

You might be surprised how many radicals and innovators have been in that boat. Thinkers and writers and playwrights who've shaped us more than we realize have looked back to Augustine across the twentieth century. You'll be reintroduced to them on the road here: Martin Heidegger, the father of existentialism, whose cascading influence across France and beyond eventually made us all seekers of authenticity; Albert Camus, who named our experience of the absurd, spent the early part of his career wrestling with Augustine, and perhaps never stopped; Hannah Arendt, who probed the nature of love and friendship in conversation with Augustine; Jacques Derrida, *enfant terrible* of postmodernism, who deconstructed and unsettled our confidence in eternal verities and would later return to consider the secrets his North African compatriot offered. There are ways in which the twentieth century was Augustinian, which makes him our contemporary in ways we haven't considered. What if he still speaks? What if Augustine is not only behind us but also ahead of us, waiting for us to arrive where he ended? Maybe it's time to consider his answer to the questions he gave us.

ORIENTATION

Wherein we find

our bearings

and meet our companion

and discover he

has been alongside us this

whole time.

HEART ON THE RUN

How to Hit the Road

It might be youth. It might be the reptilian impulses of a species with migration encoded in its DNA. It might be your inferiority complex or the boredom of small-town claustrophobia or the exhibitionist streak you've never told anyone about. It might be the hungers of ancestors whose aspirations have sunk into your bones, pushing you to go. It might be loneliness. It might be your inexplicable attraction to "bad boys" or the still unknown thrill of transgression and the hope of *feeling* something. It might be the self-loathing that has always been so weirdly bound up with a spiritual yearning. It might be the search for a mother, or a father, or yourself. It might be greed or curiosity. It might be liberation or escape. It might be a million other reasons, but we all leave.

It's like all we ever do is leave. "Honey, all I know to do is go," the Indigo Girls confess in "Leaving." You can leave without a bus ticket, of course. You can depart in your heart and take an existential journey to anywhere but the "here" that's stifling you. You can be sleeping in the same bed and be a million miles away from your partner. You can still be living in your childhood bedroom and have departed for a distant country. You can play the role of the "good son" with a heart that roams in a twilight beyond good and evil. You can even show up to church every week with a voracious appetite for idols. Not all prodigals need a passport.

We leave because we're looking. For something. For someone. We leave because we long for something else, something more. We leave to look for some piece of us that's missing. Or we hit the road to leave ourselves behind and refashion who we are. We hit the road in the hope of finding what we're looking for—or at least sufficiently distracting ourselves from the hungers and haunting absences that propelled our departure in the first place.

And the road doesn't disappoint: it offers an unending ribbon of sights and stop-offs whose flashing billboards promise exactly what you're looking for—happiness, satisfaction, joy. Indeed, the road has a strange way of showing what looks like a destination in the distance that, when you get there, points to another destination beyond it. So just when you think friendship or wealth or a family or influence was your ultimate destination, you hang out there for a while and the place starts to dim. What once held your fascination—even, for a time, seemed like it was your reason to live—doesn't "do it" for you anymore. You won't admit it to yourself for a long while. After all, you sent out all those celebratory announcements about your new existential home. You effectively told everyone you'd arrived; you believed it yourself. But at some point you'll finally be honest with yourself about the disappointment, and eventually that disappointment becomes disdain, and you can't wait to get away. Fortunately, just as you start to look around, you see the promise of a new destination down the road.

Like the crew in Kerouac's *On the Road*, we convince ourselves that "the road is life."[1] We've been shaped by a book that many of us have never read, the tale of bohemians and beatniks on a journey of self-discovery. *On the Road* chronicles their quest for experience, for authenticity. The narrator, Sal Paradise, paints a picture of the road that suggests happiness is crooking our straight paths. Like John the Baptist in negative, Sal Paradise proclaims the incessant, frantic way of his messiah, Dean Moriarty: "Dean is the perfect guy for the road because he actually was born on the road."[2] But really, who isn't?

Our road-hunger is like some leftover evolutionary habit from our ancestors. But ours is a pilgrimage without a destination—which is to say, it's not a pilgrimage at all but rather a pilgrimage deferred, not because we stay home but because we revel in the roaming, or at least try to talk ourselves into that. Our ancestors sang psalms of ascent as they marched to Zion or made the arduous hajj to Mecca or wended their way to Canterbury. We've inherited their pilgrim penchant, but it's morphed into unsettledness, a baseline antsy feeling that leaves us never feeling at home (which brings to mind the Freudian notion of the "uncanny," the *Unheimlich*, not-at-home-ness). We're always on the move, restless, vaguely chasing something rather than oriented to a destination. We're all a bit like Mississippi Gene, whom Sal meets in *On the Road*: "He had no place he could stay in without getting tired of it and because there was nowhere to go but everywhere."[3]

If the road is life, then we're not really vagabonds. To be on the way is to have arrived. Ignore "the feeling of sadness only bus stations have";[4] ignore the nights of despair and move on;[5] don't get too hung up on your recognition that "LA is the loneliest and most brutal of American cities."[6] And when you find yourself haunted by the sense that you've forgotten something and recognize this as the wake-up call of mortality, the vague way the fear of death settles over your wandering, be like Sal: find a friend who will take you to the club and numb the sound of that revenant.[7] The trick is to convince yourself that the road is life, making restlessness peace, uprootedness home, like Sal: "The car was swaying as Dean and I both swayed to the rhythm and the IT of our final excited joy in talking and living to the blank tranced end of all innumerable riotous angelic particulars that had been lurking in our souls all our lives."[8]

Whether we can really pull this off is the question considered in *Up in the Air*, a George Clooney film based on the novel by Walter Kirn. Ryan Bingham, played by Clooney, has shed all attachments. He lives on airplanes and is "at home" in airports. His quest isn't a destination but incessant journeying: he wants to be a million miler. In fact, he has made a career of telling people to shed everything that would hold them down. As a motivational speaker with a gimmicky prop—a backpack filled with all the things that weigh us down, especially relationships—Bingham counsels up-in-the-air independence. But when his assistant finally challenges him with the question, "What do you want?" Bingham is silent ("You don't even know what you want," she spits back.) And when he achieves the sought-after million-miler status, the captain visits him, congratulates him ("We appreciate your loyalty"), and asks, "So where are you from?" Bingham's only reply is, "I'm from here." The hollowness rings in his own ears.

The question that haunts our journey, the question that Sal Paradise is confronted with early on, goes unanswered: "You boys going to get somewhere," a Nebraska farmer asks, "or just going?" Looking back, Sal now sees: "We didn't understand his question, and it was a damned good question."[9] Do we tell ourselves we're "just going" in order to guard against the disappointment of never arriving? Do we call the road "home" to avoid the pain of never being welcomed?

What if you met a saint on the road, and that saint had a map and had spent time at every stop-off that lured but then disappointed you? What if he'd already met the "you" you somehow want to be? What if he could introduce you to the person you've been looking for and lead you to a house with many rooms, where a Friend would open the door and say, "Welcome home. You can rest here"?

A YOUNG MAN meanders through the bustle of the port at dusk, his last night in Africa. His father is dead. He has eluded his cloying mother with a lie that pains him, but it is a necessary evil if he's ever going to escape her and her provincial faith. The waves of the Mediterranean lap on the coast of Carthage with hints of hope, as if carrying the transformation he's expecting in Rome. The Eternal City is now invested with the glow of his success, like Gatsby's green light blinking as a beacon of a future, hoped-for arrival. In Rome he'll finally find what he's been looking for. In Rome he'll become the man he's destined to be, the person he *deserves* to be. Augustine will have arrived.

Granted, yes, he once expected to find all this in Carthage, as close as one could get to Rome in Africa. It's where he discovered the theater. It's where he found his professional calling and started to move in literary circles. It's where he fell in love with love. It's where he found *her*. But now Carthage feels like a backwater: unsophisticated, provincial, a town not big enough for his importance. What had been a destination has now become a way station. The place he longed to reach is now just a launching pad to the new destination that promises happiness.

Just before dark, the sails begin to ripple. A fortuitous wind has arrived. Time to go. "The wind blew and filled our sails and the shore was lost to our sight."[10]

But when he gets to Rome, that beacon is still blinking. Now it's coming from Milan, seat of the emperor. The next rung on the ladder is a post as an imperial rhetor; the networks the young man has cultivated are paying off. When the job offer arrives, it comes with a promise that he will be transported via the imperial courier (*cursus publicus*). Funny how dingy Rome suddenly looks when the emperor sends Air Force One to whisk you away to his palace.

Milan for Augustine is our Manhattan or London or, well, Milan—a metropolis made of money and power. What John Foot says of contemporary Milan is true of the ancient city (and all other sites of earthly ambition): "Milan is a city obsessed by one thing, or rather by two—work and money."[11] It's the place where you either "make it" or slink home in defeat. The hopes of such urban pilgrimages are perennial: to realize the "you" that's been buried in the provincial version of yourself until now. These cities are like sculptors in a sense, unearthing the "you" that was always just beneath the surface. So you go to climb, achieve, win, conquer; you go to realize your potential and demonstrate your worth; you go to enjoy the good life and inhale the energy of influence, the freedom that comes with privilege; you go to remake yourself, but in so doing you expect to find the "you" you always knew you could be. It's why you "find yourself" someplace else. The road is the road to that "you."

Which is why this young man is so rattled when Milan disappoints him. Milan was supposed to be the end of the road, the destination he had envisioned as synonymous with happiness. Working in the precincts of the imperial palace, unleashing his creative energy and expertise, mingling with the great and the good, he would be seen for who he was: Augustine, the precocious provincial, the African from the edge of the empire who'd made it to the center. The happy life had a zip code, and Augustine now lived there.

So why didn't he feel at home? Why did the *Unheimlich* still haunt him? He thought he was coming to Milan to get close to the emperor; he didn't expect to fall for a bishop.

Augustine is a saint who's been down that road we still travel, fueled by ambition, trailing our hopes behind us. He's familiar with all the things we carry.

IN SAN GIMIGNANO, a Tuscan hill town south of Florence—not far from the path that would have taken Augustine from Rome to Milan—is a small Augustinian church from the thirteenth century. Not to be confused with the magnificent Duomo in the center of town, the Chiostro di Sant'Agostino is a humble affair just inside the north wall. On the day we visited, our heels clopped on quiet, narrow streets. We seemed to have the place to ourselves. A bright spring sun turned the sky neon indigo, the heavenly ceiling for a memorable alfresco meal of Tuscan pici and lamb ragù at the Locanda di Sant'Agostino Osteria next door.

But we were here for the frescoes inside the church. In the apsidal chapel is a stunning series of paintings that capture Augustine on the road. Painted by Benozzo Gozzoli in the fifteenth century (1464–65), the images narrate the life of Augustine from his childhood education in Thagaste to his death in Hippo. The cycle of seventeen episodes, circling from left to right, bottom to top, is a bit like staging Shakespeare as a hip-hop drama: Gozzoli's realism transposes Augustine to Renaissance plazas adorned in fifteenth-century attire. The realism demystifies the saint. Because we can imagine him being like us, a solidarity that is at the heart of the *Confessions*, it encourages imitation. When fourth-century Carthage looks like thirteenth-century Florence, and ancient Hippo looks like medieval Milan, it might help us see why the aspirations of ancient Rome aren't so different from those of contemporary Los Angeles.

Gozzoli's rehearsal of Augustine's life is inflected with intriguing emphases. Education and teaching dominate the cycle, from Augustine's own boyhood education in Africa to his role as teacher in Rome, Milan, and Hippo. This is Augustine the humanist rediscovered in the Renaissance—the Augustine who read Plato, reformed rhetoric, and championed the liberal arts. Not surprisingly, his mother Monica appears in five of the scenes, including a heartrending scene of her being left behind.[12]

But utterly singular is Gozzoli's fascination with Augustine's various journeys. The frescoes might as well have been called "On the Road with Augustine." Gozzoli paints Augustine on the move. We see Monica praying he won't leave, and then immediately beside it Augustine's journey to Rome, Monica now at the left with hand upstretched in prayer over the saint at sea.

We see him landing at the port in Ostia, en route to the Rome that will disappoint him. The cycle later brings us back to Ostia to witness the death of Monica. But in Gozzoli's unique attempt to convey temporal dynamism in a single static frame, through the columns on the right we see Augustine set sail, returning to the Africa he'll never leave (see figure 1, top). True to one of the most enduring aspects of Augustine's character, he never travels alone.

The panel that most captivated me, though, depicts Augustine's departure from Rome for Milan. Augustine has acquired relationships of note. Dignitaries attend his departure. Medieval Rome is in the distance behind him, the Tuscan hills lie before them, and over the horizon lies Milan (figure 1, bottom).[13] The regal transport of the imperial courier means he can travel on horse. The beasts are stately, powerful, and—curiously—looking right at us. Are you coming? their eyes seem to ask. Have you considered this road? Do you know where this leads? Does *he*?

It is perhaps ironic, and a sign of how far he'd come, that a decade after his move to Milan the middle-aged Augustine who had roamed in search of happiness found that the blinking beacon of hoped-for joy kept receding despite his pursuit. This might explain why he would come to identify happiness with *rest*.

If the young Augustine was tempted to imagine that "the road is life," that happiness was synonymous with adventure, with going out, with departing for distant shores and escaping the strictures of home, then his midlife *Confessions* reveal a U-turn of sorts. If the aspiring Augustine was looking to Virgil as a model, imagining himself on his own odyssey of conquest in Italy, only later will Augustine see a different pattern emerge in his wanderings: the prodigal who comes home.

This might not be the prodigal you know. This is the existential prodigal, the wayward son filtered through philosophy, hearing the Gospel of Luke through Platonic ears as a cautionary parable of human existence. It is the tale of an ungrateful son who runs off with his premature inheritance, having effectively told his father, "I wish you were dead." And this odd, surprising Father acquiesces: "Here you go," he says. "I love you." The son takes his Father's property (*ousia*) and departs for a distant country, squandering it in "dissolute living" and ending up with nothing—and nothingness.

How could Augustine resist reading this as a parable of human existence itself? Being (*ousia*) is gifted to us by our Creator, but we take the gift as if there were no Giver, and we set off to "live" according to our best lights. The result? You, a good Jewish boy, wake up one morning and realize that even the pigs are eating better than you are, and you start to ask yourself some questions, like "What the hell am I doing?" And "Who am I?" And "*Whose* am I?" So despondent you can't even voice it, you nonetheless wonder, timidly, desperately: "Would my father ever take me back?" By some grace inexplicable, you start on your way back home. And as you're yet again rehearsing a long speech that is three parts apology and two parts legal plea for reinstatement, you're bowled over when that Father of yours comes running and gathers you up in his arms while your head is down, and your mother later tells you, "He walked to the end of the road every single day waiting for you."

This is the road trip in which Augustine finally saw himself, and it becomes the literary skeleton of the *Confessions*, a travelogue of the human heart. The reason Augustine tells *his* story is that he thinks it is simply an example of the *human* story—that we are all prodigals—and he wants us to ask ourselves a question: "What if I went home?"

For Augustine, psychology is cartography: to understand oneself is a matter of mapping our penchant to look for love in all the wrong places. The range of our exterior wandering is mirrored by the interior expanse of the soul. "A human being as such is a huge abyss," he would later muse to his God. "You know the number of hairs on his head, Master, and in you there's no subtraction from that number; but it's easier to count his hairs than his moods or the workings of his heart."[14] One's own heart can be foreign territory, a terra incognita, and this lack of at-home-ness with oneself generates our propensity to run. We still can't find what we're looking for because we don't know what we want. If we never seem to arrive, growing tired of every place that promised to be the end of the road, it's because the terrain of our interior life is a wilderness of wants. When we leave home looking for happiness, we're in search of the self we never knew.

That's why, Augustine suggests, you can be prodigal without moving an inch. What we're mapping here is the geography of desire. It took running from Carthage to Rome to Milan for Augustine to realize that his exile was inward:

> One does not go far away from you or return to you by walking or by any movement through space. The younger [prodigal] son in your Gospel did not look for horses or carriages or ships; he did not fly on any visible wing, nor did he travel along the way by moving his legs when he went to live in a far country and prodigally dissipated what you, his gentle father, had given him on setting out, showing yourself even gentler on his return as a bankrupt.[15]

When Augustine put on this prodigal lens to look at himself, he had an epiphany. This narrative frame would reframe everything and explain what had puzzled him; it would give him concepts to name what had been gnawing away at him and permission to be honest about his disappointment with what everyone else saw as "success." What looks like attainment in Milan—success, conquest, arrival—was experienced as one more letdown. What looks like the good life is experienced as loss of nothing less than one's self. Just as the prodigal son spends down his inheritance to nothingness, so the wandering, ravenous soul consumes everything and ends up with nothing: no identity, no center, no self. The "distant country" where the prodigal ends up isn't just far off and lonely. It dissolves. It fragments. It liquefies. "I was storm-tossed, gushing out, running every which way, frothing into thin air in my filthy affairs."[16] The frantic pursuit of the next place is symptomatic of his self-alienation. "I had left myself and couldn't find me," Augustine recalls. "I turned myself into a famished land I had to live in."[17]

The road, the journey, the quest not only organizes his *Confessions*; it is a dominant metaphor of Augustine's spirituality. In *Teaching Christianity*, his manual for preachers, he describes a heart on the run. Where we rest is a matter of what and how we love. Our restlessness is a reflection of what we try to "enjoy" as an end in itself—what we look to as a place to land. The heart's hunger is infinite, which is why it will ultimately be disappointed with anything merely finite. Humans are those strange creatures who can never be fully satisfied by anything created—though that never stops us from trying. The irony, Augustine points out, is that we experience frustration and disappointment when we try to make the road a home rather than realizing it's leading us home, when we try to tell ourselves "the road is life." Then we foist infinite expectations upon the finite. But the finite is given as a gift to help us get elsewhere.

> This we should be making use of with a certain love and delight that is not, so to say, permanently settled in, but transitory, rather, and casual, like love and delight in a road, or in vehicles, or any other tools and gadgets you like, or if you can think of any better way of putting it, so that we love the means by which we are being carried along, on account of the goal to which we are being carried.[18]

There is joy in the journey precisely when we don't try to make a home out of our car, so to speak. There is love on the road when we stop loving the road. There are myriad gifts along the way when we remember it's a *way*. There is delight in the sojourn when we know where home is.

But how to get home? Is there really hope of rest? What if the road is long and we're sick and tired of rest-stop food and the cheap motels we called "success," and the pleasures of this journey have turned stale? What if we can see through the finite, and we have some inkling of another shore but despair of ever getting there? What if we've gotten just far enough to see that no place will make us happy and so have given up the quest altogether?

Augustine has been there. Later in his life, in a sermon on the African shore in Hippo, he would revisit this with his congregation. When you've tried everything but keep finding that what you grasped as ultimate bleeds through your fingers as finite, he says,

> It is as if someone could see his home country from a long way away, but is cut off from it by the sea; he sees where to go, but does not have the means to get there. In the same way all of us long to reach that secure place of ours where that which is *is*, because it alone always *is* as it is. But in between lies the sea of this world through which we are going, even though we already see where we are going (many, however, do not see where they are going).[19]

The brutal truth: *You* can't get there from here. Not even a map is enough. You might already have realized where you need to go, but the question is how to get there.

What if God sent a boat? What if the Creator captained a ferry from that other shore?

"So that we might also have the means to go, the one we were longing to go to came here from there. And what did he make? A wooden raft for us to cross the sea on."[20] God sends a raft from home: "For no one can cross the sea of this world unless carried over it on the cross of Christ." Get on, God invites. Hang on. I'll never let you go.

It's not just a matter of finally settling down or coming to the end of the road. We find rest because we are found; we make it home because someone comes to get us. The prodigal's story reframes everything because of how it ends: "While he was still a long way off, his father saw him and was filled with compassion for him; he ran to his son, threw his arms around him and kissed him" (Luke 15:20). The wayward son is not defined by his prodigality but by the welcome of a father who never stopped looking, who is ever scanning the distance, and who runs to gather him up in an embrace. God is not tapping his foot judgmentally inside the door as you sneak in, crawling over the threshold in shame. He's the father running toward you, losing his sandals on the way, his robes spilling off his shoulders, with a laughing smile whose joy says, "I can't believe you came home!" This is what grace looks like.

Meditating on the incarnation, on God becoming human in Jesus, Augustine describes the God who runs to meet us: "He lost no time, but ran with shouts of words, acts, death, life, descent, ascent, all the time shouting for us to return to him."[21] Jesus is the shout of God, the way God runs out to meet us. Augustine shares the story of his prodigality as an invitation to find ourselves in the end of the story. To map our roaming like that of the prodigal is not a cartography of despair or self-loathing and shame; to the contrary, it is a geography of grace that is meant to help us imagine being welcomed home.

"Oh, the twisted roads I walked!" Augustine recalls. "But look, you're here, freeing us from our unhappy wandering, setting us firmly on your track, comforting us and saying, 'Run the race! *I'll* carry you! *I'll* carry you clear to the end, and even at the end, *I'll* carry you.'"[22]

WHOSE HEART ISN'T prodigal? One of the gifts Augustine offers is a spirituality for realists. Conversion is not a "solution." Conversion is not a magical transport home, some kind of Floo powder to heaven. Conversion doesn't pluck you off the road; it just changes how you travel.

One of the reasons I've found Augustine a comforting companion on the way is that he is honest about how hard the road is even once you know where home is. His pastoral realism recognizes something I hear in the music of Jason Isbell about winding roads and ditches that seem to have a magnetic pull about them. You can hear it in "Heathens," a song he performed with his earlier band, the Drive-By Truckers:

> It just gets so hard to keep between the ditches
> when the roads wind the way they do.

Or in Isbell's solo work, like "Flying over Water":

> From the sky the highway's straight as it could be.
> A string pulled tight from home to Tennessee.
> And still somehow those ditches took a better part of me.

Augustine doesn't write from the sky; he writes from the road. He knows ditches, and as he'll confess in book 10 of the *Confessions*, not even a bishop can avoid them. We are still *on the way*. He comes to this realization not long after his own conversion. As he points out in one of his early dialogues, "Just as the soul is the whole life of the body, God is the happy life of the soul. While we are doing this, until we have done it completely, we are on the road."[23] Peter Brown, Augustine's magisterial biographer, captures this creeping realization:

> For some years, he remained perched between two worlds. There was no more talk of an "ascent" in this life. "Remember . . . you have postponed your vision" [*On the Free Choice of the Will* 2.16.42]. A new image will make its appearance: that of a long highway, an *iter*. The moments of clear vision of truth that the mind gains in this life, are of infinite value; but they are now the consolations of a traveller on a long journey: "While we do this, until we achieve our aim, we are still travelling." These moments are no more than points of light "along this darkening highway" [2.16.41]. Augustine, himself, always resented travelling: he always associated it with a sense of protracted labour and of the infinite postponement of his dearest wishes; and these associations will colour the most characteristic image of the spiritual life in his middle age.[24]

There are two very different kinds of dissatisfaction or restlessness. One is engendered by disappointment, by not knowing where home is, by thinking you've arrived only to later become tired of the place or realize it's not home in the way you thought it was. In this case the road is the endless exhaustion of continuing to try to locate home, the frantic search for rest. That is the angst of the prodigal still in exile.

But there is another kind of restlessness that can be experienced on the road, a fatigue that stems from knowing where home is but also realizing you're not there yet—a kind of "directed" impatience.[25] The first is a baseline aimlessness that keeps looking for home; the second is the weariness of being en route, burdened by trials and distracted by a thousand byways and exhausted by temptations along the way that sucker you into forgetting where home is.

Augustine's spiritual realism doesn't shrink from honesty about this ongoing struggle.[26] You can hear this counsel in his sermon on Psalm 72, reflecting on Israel's experience after the exodus, its liberation through the sea. "Notice this point, brothers and sisters," he admonishes. "After crossing the Red Sea the Israelites are not given their homeland immediately, nor are they allowed carefree triumph, as though all their foes had disappeared. They still have to face the loneliness of the desert, and enemies still lurk along their way." Here is a template for the experience of a converted life: "So too after baptism Christian life must still confront temptations. In that wilderness the Israelites sighed after their promised homeland; and what else do Christians sigh for, once washed clean in baptism? Do they already reign with Christ? No; we have not reached our homeland yet, but it will not vanish; the hymns of David will not fail there." The key is to know where we are, and whose we are, and where we're headed, and not be surprised by the burdens of the road. "Let all the faithful listen and mark this; let them realize where they are. They are in the desert, sighing for their homeland." The Egyptians might not be pursuing us anymore, but that doesn't mean there aren't new threats on the way, "lying in ambush along our path."[27] To know where you're headed is not a promise of smooth sailing.

This is why book 10 of Augustine's *Confessions* is such a gift: it is the testimony of a broken bishop in the present. You realize Augustine isn't just narrating past temptations he has escaped; he's confessing all the ways he's still tempted to camp out in alcoves of creation as if they were home. "I struggle every day," he admits, and I love him for doing so.[28]

This is the authenticity we should value. As Jay-Z puts it in his memoir, *Decoded*:

> This is one of the things that makes rap at its best so human. It doesn't force you to pretend to be only one thing or another, to be a saint or sinner. It recognizes that you can be true to yourself and still have unexpected dimensions and opposing ideas. Having a devil on one shoulder and an angel on the other is the most common thing in the world. The real bull—— is when you act like you *don't* have contradictions inside you, that you're so dull and unimaginative that your mind never changes or wanders into strange, unexpected places.[29]

Any version of Christianity that isn't honest about this is not Augustinian. As French philosopher Jean-Luc Marion points out, conversion doesn't solve temptation; rather, it heightens temptation, because conversion creates resistance. In some sense, the tension of time is experienced more intensely by the soul that is on its way home. In conversion I find myself; I'm pulled together from the liquefaction of disordered loves and distractions that dissolved me. But conversion introduces a new kind of tension in my experience: "resistance of what I have become to what I used to be." Even if, by grace, I find wholeness, find *myself*, the experience of conversion—of reordering, reorienting—"renders me different from myself."[30] "Coming to myself" isn't an escape; instead, it makes the struggle more quotidian: every day I'm haunted. Selfhood is an ordeal not just before conversion but *because of* conversion. It is the converted, baptized, ordained Augustine who confesses, "*Onus mihi, oneri mihi sum*": "I am a burden to myself."[31]

The question is *how* to bear this burden. As Marion rightly comments, this "weight of the self," this burden of conversion, means "deciding between two burdens: that of the self reduced to itself, the weight of a deadweight, or that which I would love and which would lighten me."[32] There is a burden that actually takes the weight off, a yoke that liberates.

Augustine invites his parishioners to consider giving themselves over to one who gave himself for them, the Christ who assures them, "My yoke is kindly and my burden light" (Matt. 11:30). "Every other burden oppresses you and feels heavy, but Christ's burden lifts you up; any other burden is a crushing weight, but Christ's burden has wings."[33] Not only can you make it home; you can fly.

AUGUSTINE OUR CONTEMPORARY

How to Find Yourself

We are philosophical heirs even if we don't realize it. We have inhaled invisible philosophies in the cultural air we breathe. Our everyday quests for authenticity and identity are grooves in the heart laid down by the ripple effects of an existentialism we've perhaps never heard of.

In her wonderful introduction to twentieth-century philosophy, *At the Existentialist Café*, Sarah Bakewell pictures the mélange of existentialists—Jean-Paul Sartre and Simone de Beauvoir, Albert Camus and Martin Heidegger, Karl Jaspers and Gabriel Marcel—seated "in a big, busy, café of the mind, probably a Parisian one, full of life and movement, noisy with talk and thought." She pictures the scene that her book eavesdrops upon:

> When you peer in through the windows, the first figures you see are the familiar ones, arguing as they puff their pipes and lean toward each other, emphasizing their points. You hear clinking glasses and rattling cups; the waiters glide between the tables. In the largest group in front, a dumpy fellow and an elegant woman in a turban are drinking with their younger friends. Towards the back, others sit at quieter tables. A few people are on

the dance floor; perhaps someone is writing in a private room upstairs. Voices are being raised in anger somewhere, but there is also a murmuring from lovers in the shadows.[1]

They are talking about freedom and authenticity, being and nothingness. Sartre dominates the conversation, though Beauvoir is the sharper mind. Camus is at times boisterous, at other moments unsure of himself. This is a philosophy that is engaged, concrete, even erotic. There are cocktails and cigarettes.

Amid the tables in the back, assiduously avoiding the dance floor, there is another African, a compatriot of Camus. He listens with interest, sometimes leaning in to grasp a finer point, sometimes grimacing at a conclusion. He is a silent patron of the café and, truth be told, a catalyst of the conversation, even if it's taken a turn that pains him. He recognizes himself in many of them. In their conversation he relives the frustration, the alienation, the burden of being free. Which is why, as the night winds down, Augustine quietly picks up the check before he slips out.[2]

SOME OF AUGUSTINE'S most interesting journeys were posthumous. He shows up in places you wouldn't expect. His influence is in the water, so you don't notice it.

This struck me once when we were staying in Santa Monica, California—the city named for Augustine's mother. Thousands of miles and a world away from Hippo, in a city whose coast and light would have felt familiar to Augustine, his mother is mostly unknown to those who now envision "Santa Monica"—its palm trees and promenade, its glistening beaches and glittering stars. Santa Monica almost looks like an Augustinian monastery in negative. And yet his mother, praying over the son of her tears, covers the city.[3]

Santa Monica lies at the end of a famous road: the fabled ribbon of pavement known as Route 66, whose terminus is the Santa Monica pier. The frivolity of the pier's amusements are the sorts of circus distractions Monica's son would criticize in his *Confessions*. But just a few blocks from the pier, as you walk by shops on the promenade like "True Religion" and "Saints Hair Salon," you'll find St. Augustine by-the-Sea parish, an Episcopal church on Fourth Street. Located in the heart of the city, the white building reflects a 1960s modernism with a vaguely Spanish accent. Simple white walls inside are made dazzling by stained glass refracting the California sun.

On the Sunday morning we visited, the sanctuary was animated by a healthy, vibrant congregation, notably diverse and affirming, with a clear sense of belonging, of family. Indeed, I was struck by the gay couple in front of us: in secularized California, in liberal Santa Monica, they don't "need" to be here. There's no social capital to be gained, and perhaps not a little to be lost. And yet here they are: hungry, open, welcomed, worshiping. This is the Augustinian journey, replayed in the twenty-first century in a California sanctuary where a banner hangs with a heart aflame, *Veritas* inscribed across it. Still seeking. Still on the road with the saint.

The city named for his mother embodies the cross-pressures and complexities of faith in a secular age, where transcendence still haunts but where consumerism threatens to domesticate everything. In the incubator of LA narcissism and its cult of the image, even Augustine's legacy can be reduced to a veneer, like the façade of a film set. This was my sense one afternoon as I was writing at Holy Grounds, the café in St. Monica Catholic Church on the corner of California Avenue and Lincoln Boulevard, not far from St. Augustine by-the-Sea. The church, together with St. Monica Catholic High and Elementary, elite parochial schools, formed its own complex nestled in a bougie enclave. I was on the patio of the café when school let out. Coiffed moms and dispatched nannies arrived in BMWs to pick up children of privilege—children receiving the sort of elite education that Augustine's parents desired for him, come to think of it. It was an odd mix of handbags and high heels, backpacks and sneakers, suffused with an air of aspiration and ambition and not a little entitlement, all under the guise of Monica's legacy. But then again, you'll find this perplexing concoction of sacred and profane in the *Confessions* too. And this world isn't so unlike the world reflected in Augustine's sermons and letters, counseling the *corpus permixtum*, the mixed-up body of Christ who are supposed to be *in* the world but instead seem very much *of* it. Augustine doesn't just help us understand saints; he will help us make sense of La-La Land.

This secular stew seemed to find its quintessential expression as I began walking home. I peeked inside the sanctuary of St. Monica's church where the music of a wedding rehearsal resonated softly. Augustine the bishop presides to the left of the altar; his mother Monica prays on the right. I listened and prayed, and as I turned to leave, a statue outside on the corner of the block caught my eye. A slender, youthful, bronze Monica, hands outstretched in welcome and prayer, was surrounded by fresh flowers, white lilies and pink ranunculus, withering yellow carnations, and a lone pink rose laid at her feet. Votive candles were interspersed among prayer notes. One prayer was written on a paper airplane; another had been folded into a paper boat. Prayers for the journey, prayers from the road, missives of devotion and intercession. In stone under the statue was a word about its provenance: "Dedicated to the priests and people of St. Monica's who inspired the making of the 1944 film, 'Going My Way.'"

JUST UP THE street from the Santa Monica pier, where Route 66 dreams of freedom and the open road crash into the Pacific Ocean, there is another statue of Augustine's mother, at the foot of Wilshire Boulevard. The art deco sculpture was a New Deal public works project completed in 1934. Her back to the ocean, looking over the city, Monica stands serenely in Pacific Palisades Park, hands folded over her bosom in prayerful contemplation.

If you were to follow Monica's gaze and make your way up Wilshire Boulevard, perhaps taking the 720 bus downtown, you would pass through Brentwood and past UCLA, curving around the Beverly Hilton before crossing Rodeo Drive and perhaps catching sight of incognito stars dining at Spago or the Four Seasons. Just after skirting the north edge of Little Ethiopia, you would arrive at the Los Angeles County Museum of Art (LACMA). There, amid midcentury modern design and contemporary transgression, you will find an iconic image of Monica's son (see figure 2).

Her son has aged, but his eyes remain bright, hungry, illuminated by the light of truth, his heart aflame with love. In his right hand is a quill, the tool of this verbose doctor of the church who penned volumes. We find him in the place where, in many ways, he's most at home: his study, surrounded by his library, books open all around him (save the volumes of Caelestius, Pelagius, and Julian on which he stomps with his blue suede shoes!). One imagines Augustine would be somewhat uncomfortable in the gilded vestments that the artist, Philippe de Champaigne, has cloaked him with. And his face looks more northern European than North African.[4] His face is turned toward the Word, looking expectantly for revelation. But situated here on Wilshire Boulevard, in the City of Angels, it almost seems like he's looking back toward Santa Monica, to his mother on the coast, a new-world Ostia.

We visit LACMA every year when we spend time in Los Angeles, and each time I make a pilgrimage to Champaigne's Augustine as an exercise in cultural vertigo. LACMA is a place you go not only to see but to be seen. *Urban Light*, the forest of street lamps just outside the entrance, is a perfectly Instagrammable backdrop. Ray's and Stark Bar on the museum's plaza is a hip space for sipping fifteen-dollar cocktails and schmoozing on jazz nights. The museum is a place where the stars turn out; as we've toured the galleries we've bumped into Will Ferrell, Minnie Driver, and others. And with typical LA nonchalance, everyone treats their proximity to fame casually, even while incessantly watching. (In LA everybody *looks* like they could be famous.) To visit LACMA is to make a secular pilgrimage where being seen seeing art is like an Escher illusion of devotion.

And then you run into Augustine: ancient, devout, looking past you, beyond you, oblivious to your stare (or oblivion). He's so anachronistic he could be avant-garde (you think Beyoncé doesn't want a cape like that?), and his presence here in Los Angeles is an opening for a conversation.

Indeed, I've sometimes wondered if there isn't a tacit conversation happening in the gallery itself. If you make your way out of the Thomas V. Jones Gallery that is home to Augustine, wander past works by Monet, Pissarro, and Cézanne (who, like Augustine, was interested in the invisible becoming visible), spanning continents and centuries, you will, in the opposite corner of the Ahmanson Building, encounter Ferdinand Hodler's 1892 painting *The Disillusioned One* (see figure 3). He is a study in contrast: wearing simple, black, monkish robes, sitting on an unadorned bench amid a barren landscape, here is the priest on the leeward side of modernity's disenchantment. There is no chorus of witnesses, no communion of saints on his shoulders, not even books to occupy him (and certainly no blue suede shoes). The loneliness and isolation are palpable in the palette and setting. His gaze is downcast, hands folded from a habit of prayer, but he's not pleading. His eyes have the glaze of dejection.

Does Augustine have anything to say to him? Or is Augustine safely benighted in his ancient world, railing against a paganism irrelevant to those of us who endured the disenchantment of modernity? We live between Augustine and the disillusioned one—except that Augustine *was* the disillusioned one. Maybe there's new light to be found by looking back?

Champaigne's *Augustine*, now at home in Los Angeles, was the fruit of one of Augustine's first posthumous journeys to France, in connection with the renaissance of interest in his work during the seventeenth century. Primarily associated with Port-Royal and figures like Blaise Pascal and Antoine Arnauld, Augustine also made a dent in the thinking of René Descartes, who would so influence the subsequent questions and conversation in modern philosophy.[5] In many ways, modernity is Augustinian. And Augustine has continued to arrive on the shores of contemporary thought, shaping us in invisible ways. This is how Augustine made it to that Parisian café, a journey to the Left Bank via German roads.

WHEN I VENTURED to the United States to pursue graduate study in philosophy, I didn't realize I wouldn't be returning home. I also didn't realize I would be joining Augustine on the road.

As a student in Toronto, it was existentialism and phenomenology that had captured my imagination. Edmund Husserl, Martin Heidegger, Paul Ricoeur, and Jacques Derrida were asking my questions—about meaning and interpretation, about authenticity and mass society, about identity and selfhood. Unlike the analytic logic games that seemed to be solving problems no one else had, this stream of continental philosophy flowing from Germany and France was grappling with difference—"the Other"— and the challenge of knowledge in pluralist societies. (One might recall that Jean-François Lyotard's famous little book *The Postmodern Condition* was commissioned as a report for the government of Quebec on "the question of knowledge in advanced industrial societies."[6]) Here were philosophers tackling fundamental questions about justice, ethics, and obligation, particularly in the wake of the Holocaust.

My gateway drug was John Caputo's *Radical Hermeneutics*, a book that was at once instructive and intoxicating.[7] A masterful teacher, Caputo engaged in exegesis of Husserl, Heidegger, Derrida, Søren Kierkegaard, and Hans-Georg Gadamer that gave a young student the confidence to tackle these texts firsthand (no mean feat). But by this time, Caputo had found his own voice, and so *Radical Hermeneutics* was also something of a manifesto for a philosophy that mattered. The introduction was titled "Restoring Life to Its Original Difficulty"; the final chapter, "Openness to Mystery." This was a postmodernism with philosophical chops and a religious heartbeat.

In the summer of 1995, my wife, Deanna, and I, along with our two children (ages three and one at the time), packed all of our worldly possessions into a Ryder truck and a 1983 Chrysler LeBaron station wagon (complete with faux wood paneling) and set out for Villanova University, where I would begin a PhD program working with John Caputo. We were the first in either of our families to move away from home, let alone move out of the country. We crossed the border armed with letters and paperwork, always aware of the capriciousness of the situation, of how subject we were to the moods and whims of border officials. ("Are you bringing more than $10,000 with you into the country?" they asked. We wished!) Working to maintain our little convoy, we barreled through upstate New York and chugged up and down the Poconos, sometimes audibly coaxing the stuttering yellow moving truck up the hill. When we finally made it to Villanova's campus, it felt like arriving in paradise, both because of the youthful thrill of getting to devote myself to studying phenomenology, but also because Villanova's campus was an idyllic setting, recognized at the time as a national arboretum. Here I arrived to study Heidegger, who was most at home in the Black Forest. Little did I realize I would end up studying Augustine.

The monks on campus should have been a sign. Villanova is a Catholic university founded by the Augustinian order and named after St. Thomas of Villanova, a Spanish friar of the Order of Saint Augustine. If it was Heidegger and Derrida that led me to Villanova, it didn't take me long to realize that Augustine was the heartbeat of the place. The philosophy department, along with the rest of the humanities division, was housed in the St. Augustine Center for the Liberal Arts, with the departments of philosophy and theology on the ground level to provide a "foundation." The president of the university was (and still is) an Augustinian friar. I had come to study deconstruction among devotees of the doctor of grace.

This would turn out to be fortuitous in ways I couldn't have imagined. That same year, the cabal in charge of publishing Heidegger's collected works—his *Gesamtausgabe*—released volume 60, *Phänomenologie des religiösen Lebens* (*The Phenomenology of Religious Life*).[8] This volume would turn out to be a revealing backstory to Heidegger's famous bombshell of a book, *Being and Time*, published in 1927. *Being and Time* unleashed some of the central concepts of existentialism that would ripple into French cafés and cinemas, eventually making their way to American universities and magazines, and even to Hollywood. It was from Heidegger, via Sartre and others, that we would learn to prize "authenticity" and seek to resist the flattening effect of mass society. Heidegger offered an account of all of this through an analysis of a strange beast he called "Dasein," his version of the self. Unlike philosophers before him who spoke of some abstract "ego" or of a vague "subject," Heidegger took up Dasein, which means "being there." The point was to remember that I am embedded in a world, heir to a history of possibilities that opened up the world, if only I could resist falling prey to the "idle talk" of "the they" (*das Man*). And so Dasein functioned like a philosophical saint of sorts, an exemplar to imitate. Could we measure up to "authentic" Dasein, seizing possibilities and resisting temptation? Could we learn to be resolute, to resolve to answer the call of being, to seize our inmost possibilities—to become the "I" that I'm destined to be? As Bakewell rightly notes, while later existentialists would frame this as a call to "be yourself," for Heidegger it was "a call to take up a self that you didn't know you had."[9]

Much of this was crammed, *in nuce*, into Heidegger's *Being and Time*, which then became something of an urtext for everyone from Sartre to Walker Percy, from Ingmar Bergman to Terrence Malick, even for renegade winemakers in Napa Valley.[10] Existentialism seeped into the postwar water and was disseminated not only in philosophy books but in film and art, perhaps especially in movies that ranged from *The Seventh Seal* (1957) to *Groundhog Day* (1993) to *I Heart Huckabees* (2004). Bakewell captures the ubiquity of this invisible philosophy in our culture:

Existential ideas and attitudes have embedded themselves so deeply into modern culture that we hardly think of them as existentialist at all. People (at least in relatively prosperous countries where more urgent needs don't intervene) talk about anxiety, dishonesty and the fear of commitment. They worry about being in bad faith, even if they don't use that term. They feel overwhelmed by the excess of consumer choice while also feeling less in control than ever. A vague longing for a more "real" way of living leads some people to—for example—sign up for weekend retreats in which their smartphones are taken away like toys from children, so that they can spend two days walking in the country landscape and reconnecting with each other and their forgotten selves. The unnamed object of desire here is authenticity.[11]

The DNA of our quest for authenticity points to the legacy of Heidegger and existentialism.

What made the 1995 publication of an obscure volume of Heidegger's works of particular interest was that it filled in the backstory of *Being and Time*, which in 1927 had seemed to come from nowhere. In fact, Heidegger had been honing its concepts and ideas for a decade. And the year I arrived at Villanova, to study the young Heidegger at this Augustinian university, volume 60 of his collected works provided its own bombshell of a revelation. The volume includes lecture notes for two courses the young Heidegger taught at the University of Freiburg that look like a first draft of *Being and Time*. But they also show us the unexpected provenance of these notions of authenticity, conformity, and the call to be.

In the winter semester of 1920–21, Heidegger taught "Introduction to the Phenomenology of Religion." After a typical survey of other scholars, the bulk of the course is devoted, almost bafflingly, to a philosophical reading of the apostle Paul's Epistles to the Thessalonians. Here we realize that what will later, in *Being and Time*, become Dasein's "being-towards-death" first finds its articulation in Heidegger's encounter with St. Paul's exhortations about the second coming of Christ. Even more significantly, we see that some of the central existential concepts of *Being and Time*—core notions like despair, "falling," throwness, and care—first emerge in Heidegger's 1921 summer semester course on (you guessed it) Augustine!

The notion of inauthenticity that will be so central to existentialism's diagnosis of our malaise is generated in the chemical reaction of Heidegger's reading of Augustine's *Confessions*. What Heidegger will later call "fallenness," our tendency to "fall prey" to the vague, mass society of "the they" (*das Man*), is something he learned from Augustine's account of our "absorption" in the world. The aversion to inauthenticity that suffuses our cultural attitude is a trickle-down from Augustine's critique of disordered love. Working through this freshly minted German text as a young doctoral student, it was dawning on me: we are more Augustinian than we realize.

THE THINKER WHO perhaps most freshly broke open Augustine for me, who taught me to read him with new eyes and to see him as a prescient analyst of our own cultural anxieties, was Hannah Arendt, whose insights into totalitarianism have received timely reconsideration of late.

Not long after the publication of Heidegger's early lectures on Augustine, Arendt's doctoral dissertation on *Love and Saint Augustine*, written under the direction of Karl Jaspers and the informal tutelage of Heidegger, was translated into English.[12] Lots of devotees of the famed New York intellectual were surprised to learn Arendt had cut her philosophical teeth on Augustine. Equally surprising was that Arendt, the political thinker, instead of focusing on *City of God* as one would expect, had focused on the central theme of love in Augustine's *Teaching Christianity*, *Confessions*, and a wide range of sermons. It was Arendt who showed me that Augustine was a cartographer of the heart.

Up to that point, my encounters with Augustine had been badly framed. Inexplicably (though not uncommon), I had been introduced to him as a "medieval" thinker who was primarily a theologian. My first brush with Augustine was citations in dogmatic theology texts, and my later interactions in philosophy classes tended to lump him with Thomas Aquinas, which meant that Thomas's late medieval scholasticism—which felt a little too much like analytic philosophy's logic-chopping—was the lens through which I anachronistically read Augustine, as if he were doing the same thing. I had been taught to read Augustine to get doctrines, dogmas, and propositional claims about sin and God and salvation. Only later did I realize what a travesty this framing was—not only the way it domesticated a protoexistentialist but also the way it dehumanized a fellow traveler.

Which is why Arendt came along at a critical point and introduced me to Augustine again for the first time. The pivot was a bold methodological move early in the work: she would try to disclose Augustine's unique genius, the incisiveness of what we might call his "psychological" insight, by bracketing doctrinal concerns. She would fixate not on *why* Augustine said *x* but on whether and how *x* proved illuminating for our experience. For the purposes of trying to grasp Augustine's insights from the inside, as it were, to get a feel for the dynamism of his thought, her interpretation of Augustine "was not dogmatically bound."[13] This was not a way of eviscerating Augustine or remaking him in our secular image. What she meant was that she would read Augustine as, well, a phenomenologist, a philosopher of experience, a protoexistentialist who, *as a philosopher*, had something to show us about ourselves.[14]

I never looked back. It was like scales fell from my eyes. A human Augustine emerged from the flat, two-dimensional caricature I'd been looking at. Arendt's suggestion, coupled with Heidegger's reframing, made the *Confessions* a new book for me. No longer merely a narrative dress-up for doctrine or the tortured machinations of an ancient Puritan, Augustine was reshelved in the philosophical canon of my imagination—moved from the medieval *A*'s alongside Aquinas and Anselm, he was bumped to the shelf with dog-eared, coffee-stained copies of Pascal, Kierkegaard, and Nietzsche, alongside Heidegger, Arendt, and Camus. They weren't at all surprised to see him.

THE CAFÉS AND theaters of postwar France were the incubators for existentialism because they were a confluence of streams from Germany and Africa, Algeria in particular (the country that now occupies the region Augustine called home). What's remarkable is that, while Sartre was unwittingly drinking from Augustinian wells via Heidegger, his friend and collaborator Albert Camus was independently wrestling with Augustine's legacy in his dissertation, *Christian Metaphysics and Neoplatonism*, submitted in 1936.[15] Camus felt a solidarity with Augustine, he emphasized, as a Mediterranean.[16] The first resonance was geographical. They shared the same sky, the same sun, the same sea. These were geographical resonances they both felt.

Camus's dissertation gives us insight into the Christianity that Camus said he couldn't believe. After World War II, in 1948, Camus gave a talk at a Dominican monastery in Latour-Maubourg, in which he made an interesting concession: "I shall never start from the supposition that Christian truth is illusory, but merely from the fact that I could not accept it."[17] In his biography of Camus, Olivier Todd recounts an episode where Camus and a friend were walking through the village of Le Chambon. After passing a Salvation Army poster that read, "God Is Looking for You," Todd says, "Camus wisecracked, 'He wouldn't be looking for me if he hadn't already found me.'"[18]

But apart from the question of God's existence, a persistent theme that has a deep Augustinian resonance weaves its way throughout Camus's corpus. It could be named in different ways: exile, alienation, strangerhood. Sartre noted this upon first reading the pairing of Camus's novel *The Stranger* and his accompanying essay on the absurd, *The Myth of Sisyphus*.

"Camus might as well have chosen the title of one of George Gissing's works, *Born in Exile*."[19] This is something like Heidegger's "thrownness," or like an Augustinian fall without Eden or eschaton. We are strangers in the world, but also strangers to ourselves. This is not unrelated to Camus's (early) notion of the absurd—a sense of being under obligation but without meaning or rationale, without hope of redemption. It's tragedy all the way down, and yet we can be (godless) saints. It's here that one wonders whether Camus's very notion of the absurd isn't itself haunted by something like Augustine. As David Bellos has remarked,

> It has often been pointed out that Camus's concept of the absurd is itself rather absurd. Why should anyone find it at all remarkable—or even more strangely, lamentable—that there is no transcendent meaning to human acts? Things would surely be far worse if the opposite were the case. If the world were not at all absurd, in Camus's sense, then things in general and acts in particular would be endowed irrevocably with "meaning." And that would make the world a very strange and inhumane place indeed.[20]

So one can wonder whether Camus's project isn't governed—or at least stalked—by something like Augustine's vision, a world that *ought* to have meaning, where evil is vanquished, where tragedy doesn't have the last word, even if Camus concludes that's not true. Conor Cruise O'Brien, for example, argues that Camus's novel *The Fall* "is profoundly Christian in its confessional form, in its imagery, and above all in its pervasive message that it is only through the full recognition of our sinful nature that we can hope for grace. Grace does not, it is true, arrive and the novel ends on what is apparently a pessimistic note. Yet the name of the narrator [Jean-Baptiste Clamence]—that of the fore-runner—hints, however teasingly, at the possibility of a sequel."[21] Augustine represents the Christianity Camus doesn't believe, which might make him more Augustinian than he realizes—and might make *us* more Augustinian than we imagined. An Augustinianism *sans* grace might nonetheless be a gateway.

SEVERAL YEARS AGO when I was in Paris, I stepped out of the university onto La Place de la Sorbonne. I was headed for the Presses Universitaires de France bookshop (sadly, no longer there) but stopped short in front of a smaller bookstore just across the street, the equally famous Librairie philosophique J. Vrin. There, in the middle of twenty-first-century France's intellectual center, was an entire display window devoted to St. Augustine. There, beside the hallowed halls of the Sorbonne—in the land of *liberté, égalité, fraternité*, and deconstruction—was a celebration of philosophical works, both ancient and contemporary, devoted to a Catholic bishop from the African provinces.

I shouldn't have been surprised. In the late twentieth century, interest in Augustine continued to be fostered by French intellectuals from colonial Africa. After Camus came Algerians Jacques Derrida and Jean-François Lyotard. Derrida's coy, playful, even somewhat sacrilegious "Circumfession" was written from his apartment in Santa Monica, while he was a visiting professor at the University of California Irvine, his mother dying on the Mediterranean coast in Nice at the time. Derrida leverages the parallels with his ancient North African forebear (Derrida grew up on Rue St. Augustin in Algiers) to wrestle with his own identity, as an exile from his homeland (even in his homeland), and how he "passes for an atheist."[22] Lyotard likewise substantively revisited Augustine in a posthumous volume. And since then, Sorbonne professor Jean-Luc Marion has published his own book on Augustine.[23] We don't need to "make" Augustine postmodern: the postmodern is already Augustinian. We are already Augustinian; we just didn't know it.

Augustine is our contemporary. He has directly and indirectly shaped the way we understand our pursuits, the call to authenticity. In some ways, he put us on the road we're on. It's why he continues to fascinate.

Mark Lilla, in a review of Robin Lane Fox's biography of Augustine, succinctly encapsulates the choice that is before us:

For a millennium Augustine's portrait of himself served as a model for self-cultivation in Christian civilization. The imitation of Christ was the ideal, but those falling short could turn to *Confessions* for help getting there. It was during the Renaissance that this conception of the self came under serious challenge, most powerfully in Montaigne's "Essays," which mocked the idea of sin and preached self-acceptance. To Augustine's anxious admission that he was a problem to himself, Montaigne simply responded, So what's the problem? Don't worry, be happy. As modern people we have chosen Montaigne over Augustine. We traded pious self-cultivation for undemanding self-esteem. But is love of self really enough to be happy? You know the answer to that, dear reader. And so did Augustine.[24]

We've been asking Augustine's questions for a century. Perhaps it's time to consider his answer.

A REFUGEE SPIRITUALITY

How to Live Between

We cultivate indifference as a cocoon. We make irony a habit because the safety of maintaining a knowing distance works as a defense. If you can't find what matters, conclude that nothing matters. If the hunger for home is always and only frustrated, decide "the road is life."

Such concession is the cultivated posture of Meursault, the antihero at the center of Albert Camus's breakout novel, *The Stranger*. He exhibits an odd aloofness from the very beginning. He can't remember which day his mother died. The day after receiving the telegram, he is laughing and frolicking with Marie in the Mediterranean Sea. Puzzled when he puts on a black tie, Marie asks in jest whether he's in mourning.

> I told her Maman had died. She wanted to know how long ago, so I said, "Yesterday." She gave a little start but didn't say anything. I felt like telling her it wasn't my fault, but I stopped myself because I remembered that I'd already said that to my boss. It didn't mean anything. Besides, you always feel a little guilty.[1]

And are.

Later in the novel, his guilt well established, Meursault is imprisoned. But this is only an intensification of how he has always experienced the burden of life. Like Socrates practicing to die, Meursault has unwittingly spent a life learning to be guilty, denied his freedom.

> When I was first imprisoned, the hardest thing was that my thoughts were still those of a free man. For example, I would suddenly have the urge to be on a beach and to walk down to the water. As I imagined the sound of the first waves under my feet, my body entering the water and the sense of relief it would give me, all of a sudden I would feel just how closed in I was by the walls of my cell. But that only lasted a few months. Afterwards my only thoughts were those of a prisoner.[2]

When all you'll see is this walled yard, decide that walking around within it is the only journey that could ever make you happy. When your only visitor is your lawyer, convince yourself hell is other people. When happiness eludes you, believe that eschewing happiness makes you happy. You can learn to stifle the stubborn suggestions otherwise, as Meursault learned. During the incessant drone of his trial, through "all the interminable days and hours that people had spent talking about my soul," he says,

> I could hear through the expanse of chambers and courtrooms an ice cream vendor blowing his tin trumpet out in the street. I was assailed by memories of a life that wasn't mine anymore, but one in which I'd found the simplest and most lasting joys: the smells of summer, the part of town I loved, a certain evening sky, Marie's dresses and the way she laughed. The utter pointlessness of whatever I was doing seized my throat, and all I wanted was to get it over with and get back to my cell and sleep.[3]

As long as he could squelch these murmurings that it could be otherwise, as long as he could convince himself that this, indeed, was all he wanted, then this stranger could make a home out of exile: "I opened myself to the gentle indifference of the world. Finding it so much like myself—so like a brother, really—I felt that I had been happy and that I was happy again."[4]

Such resignation—the consolation of alienation—is the deep bass note in Camus's corpus that makes his work resonate as contemporary. If Camus took this to be the human condition, it also echoed his experience as an Algerian expat, an émigré who never found rest in Paris. Sarah Bakewell recalls Camus's "dislocated experience as a French Algerian, caught between two countries and never fully at home in either." She continues: "Camus went on to spend much of his life in France, but he always felt an outsider there, lost without the brilliant-white Mediterranean sun."[5]

It's little wonder that this experience is enshrined in a novel about *l'étranger*—the stranger, the foreigner, the outsider.[6] It's also not surprising, then, that the human condition is considered in the language of sojourn. But for Camus, this isn't about pilgrimage; it's about *exile*. In his notebooks, Camus once wrote, "We travel to cultivate our most private instinct, which is that of eternity." We are compelled to look for home. What makes it absurd is that we've never had one.

The journey is one of our oldest tropes for the adventure of being human. In many cases, the template is Odyssean: departure and return, adventure and homecoming, from *bon voyage* to *welcome home*.[7] Even the lament of *You Can't Go Home Again* (by Thomas Wolfe) rehearses the Odyssean itinerary by trying to go back. But the adventure of Camus's exile is not Odyssean; it is Sisyphean. Joy is predicated on the impossibility of arrival.

In *The Myth of Sisyphus*, Camus describes the experience of the one for whom the illusions of rationality have been peeled back: "In a universe suddenly divested of illusions and lights, man feels an alien, a stranger. His exile is without remedy since he is deprived of the memory of a lost home or the hope of a promised land."[8] The world is inhuman, indifferent to us, and there are days, moments, seasons where its aloof strangeness swells to encompass our vision and we experience a vertigo, like looking at the Mediterranean on a cloudy day and the horizon vanishes in a bright gray. "If man realized that the universe like him can love and suffer," Camus remarks, "he would be reconciled."[9] But the world refuses.

This strange disaffection bleeds into me if I sit still long enough. "Likewise the stranger who at certain seconds comes to meet us in a mirror, the familiar and yet alarming brother we encounter in our own photographs is also the absurd."[10] "A stranger to myself and to the world, armed solely with a thought that negates itself as soon as it asserts, what is this condition in which I can have peace only by refusing to know and to live, in which the appetite for conquest bumps into walls that defy its assaults?"[11]

The condition is exile, and happiness is embracing it. Relinquishing any nostalgia for home and any hope of arrival, the "absurd one" is the one who manages to make exile what he always wanted. The feat, the trick, is to learn how "to live *without appeal*."[12] Exile *is* the kingdom: "This hell of the present is his Kingdom at last."[13]

Imagine Sisyphus as a pilgrim caught in a loop, arrival always eluding him, accomplishment perpetually undermined. Sisyphus is the absurd hero for Camus because he embraces this perpetual pilgrimage of futility. "It is during that return, that pause, that Sisyphus interests me," Camus admits. When the stone has rolled away *again*, Camus praises Sisyphus for his trudge back down the mountain. Left at the foot of the mountain, the rock rolling back every time, Sisyphus manufactures joy in the effort: "All Sisyphus' silent joy is contained therein. His fate belongs to him. His rock is his thing."[14] He's never going to arrive, never reaching the other shore, never getting to stay on the top of the mountain. But "the struggle itself towards the heights is enough to fill a man's heart. One must imagine Sisyphus happy."[15]

Must?

Like Camus, we sometimes try to remake despair as joy. Never feeling at home, we turn our estrangement into a philosophy: "The road is life" is a motto you try to convince yourself is true when you never feel at home with yourself. And yet it's hard to efface the home-hunger that even Camus admits is an impulsion.

But imagine Camus's philosophy as a message to actual migrants, to those risking their lives today in boats submerged to the gunwales, ferrying hopeful refugees across Camus's prized Mediterranean, all too often failing to arrive. Or imagine young parents, toddlers in tow, making the harrowing journey from murderous Honduras to the southern border of the United States, parched and depleted by the desert journey, trying to cross this fabled line to apply for asylum, only to be refused and returned over and over again. Are *they* to look to Sisyphus as the hero? Should refugees' hearts be filled every time they step foot onto another laden dinghy, casting out into the threats of the Mediterranean, wondering if this is the time they'll make landfall, or perish? Is scaling the fence over and over again where they should determine they'll find joy?

Or do such Sisyphean philosophies—that "the road is life"—turn out to be bourgeois luxuries indulged by those safe enough to pretend this is all there is? Does the hunger and hope of the migrant show us something more fundamentally human? Maybe our craving for rest, refuge, arrival, home is a hunger that can't be edited—the heart an obstinate palimpsest that suggests there might be another way. If there's a map inscribed in the human heart that shows where home is, the fact that we haven't yet arrived doesn't make it a fiction. It might just mean there's a way we haven't tried. Maybe Camus gave up too soon. Augustine, his fellow African, might be a better guide.

THE ALIENATION IS real. The sense of frustration, futility, of never arriving, never feeling settled with ourselves—these are not figments of the imagination to be papered over with pious assertions of homecoming. The way out of the experience of being fractured and fragmented and ill-at-ease in our own skin is neither Sisyphean redescription nor some born-again leapfrog out of the vagaries of the human condition. If there's a way out, a way home, a way to oneself, it has to be a way *through* what Camus confronts.

Of course, the most popular way to quell this unsettling sense of not-at-home-ness is by trying to make ourselves at home in the world, even if that looks like mostly distracting ourselves from the unsettling fact of our alienation. As Heidegger would put it—in a way he learned from Augustine—I am absorbed by "everydayness"; I give myself over to those "producers of bustling activity" who are more than happy to take the burden of selfhood off my hands.[16] We learn to forget our alienation by letting ourselves be taken over by the distractions and entertainments and chatter of the world. We trade one sort of self-alienation for another that gives the illusion of homey comfort: "You belong here" is the lie told to us by everyone from Disney to Vegas. We try to cover up not knowing who we are by letting everyone else sell us an identity, or at least a distraction from needing one.

This is why Camus's honesty is a gift. He names—and gives permission to voice—those irruptions that unsettle this deal we've brokered with everydayness. Like those late-afternoon business meetings where everyone around the table morphs into strangers that we either loathe or can't fathom, and we tire of the pointless monotony of it all and wonder, why bother? Or the way an airport discloses the sadness of the world and leaves us overwhelmed by the meaninglessness of the hurried endeavors of all these deluded, self-important mammals scurrying through the terminal, an allegory for the cosmos.

What Camus is honest about is what Heidegger calls *Angst*, the anxiety that emerges in such moments, calling into question everything that we consider to be the homey faux-comfort of our absorption in the world. In fact Heidegger himself, echoing Freud, describes this productive, unveiling anxiety as *Unheimlich*, "uncanny," but even more literally, "not-at-home-ness." When we've fooled ourselves into thinking we're at home with distraction, tricked ourselves into feeling "settled" only because we've sold our home-hunger for entertainments, then the irruption of the uncanny, a sense of not-at-home-ness, becomes a gift that creates an opening to once again face the question of who we are. *Angst*'s disturbing disclosure of meaninglessness is a door to walk through: it opens onto the possibility of finding yourself. Not-at-home-ness could be the place from which you finally hear the *call* to be yourself. If Camus advises us to wake up from our absorption and learn to live *without appeal*, Heidegger suggests that the wake-up call of anxiety might be how we learn to hear "the Appeal" that comes from beyond us, a transcendence calling us to something—calling us to ourselves.[17]

THE UNCANNINESS OF anxiety, the gnawing sense of not-at-home-ness, could be a gift, its own sort of invitation to discover something about ourselves. The fact that we can't shake it challenges Camus's Sisyphean response that essentially counsels: "There's no home; there's no arrival; rejoice!" And the fact that such counsel trivializes the fatal frustrations of migrants makes one wonder whether there isn't a bourgeois cosmopolitanism behind this celebration of never arriving. Bakewell's take on Sartre's notion of intentionality is telling: "We have no cosy home: being out on the dusty road is the very definition of what we are."[18] "The road is life" is an exhilarating philosophy when you enjoy the comforts of a Parisian café.

What if the human condition was understood not as Odyssean (a neat and tidy return) or Sisyphean (learning to get over your hope for home), but as being like the experience of a refugee? What if being human means being a cosmic émigré—vulnerable, exposed, unsettled, desperate, looking for a home I've never been to before? The longings of the refugee—to escape hunger, violence, and the quotidian experience of being bereft in order to find security, flourishing, and freedom—are good and just precisely because they are so deeply human. They even signal something about our spiritual condition: that our unshakable hopes of escaping a bereftness of the soul and finding the security of a home are not absurd.

The exhaustion we experience from perpetually seeking, the fatigue of trying to live as if "the road is life," the times we crumple onto the road just wishing someone could find us and take us home—the persistence of this hope almost makes us wonder if it could be realized.

This experience of the refugee, the tenuous existence of one forced to flee and wander, is movingly captured in Stefan Zweig's memoir, *The World of Yesterday*. Zweig was a Jewish émigré formed by fin-de-siècle Vienna but uprooted by tensions and monstrosities that befell Europe in the early twentieth century: World War I, the Russian Revolution, and eventually the specter of Hitler's Nazism (Zweig died in 1942). The memoir is very much an account of his uprooted life on the road, roaming the continent, migrating to London and eventually Brazil. Zweig captures what it feels like to be an émigré.

> Every form of emigration inevitably, of its nature, tends to upset your equilibrium. You lose—and this too has to be experienced to be understood—you lose something of your upright bearing if you no longer have the soil of your own land beneath your feet; you feel less confident, more distrustful of yourself. And I do not hesitate to confess that since the day when I first had to live with papers or passports essentially foreign to me, I have not felt that I entirely belong to myself anymore. Something of my natural identity has been destroyed forever with my original, real self. I have become less outgoing than really suits me, and today I—the former cosmopolitan—keep feeling as if I had to offer special thanks for every breath of air that I take in a foreign country.[19]

There is more than one way to be on the road. There is, of course, a vulnerability to this experience—an exposure, what Zweig describes as a kind of dependence that he resents, a sense that his existence is a favor granted by others, that even the air he breathes is something for which he is obligated to give thanks. But what would it mean to "entirely belong to myself"? Is self-possession the way I find security? Or could even this experience be a door to a different way of being, where my dependence is not something I resent but something that I learn is the condition of creaturehood? While this might be an affront to my autonomy, perhaps it is my autonomy that is the source of my dis-ease, not its solution. What if dependence is a gift because it means I'm not alone? What if the welcome I experience elsewhere is how I learn to be human?

In the same way that the uncanny experience of the absurd, the *Unheimlich*, the un-homey, can be its own sort of wake-up call, the experience of immigration can open up something in the self and shake loose habits that immersed us in the anonymity of "the they," as Heidegger liked to put it. Zweig recounts,

> On purpose, I set out to avoid feeling permanently settled in Vienna, and thus forming sentimental links with a particular place. For many years I thought that my deliberate training of myself to feel that everything was temporary was a flaw in me, but later on, when I was forced time and again to leave every home I made for myself and saw everything around me fall apart, that mysterious lifelong sensation of not being tied down was helpful. It was a lesson I learnt early, and it has made loss and farewells easier for me.[20]

Imagine a refugee spirituality, an understanding of human longing and estrangement that not only honors those experiences of not-at-homeness but also affirms the hope of finding a home, finding oneself. The immigrant is migrating toward a home she's never been to before. She will arrive in a strange land and, in ways that surprise her, come to say, "I'm at home here," not least because someone is there to greet her and say, "Welcome home." The goal isn't returning home but being welcomed home in a place you weren't born, arriving in a strange land and being told, "You belong here."

But that would mean the human condition is suffused with a tenuousness, tethered to a beyond that is our hope but that doesn't magically alleviate the trials of the journey. The illusion of "settling down" in the everyday, settling for here, is one way to try to imagine you've arrived. But it is doomed to disappoint if you've been made for another shore. It's not a matter of settling down in the vagaries of the present or of settling for what you can find, and it's certainly not about living with the fears and injustices that fuel the hunger for elsewhere; it's about knowing *how* to make the journey, how to adopt the posture of the refugee who travels light.

One can see an oblique illustration of this in Zweig's learning to travel light. We experience the deprivation of his enforced sojourn, but we also see hints of what an open-handed journey might look like. Zweig recalls his collection of autograph manuscripts: a page from Leonardo's sketch-book; Napoleon's orders to his soldiers at Rivoli; a novel in proofs by Balzac, "every sheet of it a battlefield of corrections"; a Bach cantata; an aria from Handel. He had hoped to leave the collection to an institution that would agree to keep adding to it. "Then it would not have been a dead thing, but a living organism refining and adding to itself for fifty or a hundred years after my lifetime, becoming an increasingly beautiful whole."[21]

But it is not granted to our much-tried generation to make such plans for the future. When the Hitler period began and I left my house, my pleasure in collecting was gone, and so was any certainty that something of what I had done would last. For a while I kept parts of the collection in safes at friends' houses, but then, remembering Goethe's warning that museums and collections will ossify if they do not go on developing, I decided that instead, since I could not devote my own efforts to perfecting my collection, I would say goodbye to it. I gave part of it to the Viennese National Library when I left, mainly those items that I myself had been given as presents by friends and contemporaries. Part of it I sold, and what happened or is now happening to the rest of it does not weigh on my mind any more. I had enjoyed creating the collection more than I enjoyed the collection itself. So I do not mourn for what I have lost. For if there is one new art that we have had to learn, those of us who have been hunted down and forced into exile at a time hostile to all art and all collection, then it is the art of saying goodbye to everything that was once our pride and joy.[22]

A refugee spirituality does not make false promises for the present. It is not a prosperity gospel of peace and joy in the present. It warns of the allure of imagining one could settle in and for the present. An émigré spirituality is honest about what is not granted to our generation, so to speak—what is not granted to the human condition in this vale of tears. Hope is found in a certain art of saying goodbye, but also in looking ahead to the day when Someone will greet us with, "Welcome home"—and knowing how to navigate in the meantime.

LIKE CAMUS, AUGUSTINE was an African who ventured to Europe looking to make a name for himself—to "arrive" in both senses of the word, thereby securing his identity. And like Camus, he found there only a new sense of alienation. A provincial in the centers of cultural influence (first Rome, then Milan), he realized the limits of his welcome into the upper echelons of power. As his biographer Peter Brown reminds us, "Even the fully Latinized African of the fourth century remained somewhat alien. The opinion of the outside world was unanimous. Africa, in their opinion, was wasted on the Africans."[23] His accent is suspect, a stubborn hayseed halo around his eloquence.[24] Even when he achieves employment in the emperor's court, he surrounds himself with old friends from Africa who provide him with an outpost of Thagaste amid the busyness of Milan. He'll never be at home here.

But when he returns to Africa, he finds himself suspect there now too. His meteoric rise through Roman channels of power is a sign to some African compatriots (Berbers and Donatists) that he's gone over to the other side. He is tainted with "foreignness" even at home now. And so he is caught between worlds, between classes, falling through the cracks of belonging by virtue of his emigration and return. Indeed, one could describe him the way Zweig describes a fellow traveler: an "amphibian between two worlds."[25]

For Augustine, this experience turns out to be a hermeneutic key to the human condition, a place from which he read the Bible, understood himself, and grasped something about humanity's cosmic sojourn. In a provocative, creatively anachronistic proposal, historian Justo González sees in Augustine the makings of a mestizo and suggests that this experience of tenuous hybridity was both a burden and a fund for theological creativity. González summarizes the concept:

> To be a mestizo is to belong to two realities and at the same time not to belong to either of them. A Mexican-American reared in Texas among people of Euro-American culture is repeatedly told that he is a Mexican—that is, that he does not really belong in Texas. But if that Mexican-American crosses the border hoping to find there his land and his people, he is soon disappointed by being rejected, or at least criticized, as somewhat Americanized—or, as Mexicans would say, for being a *pocho*.[26]

"Augustine's restlessness," González observes, "was not due only to his distance from God, as he tells us in his *Confessions*, but also to the inner struggles of a person in whom two cultures, two legacies, two world visions clashed and mingled—in short, of a mestizo."[27] Even Augustine's home was hybrid, which prepared him for his later experiences of emigration and return, all informing a theology of the Christian life as one of migration, a quest for a home one has never seen. Joy is arriving at the home you've never been to.

One can hear this paradoxical notion—a homeland where one has never lived—in a letter to Nectarius in which Augustine praises him for his devotion to his *patria*, his hometown, but urges him to look for another country, a "much finer city," "a certain country beyond." The beautiful paradox is that this heavenly city is waiting to be discovered as *another* "hometown" by Nectarius, ready to welcome him as it already welcomed his father.[28] Your hometown is the place you're made for, not simply the place you've come from. Your hometown—where joy is found—is a place you arrive at and immediately feel "at home" in, even though you've never been there before. This is not the mere joy of return; it is the joy of the refugee who has found a home. For Augustine, this isn't just the situation of the expat; it is the human condition, we sojourners navigating our not-at-home-ness *and* our built-in hunger for a home, code-switching between comfort here in the world and longing to be anywhere but here, made for another world but immersed in this one, variously asking, "Are we there yet?" and "Do we *have* to go?"

This between-ness, as Augustine imagines it, is a dynamic space of movement. I am pulled in two different directions, and the question is how I'll navigate this sense that I find myself here ("thrown" here, as Heidegger might have put it) but with an inexplicable longing for somewhere else. I'm an alien here, even though "here" is the only place I've ever lived.[29] In contrast to Sisyphus's manufactured happiness—resolving to imagine his punishment *as* joy, settling for the situation in which he finds himself—Augustine imagines the human condition like that of the émigré in search of not just the security of a home but peace, rest, joy. One of the distinguishing markers of the happy life found in God is a joy and delight that could not be achieved otherwise—a rest and contentment that stems from *being found*. The "authentic happy life," Augustine concludes, is "to set one's joy on you, grounded in you and caused by you. That is the real thing, and there is no other."[30] Those found by God find in him "the joy that you yourself are to them."

Augustine frames this search as a quest, a pilgrimage to the country called joy, where we find peace and rest because we find ourselves in the God who welcomes us home. Like the exhausted refugee, fatigued by vulnerability, what we crave is *rest*. "You have made us for yourself, and our heart is restless until it rests in you."[31] This insight in the opening paragraph of the *Confessions* is echoed at the very end of book 13: "'Lord God, grant us peace; for you have given us all things' (Isa. 26:12), the peace of quietness, the peace of the sabbath."[32] The soul's hunger for peace is a longing for a kind of rest from anxiety and frantic pursuits—it is to rest *in* God. And for Augustine, to find this rest—to entrust ourselves to the one who holds us—is to find *joy*. "In your gift we find our rest," Augustine concludes. "There are you our joy. Our rest is our peace."[33] Joy, for Augustine, is characterized by a quietude that is the opposite of anxiety—the exhale of someone who has been holding her breath out of fear or worry or insecurity. It is the blissful rest of someone who realizes she no longer has to perform; she is loved. We find joy in the grace of God precisely because he is the one we don't have to prove anything to. But it is also the exhale of someone who has arrived—who can finally breathe after making it through the anxiety-inducing experience of the border crossing, seeking refuge, subject to the capricious whims of a world and system that could turn on her at any moment. What we long for is an escape not from creaturehood but from the fraught, harrowing experience of being human in a broken world. What we're hoping for is a place where a sovereign Lord can assure us, "You're safe here."

It's not that the temporal, material world is foreign to me, as if I'm a fallen angel who's been punished by being embodied (which is closer to the Platonism Augustine ultimately refused); it's that I've been made for enchantment. The earthy, embodied, material world that is all I've known would be "natural" for me if I didn't have a penchant for treating it as an end in itself. It's precisely when I try to make creation my home—when I disenchant it as an end in itself—that it becomes a foreign country, that "distant land" of the prodigal's wandering: arid, barren, a region of nothingness even if it's filled with earthly delights. As French theologian Henri de Lubac would later put it, we are made with a natural desire for the supernatural.[34] When I try to convince myself that "nature" is all I need—when I, like Camus, try to convince myself that exile is natural, that any other home is a fiction—I am effacing a built-in desire. And the suppression and deflection of that desire generates all kinds of pretzeled, frustrating machinations of self-denial. For Augustine, those moments of "uncanniness"—of *Unheimlich* not-at-home-ness—are like postcards from the self you're called to be.

The question is whether this tension of the between becomes a catalyst for pilgrimage—prompting me, like Abraham, to answer the call and "Go!"—or whether I try to decamp in that distant country, turning my exile into arrival, suppressing my sense that there must be something more, that another shore is calling. For Augustine, so much of our restlessness and disappointment is the result of trying to convince ourselves that we're already home. The alternative is not escapism; it is a refugee spirituality—unsettled yet hopeful, tenuous but searching, eager to find the hometown we've never been to.

LIKE HIS REALIST spirituality, Augustine's refugee spirituality is an account of what the Christian life feels like. The disciple as much as anyone finds herself *between*, on the way, fatigued yet hopeful. Baptism isn't a capsule that transports us to the end of the road. Conversion is not an arrival at our final destination; it's the acquisition of a compass.

Under the stunning Duomo in Milan is an archaeological area where visitors can see the remains of the baptismal font where Ambrose baptized Augustine during the Easter Vigil of 387. The octagonal shape of the large pool speaks to the hope of "eighth-day" renewal—the hope that catechumens, upon arising from the watery "grave," would be a new creation in Christ (2 Cor. 5:17). While it was Ambrose who broke through Augustine's deepest intellectual skepticism about Christianity, what he found in Ambrose, he tells us, was a father who showed kindness, welcomed him, enfolded him.[35] Augustine, unsettled and anxious, an African outsider in Milan, was welcomed by Ambrose as by an ambassador of the country for which he was made, for which he had been sighing all these years. Perhaps that's why, while I was in the cathedral proper, I was fascinated by the Chrismon of Saint Ambrose, preserved on the wall of the sanctuary (see figure 4). Constructed of the Chi Rho (a symbol consisting of the first two letters of the Greek word for Christ) and the Alpha and Omega of Revelation 22:13, it struck me how much the Chrismon looked like a compass, and how Ambrose had led Augustine to the one who is "the Way," setting him on the road with a new orientation. He emerged from the waters of baptism as an émigré with a new passport declaring his heavenly citizenship (Phil. 3:20). He had miles to go before he'd sleep, but now he knew where home was.

The Christian isn't just a pilgrim but a refugee, a migrant in search of refuge. The Christian life isn't just a pilgrimage but a journey of emigration. Augustine, in his writings, would often use the Latin word *peregrinatio* to speak of the Christian life, and most translations of his work render the cognates of *peregrinatio* in terms of pilgrimage. But that doesn't quite fit the journey Augustine is describing. Pilgrimage often has an Odyssean itinerary: a journey to a holy site only to later return home. This mimics the Neoplatonic journey of the soul "returning" to the One. But Augustine's *peregrinus* isn't on a return journey; he is setting out, like Abraham, for a place he's never been.[36] We are not just pilgrims on a sacred march to a religious site; we are migrants, strangers, resident aliens en route to a *patria*, a homeland we've never been to. God is the country we're looking for, "that place where true consolation of our migration is found."[37]

In fact, it is important that, as *peregrini*, we are *we* and not just *me*, the solo migrant. *Peregrinatio* is a social event. "The essential characteristic of the true Christian," for Augustine, "lies in his status as *peregrinus*, as belonging to a *societas peregrina*."[38] Like Israel, like migrants everywhere, we could never brave this treacherous road alone. Conversion is joining this caravan, not setting out alone. As one scholar has recently suggested, this community, this *civitas Dei*, this *societas peregrina*, is a tent city, a refugee camp on the run.[39] It is a city, a *civitas*, Sean Hannan argues, but perhaps we'd do better to look for a model of such a city not in New York or Milan but in the refugee camps in our world today, each its own metropolis: "Think of Dadaab in Kenya (population: 245,000), Bidi-Bidi in Uganda (285,000), and (somewhat closer to Augustine's Thagaste) the Sahrawi camps in the Algerian Maghreb (50,000–100,000, depending on which authority you consult)."[40] Each is a *civitas*, structured, organized, and governed in a sense; but their tented tenuousness is perhaps a better reminder of the *peregrini* than are hulking cathedrals of stone.

The city of God as tent city, as refugee camp, speaks to the vulnerability and risk of the life of faith, bringing out an essential aspect of Augustine's understanding of our journey. If we look at Augustine's understanding of *peregrinatio* through the synonyms of his preaching, we see an arduous picture of the Christian life, M. A. Claussen points out: "It is filled with labors and burdens, it is uncertain and long, it is hunger and thirst, sedition and temptation, a desert, filled with sighing, weeping, wailing, and tribulations."[41] This is a long way from the sham Joel Osteen sells as *Your Best Life Now*. If we want a snapshot of what the Christian life looks like, don't pay attention to "the malls and the megachurch stadiums" (as Josh Ritter puts it in his song "Golden Age of Radio"): look at the suffering hopeful in Calais, France, or in McAllen, Texas. It is a vulnerability that Zweig captures:

Only at the moment when, after some time spent in the applicants' waiting room, I was admitted to the British office dealing with these matters, did I really understand what exchanging my passport for a document describing me as an alien meant. I had had a right to my Austrian passport. It had been the duty of every Austrian consular official or police officer to issue it to me as an Austrian citizen with full civil rights. But I had had to ask for the favour of receiving this English document issued to me as an alien, and it was a favour that could be withdrawn at any time. Overnight I had gone down another step in the social scale. Yesterday I had still been a foreign guest with something of the status of a gentleman, spending his internationally earned money here and paying his taxes, but now I was an emigrant, a refugee.[42]

Zweig backhandedly highlights what Augustine sees as a feature of the migrant city of God: it is well aware of its *dependence*. If these tent cities remind us of the tenuousness of the migrant family that is the body of Christ, they also remind us that the migrant soul is one that is aware of its dependence and is animated by hope.

González sees in Augustine's experiences the fuel for his theological imagination: "Augustine combined all of this with his own mestizaje—he, who was both African and Roman, and therefore both and neither one nor the other—in order to develop a philosophy of history, a vision of God's action, that did not depend on Roman civilization, and in which even the Visigoths had a place."[43] The migrant soul, a stranger in the earthly city, citizen of the heavenly city, lives lightly. Not being at home anywhere, looking for the home that is the refuge of the city of God, the Christian can also, with a kind of sanctified indifference, manage to pitch her tent anywhere. This indifference is not quietist or escapist. Indeed, it is worth noting that Augustine was particularly sensitive to those seeking sanctuary in a very concrete, temporal sense. He preserved the basilica as a place of sanctuary and erred on the side of offering refuge even when it was a risk. As he once told his congregation, "There are three types of people who take refuge in the church: the good who are fleeing the wicked; the wicked fleeing from the good; and the wicked who are fleeing from the wicked. How can such a knot be untangled? It's better to give sanctuary to one and all."[44] It's no mistake that God enjoins his peregrinating people to be especially attuned to the fate of the vulnerable: widows, orphans, and strangers.

ANTHROPOLOGISTS TALK ABOUT what they call "stranger value": "While insiders find it difficult to see the world from any point of view other than their own, the pariah has no fixed position, no territory to defend, no interest to protect. As a visitor and sojourner, as one who is always being moved on, he is much freer than the good citizen to put himself in the place of another."[45] The pilgrim and sojourner has an outsider status that brings the gift of insight. Drawing on Hannah Arendt, anthropologist Michael Jackson talks about this "visiting imagination" as "the work of exiles": "The art of ethnography is to turn this deterritorialization to good account, to make a virtue out of not being at home in the world."[46]

My goal in the rest of this book is to introduce you to Augustine as an ancient ethnographer of our present, of *us*—someone who has "stranger value" both because he is a citizen migrating to kingdom come, never quite at home in the world, and as a stranger to our time who nonetheless seems to have read our mail, so to speak. In *On the Road*, Sal thought Dean was "the perfect guy for the road because he was actually born on the road." Augustine was also born on the road, in a way; indeed, he thinks we're all born on the road, on our way into self-imposed exile, looking for home in all the wrong places. The difference between Dean and Augustine is not their experience of the road; it's what they make of it. If you still find the chase exhilarating; if you're still convinced "the road is life"; if life to you feels like an open-top joyride in pursuit of the next experience, the next thrill, the next conquest, then Dean is likely going to look like your guide and exemplar.

But if the road has beat you down; if the sights have become predictable and tired, and there are nights that you look at your friends in the car and wonder, "What the hell are we doing? Please just let me out"; if you're weary from the chase, broken by the journey, tired of the disappointment, unsettled by a sense that you'd like to find some rest not in accomplishment but in welcome, then Augustine might be the stranger you could travel with for a while. Not because he's going to blow sunshine and tell you feel-good stories, and not because he's going to fast-track you to rest (beware of any religious types who roll up in a DeLorean promising time travel to either a nostalgic past or a pristine future). Augustine is the perfect guy for the road because he's been on it and is sympathetic to all our angst on the way. There's almost nothing you're going to tell him that he hasn't already heard. You'd be surprised by what a patient listener he is. He was born on the road, and he's seen right through "the road is life" philosophy. He knows who he is, whose he is, and where he's headed, and almost everything he writes is an effort to help fellow migrants on the way find an orientation that feels like peace. You might think of Augustine as offering a hitchhiker's guide to the cosmos for wandering hearts.

DETOURS ON THE WAY TO MYSELF

Wherein we embark,

looking for ourselves,

visiting the way stations

of a hungry soul,

wondering where this all

might lead—

and if there might be an end

to our striving.

FREEDOM : *How to Escape*

What do I want when I want to be liberated?

The road is iconic because it is the symbol of liberation. From *On the Road* to *Easy Rider* to *Thelma and Louise*, the road is a ribbon that wends away from convention, obligation, and the oppression of domesticity. Freedom looks like the top down, hair whipping brazenly in the wind, refusing to be constrained, en route to "Wide Open Spaces" (Dixie Chicks). It's hitting the road and heading west, loading up the car and leaving for college, hopping on a bus to New York City, backpacking through Europe, or hitchhiking to Memphis.

While modernity has made this myth almost universal, the mythology is particularly potent in the United States, land of the free, born from a fight for independence then gobbling up a continent with a network of railways and interstate highways. When you crest the Toano Range on I-80 and the salt flats of Utah stretch a hundred miles in front of you, it can feel like the vast horizon is an expanse of possibility that keeps unfolding under vaulted skies. Your soul swells with potential. It's why getting your driver's license is a coveted rite of passage, one of the only ones left in our culture. To put the key in the ignition and roll out of the driveway is the on-ramp to independence. On the road there's room to move, unhindered by walls and, more importantly, unconstrained by "their" rules, out from the hovering, watchful eye of the Man and your mom and Mr. Wilson next door. If we worship the automobile it's because it's the glossy god that gives us our freedom. So we build altars to the Corvette, the Mustang, and the motorcycle as vehicles that liberate us, symbols of our autonomy. "Here are the keys" is a quasi-sacramental pronouncement that unleashes you to finally be yourself. The highway is my way.

OF COURSE, THE road is already somebody else's idea of where you should go. The highway is not a blank slate; it is a network of channels laid down where many others wore a path before. The irony is that even when you're alone on the open road you're following somebody. To answer the call of the asphalt is to follow "them." But we're getting ahead of ourselves.

AUGUSTINE REMINDS US how ancient the identification of freedom with leaving is. Long before there were Shelby Mustangs and Route 66 and rebels without a cause, the prodigal was itching for freedom from the scowl of his father and the scolding of his mother. If freedom is the absence of constraint, it will never be found at home.

Augustine's arrival in Carthage as a student anticipates countless fraternity and sorority rushes in the centuries to come. Unfettered, with room to get his elbows (and various other appendages) out, he swells to fill more space, chasing all kinds of new opportunities and delights. He falls "in love with love," he recalls. "I rushed headlong into love, by which I was longing to be captured."[1] It's funny how we can consider being captured as "freedom" as long as we're the ones who choose it, like every time I click "Agree" and voluntarily give myself over to the whims of Google and Apple.

So the young Augustine uses his newfound freedom to devote himself to pursuits that will conscript him. His appetites become voracious. He will be captivated by theatrical shows, giving himself over to entertainments that will enslave him to his own passions. He falls in love with love, but he also falls in love with suffering, not unlike the way we love to mourn on social media.[2] Freedom is the right to be titillated, entertained, absorbed, all on one's own terms. Freedom is freedom *from*, and the way to get *from* is to leave.

This notion of freedom is the only freedom we know now: freedom as self-determination. The freedom to decide what is my own good is enshrined in Justice Anthony Kennedy's majority opinion in *Planned Parenthood v. Casey* (1992): "At the heart of liberty is the right to define one's own concept of existence, of meaning, of the universe, and of the mystery of human life."[3] Freedom means, "Hands off, I've got this. I know what I want." I'll know I'm free when I get to decide what's good for me, when every choice is a blank check of opportunity and possibility.

In fact, we call such freedom "authenticity" and don't even realize how much this is a trickle-down effect from existentialist philosophers like Heidegger and Sartre. In the laborious prose of *Being and Time*, Heidegger sketches the outlines of many a Hollywood screenplay to follow. Buried in the Teutonic heaviness of being-towards-death, what really interests Heidegger is the way my confrontation with death can disclose *possibility* in ways I never consider when I'm immersed in conformity to the tired habits of mass society (what Heidegger calls "the they" [*das Man*], as in what "they" always say you should do). The point isn't to be fixated on death or to try to imagine what it is like to die (impossible, for Heidegger); rather, in facing up to my death there is the possibility of my realizing that nothing is set in stone for me—the horizon of possibility is endless. Being-towards-death, Heidegger says, is to live in anticipation, to live toward possibility.[4] It's the realization that what's possible is up to me and only me (my "ownmost" possibility, as Heidegger puts it): there is a potential for me to be if only I will realize it, if I will answer the "call."[5] But this call isn't coming from someone else. It isn't just another mode of conformity. I'm calling myself. And that is authenticity: realizing *some* possibility on my own terms.[6] It doesn't matter what you choose; what matters is that you choose. Freedom is getting to make up what counts as the Good for yourself.

THIS IS NOT unlike what Augustine thought freedom was when he first made his way to Carthage and later to Rome. What he hadn't anticipated, and what he tried to ignore even as he was experiencing it, was the exhaustion of it all. What he envisioned as freedom—the removal of constraints—started to feel like a punishment. The obliteration of boundaries looked like liberation to the young Augustine; but he could feel himself dissolving in the resulting amorphousness. When you're swimming in a tiny aboveground pool at your cousin's house and keep bumping up against the walls, you start wishing they weren't there. But when, in your rambunctiousness, you succeed in knocking them down, you realize the pool didn't get bigger: it just disappeared. You're left in the soggy ruins. "I was storm-tossed," Augustine confesses in retrospect, "gushing out, running every which way, frothing into thin air in my filthy affairs."[7] Freedom to be myself starts to feel like losing myself, dissolving, my own identity slipping between my fingers.

What's emerging here isn't just an admission of failure; rather, it's the problem of getting exactly what you want. In the reframing of his experiences, Augustine comes to a radically different way of thinking about freedom. When you've been eaten up by your own freedom, and realize the loss of guardrails only meant ending up in the ditch, you start to wonder whether freedom is all it's cracked up to be—or whether freedom might be something other than the absence of constraint and the multiplication of options. For Patty Berglund in Jonathan Franzen's novel *Freedom*, this illusion of freedom is pulled back in a moment of self-pity. "Where did the self-pity come from? The inordinate volume of it? By almost any standard, she led a luxurious life. She had all day every day to figure out some decent and satisfying way to live, and yet all she ever seemed to get for all her choices and all her freedom was more miserable. The autobiographer is almost forced to the conclusion that she pitied herself for being so free."[8]

The luxury of unfettered agency coupled with the multiplication of options should be a formula for liberation. But Patty, like so many others, finds that this only leads to a different kind of misery. For a long while, the pleasures offered by such "freedom" can give the allure of fullness; imagining ourselves denied for so long, the new possibilities opened up by taking off the yoke feel like the realization of new potential—like *this* is what it's all about, what we're made for, what freedom feels like. But then, like the child on a field trip sidling up to the dinner buffet without his mother curtailing his appetite, he slowly reaches the point where his freedom feels like nausea. Engorged, he's rethinking his choices. On the far side of such freedom, sometimes a long way down the road, is regret. The shadow cast by this kind of freedom can be very dark. "I loved my own ways, not yours," Augustine realized. "The liberty I loved was merely that of a runaway."[9] Hounded, haunted, pursued, exhausted: sounds like an ugly sort of freedom.

In fact such freedom often slides back into its own form of enslavement. In his Carthage revel, Augustine made his way "to the shackles of gratification, and was gleefully trussed up in those afflicting bonds."[10] This dynamic of freedom lost—especially a lost freedom experienced *as if* it were liberation—would occupy Augustine for the rest of his life. Indeed, when he recalls the cataclysm of his conversion, the revolution of love that grace brought about, it comes down to a question of freedom because he had ultimately come to see himself in chains. If he had hoped to find himself—and freedom—by escaping the constraints of home, by the time he's in Milan, Augustine realizes he is his own worst master. His only hope is to escape, but he has concluded that is impossible. He is Sisyphus. But he gave himself the stone.

It is a terrible and terrifying thing to know what you want to be and then realize you're the only one standing in your way—to want with every fiber of your soul to be someone different, to escape the "you" you've made of yourself, only to fall back into the self you hate, over and over and over again. After the thrill of independence and experiments in self-actualization, drinking your so-called "potential for Being" to the dregs, when the exhaustion starts to set in and then eventually morphs into a kind of self-disgust, you can reach a point where you *know* you want a different life but are enchained to the one you've made.

This was the point Augustine eventually reached. When he glimpsed a different way of life, seeing the example of peers who had chosen the Way and relinquished power and privilege and success to follow the One humiliated on a cross, he found new desires bubbling up within him: "I sighed after such freedom," he recalls, "but was bound not by an iron imposed by anyone else but by the iron of my own choice."[11] He's back to feeling bound, hemmed in, constricted. But now the culprit isn't Mother or the Man; *c'est moi*. The freedom he chased was a chain in disguise. What Augustine offers now is a rereading of his own so-called freedom.

How did his freedom end up being a prison? Augustine identifies the links in the chain that read like a chronicle of the road he's been on. "The consequence of a distorted will is passion. By servitude to passion, habit is formed, and habit to which there is no resistance becomes necessity. By these links, as it were, connected one to another (hence my term a chain), a harsh bondage held me under restraint."[12] The first link in the chain that binds him was his own free choice. The trajectory here will feel familiar: the night he made that choice, he caught a taste for blood, as it were, a taste for flesh, a passion that primed him to try again. Eventually, that satisfaction of the passion settles into the predictability of a habit—probably just about the time that it's no longer a pleasure. The honeymoon is over; the thrill has lost the sheen of novelty; one hit isn't enough. But by then the habit has become a necessity and what I *want* is a moot point: this is what I'll chase because this is what I need.

At first it looks like he's blaming someone else. "The enemy had a grip on my will and so made a chain for me to hold me prisoner." But that's only because he gave the enemy the key. "I was responsible for the fact that habit had become so embattled against me; for it was with my consent that I came to the place in which I did not wish to be."[13] I am my own jailer.

WHAT AUGUSTINE DESCRIBES is the "freedom" of the addict. The habit that becomes a necessity, the sighing after an impossible freedom, the longing for a new will, the despair of ever overcoming it. Indeed, he goes on to draw a picture of someone who can't get out of bed, and it sounds a lot like an existential hangover: "The burden of the world weighed me down with a sweet drowsiness such as commonly occurs during sleep." He felt like "those who would like to get up but are overcome by deep sleep and sink back again." He hates himself for doing it, but at the same time "he is glad to take a bit longer."[14] But then he realizes this isn't just laziness; it's a kind of involuntary paralysis, like waking up to find your limbs heavy, foreign, unresponsive to your wishes. Unable to say what you want, even your screaming is internal, and you wonder if someone will find you and deliver you from the tomb that is your bed. This is what the Fleet Foxes call "helplessness blues."

To read Augustine in the twenty-first century is to gain a vantage point that makes all of our freedom look like addiction. When we imagine freedom only as negative freedom[15]—freedom *from* constraint, hands-off liberty to choose what I want—then our so-called freedom is actually inclined to captivity. When freedom is mere voluntariness, without further orientation or goals, then my choice is just another means by which I'm trying to look for satisfaction. Insofar as I keep choosing to try to find that satisfaction in finite, created things—whether it's sex or adoration or beauty or power—I'm going to be caught in a cycle where I'm more and more disappointed in those things *and* more and more dependent on those things. I keep choosing things with diminishing returns, and when that becomes habitual, and eventually necessary, then I forfeit my ability to choose. The thing has me now.

In her remarkable book *The Recovering*, Leslie Jamison provides both an insider account of addiction (and recovery) and a curated anthology of how writers have borne witness to their captivity. Addiction, she says, "is always a story that has already been told, because it inevitably repeats itself, because it grinds down—ultimately, for everyone—to the same demolished and reductive and recycled core: *Desire. Use. Repeat.*"[16] As a clinician later described it to her, addiction always ends up as a "narrowing of repertoire": life contracts to a fixation on what you can't live without, and the rhythms of a day, a life, are engineered to secure this thing that never satisfies, is never enough.[17] The shame of this has its own perverted delusion: an addict's pride in the genius it takes to satisfy an addiction.

But you can't self-help your way out of this. Every addict who breaks free of this bondage comes to that realization. "The Big Book of AA," Jamison notes, "was initially called *The Way Out*. Out of what? Not just drinking, but the claustrophobic crawl space of the self."[18] Coming to the end of oneself is the way out of disordered freedom. And so the irony: my freedom of choice brings me to the point where I need someone else to give me a will that is actually free. And not merely free to choose—since that's what got me here in the first place—but free to choose the good. If freedom is going to be more than mere freedom *from*, if freedom is the *power* of freedom *for*, then I have to trade autonomy for a different kind of dependence. Coming to the end of myself is the realization that I'm dependent on someone other than myself if I'm going to be truly free. Jamison recalls her own epiphany in this regard: "I needed to believe in something stronger than my willpower." Her own willpower was inadequate to secure her liberation. "This willpower was a fine-tuned machine, fierce and humming, and it had done plenty of things—gotten me straight A's, gotten my papers written, gotten me through cross-country training runs—but when I'd applied it to drinking, the only thing I felt was that I was turning my life into a small, joyless clenched fist." The turning point of recovering was her coming to the end of herself, turning outward and upward to what AA simply calls the Higher Power: "The Higher Power that turned sobriety into more than deprivation was simply *not me*. That was all I knew."[19]

A reflection from Augustine is poignant and encouraging here: "To desire the aid of grace is the beginning of grace."[20] If you come to the end of yourself and wonder if there's help and are surprised to find yourself at times hoping for a grace from beyond, it's a sign that grace is already at work. Keep asking. You don't have to believe in order to ask. Here's the thing: You can ask for help believing too. Wanting help is its own nascent trust. The desire for grace is the first grace. Coming to the end of your self-sufficiency is the first revelation.

THIS OUTWARD, UPWARD turn is Augustinian. It is the posture of a dependence that liberates, a reliance that releases. Once you've realized you need someone *not you*, you also look at constraint differently. What used to look like walls hemming you in start to look like scaffolding holding you together. If freedom used to look like the no-obligation bliss of self-actualization, once that unfettered freedom has become its own bondage you look at obligations as a restraint that gives you a purpose, a center, the rebar of identity. When Augustine looks back at the way his younger self poured his soul out into sand, he cries: "If only someone could have imposed restraint on my disorder. That would have transformed to good purpose the fleeting experiences of beauty in these lowest of things, and fixed limits to indulgence in their charms." Instead, "I in my misery seethed and followed the driving force of my impulses, abandoning you. I exceeded all the bounds set by your law."[21]

We might be surprised by how many people are hoping someone will give them boundaries, the gift of restraint, channeling their desires and thereby shoring up a sense of self. Indeed, there may be a generational dynamic to this, where boomers—whose revolution of negative freedom remade the world—imagine younger generations wanting the same but instead hear those young people asking for the gift of constraint, the charity of boundaries.[22]

This is not unlike Augustine's frustration with his father. Rather than encouraging his son to channel his desires, Augustine's father only encouraged his frizzante dissolution with "the sort of tipsy glee in which this sorry world has forgotten you, its creator, and fallen in love instead with something you've created; it's from the unseen wine of a self-willfulness distorted and tipped down into the depths."[23] He was being parented by someone still drunk on negative freedom, who hadn't yet reached the point of realizing this wasn't freedom at all. As he'll later write to some monks in North Africa, "Free choice is sufficient for evil, but hardly for good."[24] Free choice got me into this mess, he realizes, but it can't get me out.

Augustine needs help. The most revolutionary hope would be a new will—one with not only the desire but the *power* to choose the good. But the help Augustine needs can't come from just anyone; it has to come from Someone who has the power to give him this power, Someone with the mercy to share, Someone who is a giver. He needs Someone like the prodigal's father, who was a giver from the get-go. And so, back in a garden once again, he can see home, as it were, from a long way off.

But to reach that destination one does not use ships or chariots or feet. It was not even necessary to go the distance I had come from the house to where we were sitting. The one necessary condition, which meant not only going but at once arriving there, was to have the will to go—provided only that the will was strong and unqualified, not the turning and twisting first this way, then that, of a will half-wounded, struggling with one part rising up and the other part falling down.[25]

Augustine needs the help of Someone who can resurrect a will, gift him with a freedom he's never had. He's tried the alternative and is exhausted: "Without you, what am I to myself but a guide to my own self-destruction?"[26] Do you really trust yourself with yourself?

Augustine's account honors the complexity of our experience. He recognizes that *knowing* what to do isn't enough. He names that experience of feeling divided, like there are two (or more!) of me. "The self which willed to serve was identical with the self which was unwilling. It was I. I was neither wholly willing nor wholly unwilling. So I was in conflict with myself and was dissociated from myself." But even this dissociation and self-alienation "came about against my will."[27] In one of his earliest works, shortly after his conversion, Augustine framed this as the paradox of our unhappiness: "How does anyone suffer an unhappy life by his will, since absolutely no one wills to live unhappily?"[28] They're unhappy, not because they choose to be but because their will is in such a condition that it can't choose what would ultimately make them happy.

He's "torn apart" in this painful condition; "old loves" hold him back; "the overwhelming force of habit was saying to me: 'Do you think you can live without them?'" His heart is a battleground of loves, manifesting in a body that is contorted and weeping.[29] Is there a *Way Out*, as the recovery program put it?

GRACE IS THE answer to that question. Grace is the answer to the call for help. Grace isn't just forgiveness, a covering, an acquittal; it is an infusion, a transplant, a resurrection, a revolution of the will and wants. It's the hand of a Higher Power that made you and loves you reaching into your soul with the gift of a new will. Grace *is* freedom.

But the paradox (or irony)—especially to those of us conditioned by the myth of autonomy, who can imagine freedom only as freedom *from*—is that this gracious infusion of freedom comes wrapped in the gift of constraint, the gift of the law, a command that calls us into being.[30] This was Augustine's experience: in that fabled garden, he hears children chanting a curious song, "Pick up and read, pick up and read." The fateful moment is hermeneutic: "I *interpreted* it solely as a divine command."[31] The tortured soul will be called into new life by obeying a command. And what was that command? To read. And so Augustine, in a way that is almost cartoonish, picks up the volume of Paul's epistles lying nearby, breaks it open, and seizes on the first verse he sees—which, not unsurprisingly, is also a command: "Not in riots and drunken parties, not in eroticism and indecencies, not in strife and rivalry, but put on the Lord Jesus Christ" (Rom. 13:13–14). "I neither wished nor needed to read further," Augustine recalls. "At once, with the last words of this sentence, it was as if a light of relief from all anxiety flooded into my heart."[32]

Augustine deconstructs our false dichotomies between grace and obedience, freedom and constraint, because he has a radically different conception of freedom that we've forgotten in modernity: freedom not as permission but as power, the freedom of graced empowerment, freedom *for*. Such freedom doesn't expand with the demolishing of boundaries or the evisceration of constraints; rather, it flourishes when a good will is channeled toward the Good by constraints that are gifts. That's not the shape of a ho-hum life of rule-following; it's an invitation to a life that is secure enough to risk, centered enough to be courageous, like the rails of a roller coaster that let you do loop after loop. It's the grace that guards your being, the gift that gives you your self again. It's why the father exclaims upon the prodigal's return: "This son of mine was dead and is alive again" (Luke 15:24).

THERE IS A scandal here for our autonomous sense of entitlement: this new will, this graced freedom, is sheer gift. It can't be earned or accomplished, which is an affront to our meritocratic sensibilities. "The human will does not attain grace through its freedom, but rather attains its freedom through grace."[33] If Augustine spent half his life battling the heresy of Pelagianism—the pretension that the human will was sufficient to choose its good—it's because he saw it as the great lie that left people enchained to their dissolute wills. And no one is more Pelagian than we moderns.

But it's a long way from that garden to kingdom come. Augustine has many miles to go before he sleeps. If he might have first been enthused about some here-and-now attainment of perfection, then eventually his own experience, and the realities of pastoral care, disabused him of any illusions that this struggle is over. What we see across his letters and sermons and subsequent writing is an understanding of renewed freedom that reflects the temporal journey of the pilgrim soul. The story of the soul is still unfolding. Grace is a game-changer, not a game-ender. I'm not who I used to be; I'm on the way to being who I'm called to be; but I'm not there yet, Augustine counsels. His spiritual realism harbors no illusions about hasty arrival even as it nourishes his unflagging hope of getting there.

The graced soul gifted with freedom is still on the way, still sighing after an ultimate release from the parts of myself I hate and hide. This longing, for Augustine, is eschatological—a kingdom-come hunger: "What shall be more free than free choice when it is unable to be enslaved to sin?"[34] It's not that nothing's changed. Grace gives a power I couldn't have found in myself. So now I'm on this road strung between the Fall and the Parousia. I'm better off than Adam, but I'm not yet home. "The first freedom of the will was therefore to be able not to sin; the final freedom will be much greater: not to be able to sin."[35] My graced freedom in Christ now is better than that "first freedom" given at creation, though even that first freedom was a grace.[36] A "second grace . . . more potent" has made it possible for me, even now, to choose the good: a grace "by which it also comes to pass that one wills, and wills so greatly, wishing with so strong an ardor, that he overcomes."[37] But I'm still awaiting a "final" freedom, when the vestiges of my old will are eviscerated, and there are no more mornings when I wake up hating myself, ashamed, even if I "know" I'm forgiven. That grace has already broken in like a dawn; I'm waiting for the splendor of its noontide light that never ends and for the shadows of my old self to dissolve.

The Christian life is a pilgrimage of hope. We live between the first and the final freedom; we are still on the way. Grateful for the second grace, we await the final.[38] And we are emboldened in our waiting on the way by the example of the martyrs. They give us hope that we might find the power to choose well.

> In fact, greater freedom is necessary against so many great temptations that did not exist in Paradise—a freedom defended and fortified by the gift of perseverance, so that this world, with all its loves and terrors and errors, may be overcome. The martyrdom of the saints has taught us this. In the end, using free choice with no terrors and moreover against the command of the terrifying God, Adam did not stand fast in his great happiness, in his ready ability not to sin. The martyred saints, though, have stood fast in their faith, even though the world—I do not say "terrified" them, but rather savagely attacked them—in order that they not stand fast. . . . Where does this come from, if not by God's gift?[39]

These martyrs give us hope because, in fact, they are just like us: although their wills had been enslaved, they were "set free by Him Who said: 'If the Son sets you free, then you shall truly be free' [John 8:36]."[40]

WHAT DOES IT look like to live in such hope on the way? It takes practice. It is a life characterized by clear-eyed self-knowledge, for starters. Such self-knowledge Augustine learned from Ambrose. As he wrote to a group of monks in Marseille, citing the Bishop of Milan, "'Our hearts and our thoughts are not in our power.' Everyone who is humble and genuinely religious recognizes that this is entirely true."[41] At the end of the tract, he returns to this insight from Ambrose with further practical advice, pointing out that the same person who said, "our hearts and our thoughts are not in our power" also says, "Who is so happy as one who always ascends in his heart? But without divine assistance who can make it happen?"[42] And where do we learn to turn our hearts upward?

The language would have been all too familiar: this is the *sursum corda*, the opening invocation of the Eucharist: "Lift up your hearts. We lift them up to the Lord!" Where do we learn to live into this freedom on the way? Where do we learn the graced dependence that sets us free? It's not magic, Augustine counsels: look no further than "the sacraments of the faithful."[43] The cadences of worship are the rhythms where we learn to be free.

Freedom takes practice; the liberation of dependence has its own scripts. This has nothing to do with ritualistic earning, let alone with some bottom-up willpower on our part. To the contrary, the point of the sacraments is that they are embodied conduits of grace that nourish new habits.[44] We can see the echo of this insight in Jamison's account of AA meetings:

> Meetings worked in all kinds of different ways. Some had a speaker who gave her story, and then other people shared in response. Others started with everyone taking turns reading paragraphs of an alcoholic's story from the Big Book, or with someone choosing a topic: Shame. Not forgetting the past. Anger. Changing habits. I began to realize why it was important to have a script, a set of motions you followed: First we'll say this invocation. Then we'll read from this book. Then we'll raise hands. It meant you

didn't have to build the rituals of fellowship from scratch. You lived in the caves and hollows of what had worked before.[45]

A bit like following a path someone has already blazed for you. On the road, you're always already following somebody. The question is: Who are you following and where are they headed?

This deconstructs the myth of authenticity bound up with negative freedom. In that story, I'm authentic if I'm "sincere," and I'm only sincere if I act as if I'm making things up from scratch, expressing something "inside" me that's all my own. Augustine—and Jamison—are turning that on its head. You *do* to *be*. Jamison realized that learned dependence on a Higher Power required the awkward, messy business of getting on her knees to pray. "I understand arranging my body into a certain position twice a day as a way to articulate commitment rather than a bodily lie, a false pretense."[46] She had to overcome her nagging sense that she shouldn't say what she didn't already believe.

> Years later, recovery turned this notion upside down—it made me start to believe that I could do things *until* I believed in them, that intentionality was just as authentic as unwilled desire. Action could coax belief rather than testifying to it. "I used to think you had to believe to pray," David Foster Wallace once heard at a meeting. "Now I know I had it ass-backwards." . . . Showing up for a meeting, for a ritual, for a conversation—this was an act that could be true no matter what you felt as you were doing it. Doing something without knowing if you believed it—that was proof of sincerity, rather than its absence.[47]

How do you practice your way into freedom, depending on the grace of the God who loves you, turning your heart out and up? Join the community of practice that is the body of Christ, lifting up your heart to the One who gave himself for you. You might be surprised to see how committing yourself to such a ritual, keeping such an obligation, translates into freedom and liberation.

IN GRETA GERWIG'S moving film *Lady Bird*, we meet a young woman who embodies the quest for freedom as escape. Tired of the bored, backward backwaters of Sacramento, bristling at the nagging authority of her mother, embarrassed by her father's lack of ambition, the young heroine refuses even the name she was given, imposition that it is. Demanding to be called "Lady Bird" is just one of her acts of defiance as she chomps at the bit to get away to college, anywhere but Sacramento. ("Is that your given name?" a teacher asks her. "I gave it to myself. It's given to me by me." Freedom is receiving gifts from yourself.)

But at the end of the film she "comes home" without leaving her college campus. She calls her parents and leaves a voicemail. "Hi Mom and Dad. It's me, Christine. It's the name you gave me. It's a good one." Maybe the imposition was a gift after all. Maybe being named without your choosing is a sign that you're loved.

She then speaks more directly to her mother. As she does, images of Sacramento bathed in golden light are accompanied by the plaintive soundtrack of "Reconcile" by Jon Brion. "Hey, Mom, did you feel emotional the first time you drove in Sacramento? I did, and I wanted to tell you, but we weren't really talking when it happened. All those bends I've known my whole life, and stores and . . . the whole thing."

We next see images of Christine driving around Sacramento, quietly awed and grateful, spliced with images of her mother doing the same. "I wanted to tell you. I love you. Thank you. I'm . . . thank you."

Turns out, the "confines" of Sacramento were the scaffolding that gave her an identity; it was her Catholic school that made her compassionate; it was the "imposing" love of her mother that gave her the confidence to be herself. Home made her free.

Augustine found a Father waiting for him after he ran away. "You alone are always present even to those who have taken themselves far from you . . . after travelling many rough paths," he testifies. "And you gently wipe away their tears, and they weep yet more and rejoice through their tears. . . . Where was I when I was seeking for you? You were there before me, but I had departed from myself. I could not even find myself, much less you."[48] But then it turns out that being free isn't about leaving; it's about being found.

Gabriel Marcel, a Christian among the existentialists, appreciated our road-hunger. Marcel described humanity as *homo viator*, "itinerate man." But he was staunchly critical of Sartre's view of freedom. Freedom isn't digging a tunnel to escape, he counseled; it's digging down into yourself. In a 1942 lecture, Marcel appeals to the wisdom of Gustave Thibon, friend of Simone Weil.

> You feel you are hedged in; you dream of escape; but beware of mirages. Do not run or fly away in order to get free: rather dig in the narrow place which has been given you; you will find God there and everything. God does not float on your horizon, he sleeps in your substance. Vanity runs, love digs. If you fly away from yourself, your prison will run with you and will close in because of the wind of your flight; if you go deep down into yourself it will disappear in paradise.[49]

Or, as an itinerant Rabbi once said, "Whoever loses their life for my sake will find it" (Matt. 10:39).

AMBITION : *How to Aspire*

What do I want when I want to be noticed?

Ambition is a many-splendored, much-maligned thing. Your take depends on what demons you're trying to exorcise. If you're surrounded by prideful, power-hungry egomaniacs bent on making a name for themselves through Babelian endeavors, ambition looks ugly, monstrous, and domineering. But if you're surrounded by placid, passive, go-with-the-flow, aw-shucks folk who are leaving unused gifts on the table and failing to respond to their calling, then ambition looks like faithfulness. Sometimes ambition is ugly; sometimes the critique of ambition is uglier, as when powerful white men worry that others (brown women, say) are getting "uppity."

Ambition isn't any single thing; it can't be simply celebrated or de-monized. A recent collection of meditations on ambition by writers and poets gets at its many facets. If we were to think of ambition as a jewel, we could thus envision these different writers donning their loupes to consider it from different angles, approaching the phenomenon from their own personal histories. Some find an enticing glint, as in Jeanne Murray Walker's meditation on the gift of encouraging ambition in young women, drawing on her own experience when she was young. "It was my mother's ambition for her children to have ambition," Walker recalls, for example. "My ambition is to write poetry that defeats time. . . . This ambition isn't a drive for power in the world," she continues. "It feels more like a journey driven by curiosity." Here is ambition that should be stewarded and fanned into flame. "Either we are called to greatness," Scott Cairns remarks, "or we are not called at all."[1]

Others peer closer and see impurities, even fakes—as when Emilie Griffin gazes closely at the alleged diamond of ambition and finds only the zirconia of a hunger for fame. There is a shadow side of such aspiration. "On reflection," confesses Eugene Peterson, "I realized that I had become busy, a bastard form of ambition." "Ambition carries us into terrible places," suggests Erin McGraw (and I want to encourage her to add the qualifier "can"). Luci Shaw wards off "celebrity and fame, the bastard offsprings of unfettered ambition," while Griffin warns us about the "goddess" of fame—warnings that are especially germane for an evangelical subculture so susceptible to the cult of celebrity.[2]

If you keep walking around the phenomenon of ambition, you'll start to note a couple of features. First, the opposite of ambition is *not* humility; it is sloth, passivity, timidity, and complacency. We sometimes like to comfort ourselves by imagining that the ambitious are prideful and arrogant so that those of us who never risk, never aspire, never launch out into the deep get to wear the moralizing mantle of humility. But this imagining is often just thin cover for a lack of courage, even laziness. Playing it safe isn't humble. Second, it is the *telos* of ambition that distinguishes good from bad, separating faithful aspiration from self-serving aggrandizement. Augustine never stopped being ambitious. What changed was the target, the goal, the *how* of his striving. What do I love when I long for achievement? That is the Augustinian question.

AUGUSTINE DRANK IN ambition with his mother's milk. If the scrappy provincial was hankering to make it in Carthage, then Rome, climbing the ladder of recognition all the way to Milan, it's in no small part because he was propelled by his parents. Like many before and after him, the map of Augustine's aspiration was drawn by his parents. His ambition was imposed by the expectations of parents with their own ambitions. One of the only times you'll hear a criticism of his mother is when Augustine thinks back to why his parents sent him to school. "They gave no consideration to the use that I might make of the things they forced me to learn. The objective they had in view was merely to satisfy the appetite for wealth and for glory, though the appetite is insatiable, the wealth is in reality destitution of spirit, and the glory something to be ashamed of."[3] That this endangered his soul was hardly their concern. "My family did not try to extricate me from my headlong course. . . . The only concern was that I should learn to speak as effectively as possible."[4] Like Andre Agassi, who hated tennis because it was his father's dream, Augustine hated learning in no small part because his parents treated it so instrumentally, as a means to fulfill their own ladder-climbing hopes, living vicariously through the son who had no choice but to endure it.

When he was fifteen, Augustine was called home from his studies in Madauros so that his family could save up for a better education—the next rung—in Carthage. His recounting of the situation is dripping with disdain: "During that time funds were gathered in preparation for a more distant absence at Carthage, for which my father had more enthusiasm than cash." Many who were wealthy didn't invest in their children's education in this way, and so neighbors praised Patrick for this investment. "But this same father did not care what character before you I was developing, or how chaste I was so long as I possessed a cultured tongue—though my culture really meant a desert uncultivated by you, God."[5]

Justo González sees in this an experience that is familiar to immigrant children—a vicarious, imposed ambition. "One may see in Monica signs of a social mestizaje that was taking place—a mestizaje in which some among the 'Africans' sought to climb within the social Roman ladder, very much as immigrants today who, while insisting in the value of their ancestral cultures, insist also in having their children learn the language of their adopted country and leave aside their own culture, so that they may have a great chance at social and economic success."[6] Monica the tiger mom.

But imposed ambition can come from elsewhere. In Wallace Stegner's *Crossing to Safety*, his micro-epic novel about two academic couples across a lifetime, he traces the ambition that Charity, the daughter of an eminent classics professor, channels into her husband, Sid, a young English professor whose fault, in her eyes, is that he loves literature rather than the tenure game. Their best friends, Larry and Sally Morgan, reflect on what this imposed ambition has done to Sid. "He's always comparing himself, or getting compared to other people," Sally observes. "Charity sometimes compares him to you, and it isn't fair. You're a producer, he's a consumer, a sort of connoisseur."[7] When Charity reasserts her expectations of Sid, giving him a to-do list of ambition that would have him spend his summer writing criticism of Browning, Sid just wants to write poetry and learn Italian well enough to revere Dante in the original. At heart he is a dilettante in the truest sense: he just wants to *delight* in these things. In an earlier discussion, Larry tells Sally that Sid's articles on Browning are unremarkable: "'What's the matter with them?' Sally asks. 'Nothing in particular. Everything in general. His heart isn't in them. Only her heart is.'"[8]

The saddest thing about imposed ambition is that it nonetheless forms us. Our resentment doesn't inoculate us. Just because others set the path for our hearts doesn't mean we don't run there.

EVEN IF THE son's ambition was originally imposed by his parents, it eventually came to be owned by the son. "I wanted to distinguish myself as an orator for a damnable and conceited purpose, namely delight in human vanity."[9] In his twenties, the chase is all his. As a "teacher of the arts they call liberal," he was really after something else: "We pursued the empty glory of popularity, ambitious for the applause of the audience at the theatre when entering for verse competitions to win a garland of mere grass."[10] What are we looking for in our ambition? What do we hope to find at the end of our aspirations? In Augustine's experience—like our own—the answer is complicated. There is a bundle of hopes and hungers bound up with our ambitions, but so often they boil down to the twin desires to win and to be noticed, domination and attention—to win the crown and be seen doing it.

Augustine's map of this particular terrain of the hungry heart is as useful as ever because so little has changed. When Augustine reflects on ambition, he's really delving into the dynamics of *fame*. Could anything be more contemporary? We live in an age where everybody's famous. We've traded the hope of immortality for a shot at going viral. What is Instagram if not a platform for attention? Arcade Fire's song "Creature Comfort" is a chilling assessment of the extent to which the quest for attention has almost become synonymous with the *conatus essendi*, our reason to be. And if we can't have it, we'd rather not be. We

> Stand in the mirror
> and wait for the feedback
> Saying God, make me famous
> If you can't, just make it painless.

But naming the symptoms is easy. The challenge is diagnosing the disease. The question is: What do we want when we want attention? What are we hoping for when we aspire to win this game of being noticed?

For Augustine, the only way to get to the root of this desire is to understand it as a spiritual craving. That's why we can only truly understand disordered ambition if we read it as a kind of idolatry. If our ambition becomes a roadblock to peace, an inhibitor that robs us of the rest and joy we're looking for, it's because we've substituted something in place of the end for which we were made.

The point of discussing ambition in terms of idolatry isn't denunciation; it's diagnostic. Our idolatries are less like conscious decisions to believe a falsehood and more like learned dispositions to hope in what will disappoint. Our idolatries are not intellectual; they are affective—instances of disordered love and devotion. Idolatry is caught more than it is taught. We practice our way into idolatries, absorb them from the water in which we swim. Hence our idolatries often reflect the ethos of our environments. To consider ambition through the lens of idolatry is not to wag our finger in judgment but to specify the theological and spiritual nature of disorder. Augustine wants you to consider: What if, buried in your ambition, is a desire for something more, someone else? Might that explain the persistent disappointment?

For Augustine, we are made for joy. Joy is another name for the rest we find when we give ourselves over to the One who, for the joy that was set before him, gave himself for us. We find joy when we look for the satisfaction of our hungers in the Triune God who will never leave us or forsake us, when we find our enjoyment in an immortal God whose love is unfailing. That is rightly ordered love, and it is rightly ordered worship.

What, then, is idolatry? Idolatry, on this account, isn't just a problem because it's "false" worship, on the register of truth, or merely a transgression of a commandment (though it is both of those). Existentially, the problem with idolatry is that it is an exercise in futility, a penchant that ends in profound dissatisfaction and unhappiness. Idolatry, we might say, doesn't "work"—which is why it creates restless hearts. In idolatry we are enjoying what we're supposed to be using. We are treating as ultimate what is only penultimate; we are heaping infinite, immortal expectations on created things that will pass away; we are settling on some aspect of the *creation* rather than being referred through it to its *Creator*. Augustine describes this by using the metaphor of a journey: disordered love is like falling in love with the boat rather than the destination.[11] The problem is that the boat won't last forever and is going to start to feel claustrophobic. Your heart is built for another shore.

When our ambition settles, as it were, for attention or domination—when we imagine that our goal is to be noticed or to win, or both—we are actually *lowering* our sights. We are aiming low. The arc of our ambition hugs the earth, and we expect to find fulfillment from people looking at us, from beating everybody else in this competition for attention.

But what happens when their attention turns away, fleeting as it is? What happens after you get the grass garland, the medal, the scholarship, the promotion? How many "likes" is enough? How many followers will make you feel valued?

What if you're wired not to be "liked" but to be loved, and not by many but by One? Could that explain why all the attention is never enough? Or why a kind of postpartum depression sets in after every "win," every time you make it to the top of what you thought was the mountain of achievement? Why does winning leave you feeling so restless?

WHAT DO I want when I want to win? Sometimes ambition is just about competition. Then aspiration becomes just another form of the *libido dominandi*, the lust for domination. At some point you stop caring about the specifics of what you're trying to accomplish and only care about doing it first, doing it best, doing it better than the others who are trying to do it. Standing on the top of the podium or sitting in the corner office will be evidence of your arrival.

Won't it?

The story of a frequent flier named Ben Schlappig could be a cautionary tale in this respect. As Ben Wofford recounts in an engaging *Rolling Stone* profile, Schlappig, who was twenty-five at the time, "is one of the biggest stars among an elite group of obsessive flyers whose mission is to outwit the airlines. They're self-styled competitors with a singular objective: fly for free, as much as they can, without getting caught."[12] Schlappig is a master of travel hacking, which he and his community of mileage hoarders simply call "the Hobby." "His fans aren't just travel readers," Wofford observes. "They're gamers, and Schlappig is teaching them how to win."

In April 2014, at the end of his lease on a Seattle apartment, he walked into Sea-Tac Airport and, as Wofford wryly remarks, "hasn't come down since." In the past year, "he's flown more than 400,000 miles, enough to circumnavigate the globe 16 times. It's been 43 exhausting weeks since he slept in a bed that wasn't in a hotel, and he spends an average of six hours daily in the sky." But Schlappig doesn't consider himself a nomad. "The moment he whiffs the airless ambience of a pressurized cabin, he's home."

His passion for flying was born of heartbreak: Ben, when he was just three years old, lost his oldest brother, who was fourteen. Ben's brother had been a stand-in for a largely absent father, but now even he was gone. Ben was undone. He was eventually dismissed from preschool because he wouldn't stop screaming. "On the worst days, Barbara [his mother] did the only thing that seemed to calm her son. They drove to the airport and sat together in silence, watching the airplanes take off and land." What's he chasing there, up in the air?

Schlappig became a master of the game of turning air miles into currency, maximizing the return on investment like a Wall Street hedge fund manager. He distinguished himself, gathered a fan base through his blog, and became a millionaire. Known the world over, Schlappig is welcomed giddily by airline attendants and is familiar to the hosts of first-class lounges. But Wofford notes a telling absence: "His trip reports betray a theme, in photo after photo entirely devoid of human companionship: empty lounges, first-class menus, embroidered satin pillows—inanimate totems of a five-star existence." But he's winning.

"Schlappig repeatedly insists that his life can go on forever this way. But he also announces, genuinely, that he wants to settle down one day."

He longingly recalls the scenes he's witnessed in Delhi's Indira Gandhi International Airport: "You see a whole family, 20 people, picking up someone at the airport. People with signs, people with balloons, with flowers. There's something beautiful about that." But of course, those greetings are always when people are welcomed *home*.

"'The world is so big, I can keep running,' Schlappig says. 'At the same time, it makes you realize the world is so small.' After a long pause, he continues, 'I want what I can't have. There's nothing gratifying about that. . . . I'd still like to think I'm a reasonably happy person.' He grins. 'Despite all that.'"

IT WAS AMBITION that brought Augustine to Milan, but it was attainment that unsettled him. Augustine's Milan is not so different from contemporary Milan. Or London or New York or Washington, DC, for that matter. The cities of our ambition are perennial. They are always places to be seen. If, in Augustine's day, the goal was to be noticed by the emperor and noticed rubbing shoulders in the court, then contemporary Milan is not so different. As the center of fashion and design, it's the place that drapes people in ways they'll be noticed and envied. The fashion district's "block of gold" is just the latest outpost of our arenas for being noticed. The Pirelli Tower is a manifestation of architectural ambition, rivaling the cathedral as the center of the city. The prophetic films of Pier Paolo Pasolini, critical of the consumerism of postindustrial Milan, are almost like updated versions of the *Confessions* in this respect: "All the deep cultural values of the popular classes," John Foot summarizes, "had been reduced to one cultural model: to decide whether to dream of having a Ferrari or a Porsche . . . with the pretence of being 'free.'"[13]

Plus ça change, as they say. Every age has its Milans—the dense centers of our aspiration that collect all the more people to see us, the urban arenas of attention. If we're chomping at the bit to get out of the provinces, it's in no small part because there's no one to see us in our lonely backwaters.

Augustine comes to Milan with that sort of ambition: "I aspired to honours, money, marriage"—marriage being another way to secure money—"and you laughed at me. In those ambitions I suffered the bitterest difficulties; that was by your mercy."[14] The difficulty didn't stem from failure but from success. He wasn't unhappy because he didn't make it; he was unhappy where he "made it." And he was becoming less and less adept at pretending otherwise.

The consciousness of his own unhappiness snapped into focus on the day of one of his most hoped-for achievements: the day he delivered a panegyric on the emperor—a public speech of notoriety that all the networks would broadcast, so to speak. He was a long way from Thagaste. He'd made it. His mother couldn't be prouder.

"How unhappy I was!" he recalls. "The anxiety of the occasion was making my heart palpitate." While pacing the Milan streets before the event, sweating and sick to his stomach with worry, he passed a destitute beggar on the street. "Already drunk, I think, he was joking and laughing." On the day he's realizing a lifelong dream, Augustine is stopped short with a realization: "In all our strivings such as those efforts that were then worrying me, the goads of ambition impelled me to drag the burden of my unhappiness with me, and in dragging it to make it even worse; yet we had no goal other than to reach a carefree cheerfulness. That beggar was already there before us, and perhaps we would never achieve it."[15] There's the beggar, a "failure," laughing in the morning while Augustine, a "success," is racked with anxiety. "He had no worries; I was frenetic." It's funny, he remarks in retrospect, how we choose anxiety and fear over simplicity and merriment. It's as if we imagine our frantic ambition will bring joy.

"To hell with all of this!" Augustine and his friends would sometimes think.[16] A philosophical inkling was rumbling in them. They were starting to care about different things. The learned, welcoming Ambrose even had them considering Christianity. Like Dartmouth frat boys who've been headed to Wall Street or K Street but are befriended by a gentle Plato scholar, there would be nights when they'd muse about chasing other things. A seed of doubt was planted on their road to "success." A different kind of ambition was bubbling up in them.

Then the morning would come and the old habits of ambition would reassert themselves under the guise of pragmatism. "But wait," they'd remind one another.

> This stuff itself is pleasant; it's got quite a bit of its own sweetness. It's not a straightforward thing to cut off our pursuits in that direction; it would be very embarrassing to go back to them. And just think how much progress there's been already toward an appointment to some high public office. What more is there to wish for in this world? Plenty of powerful friends are backing us; provided that we pour our effort—a lot of effort—into one thing, we could even be granted a lower-ranking governorship.[17]

Then Augustine hears a story of others who actually recalibrate their compass of ambition. Ponticianus, a fellow African, visits him and his friends. Ponticianus notices a copy of the epistles of Paul lying on top of their gaming table—a bit like seeing a copy of Augustine's *Confessions* sitting on top of the Xbox in the frat house. These young men are perhaps more complicated than Ponticianus would have guessed. So he proceeds to tell them a story about a pivotal experience in his own life when he was a younger man living in Trier, with the same ambitions as Augustine and his friends, working in a special branch of the imperial government.[18] One morning, "when the emperor was detained by a circus spectacle" (shade thrown!), Ponticianus and a few of his friends went for a stroll outside the city walls. They broke up into pairs, and the other two wandered afield and came across a small, humble house that was home to some monks. Welcomed inside, one of Ponticianus's friends, scanning the shelves, picked up *The Life of Antony*, a biography of the Egyptian monk by Athanasius. He was immediately pulled in by the book and "set on fire."

> Suddenly he was filled with holy love and sobering shame. Angry with himself, he turned his eyes on his friend and said to him: "Tell me, I beg of you, what do we hope to achieve with all our labours? What is our aim in life? What is the motive of our service to the state? Can we hope for any higher office in the palace than to be Friends of the Emperor? And in that position what is not fragile and full of dangers? How many hazards must one risk to attain a position of even greater danger? And when will we arrive there? Whereas, if I wish to become God's friend, in an instant I may become that now."[19]

What is our aim in life? What are we aiming for when we aim our lives at some aspiration?

The question isn't *whether* we aim our lives. Our existence is like an arrow on a taut string: it will be sent somewhere. It's not a matter of quelling ambition, of "settling," as if that were somehow more virtuous (or even possible). The alternative to disordered ambition that ultimately disappoints is not some holy lethargy or pious passivity. It's recalibrated ambition that aspires for a different end and does so for different reasons.

What is the arc of a life whose aspiration is to be a friend of God? What difference would that make? This young striver already senses one difference: this is the only ambition that comes with security, with a rest from the anxiety of every other ambition. Because all other ambitions are fragile, fraught. The attention of others is fickle. Domination of others is always temporary; you can't win forever (just ask Rocky). Attainment is a goddess who quickly turns a cold shoulder. To aspire to friendship with God, however, is an ambition for something you could never lose. It is to get attention from someone who sees you and knows you and will never stop loving you. In short, it's the opposite of fickle human attention, which is temporal and temperamental. God's attention is not predicated on your performance. You don't have to catch God's notice with your display. He's not a father you have to shock in order to jar his attention away from the game, crying out,

"Look at me! Look at me!" God's attention is a place where you can find rest and where, "in the father's lap," as Augustine later puts it, you don't have to be worried about getting attention from anyone else.[20] You can rest.

At the end of his moving memoir, *Open*, Andre Agassi recalls a scene before his last professional match at the 2006 US Open. The story has been one of imposed ambition and a lifetime of alienation from his father who forced him to play tennis. And now, on the cusp of his retirement:

> I'm hobbling through the lobby of the Four Seasons the next morning when a man steps out of the shadows. He grabs my arm.
>
> Quit, he says.
>
> What?
>
> It's my father—or a ghost of my father. He looks ashen. He looks as if he hasn't slept in weeks.
>
> Pops? What are you talking about?
>
> Just quit. Go home. You did it. It's over.[21]

Our culture of ambition has only two speeds: either win or quit. But perhaps our ambition to win is a hunger to be noticed—maybe even a lifelong, unarticulated hunger to be noticed by a father, to hear him say, "Well done. You did it."

But that's not why he loves you. You don't have to win, but you also don't have to quit. You only have to quit performing, quit imagining his love is earned. You can rest, but you don't have to quit. You just need to change why you play.

BUT, OF COURSE, you can't change your game overnight. The habits of attention-seeking domination have deep roots, and often our attempts to weed them out, even with the grace of the Spirit, don't seem to pull them up. They keep sprouting.

One of the things I most love Augustine for is his honesty about his continued struggles with ambition and the unique pride that feeds off of being noticed and garnering praise. The shadow side of ambition is a constant companion of even reordered aspiration in this mortal life. A later Augustinian, Blaise Pascal, named this with the same sort of self-knowledge: "Vanity is so anchored in the human heart," he observed, "that a soldier, a cadet, a cook, a kitchen porter boasts, and wants to have admirers, and even philosophers want them, and those who write against them want the prestige of having written well, and those who read them want the prestige of having read them, and I, writing this, perhaps have this desire, and those who will read this . . ."[22]

This is the sort of self-doubt that would plague someone who dared to write something like the *Confessions*. He admits it. The risk of self-aggrandizement is a constant worry for Augustine.[23] This is why the turn in book 10 from past to present is oddly encouraging. Because here is Augustine the bishop confessing to his continued struggles and temptations—his love still falling for fool's gold, his aim still unsteady as he finds himself settling for earthbound targets.

Meditating on John's injunction to avoid worldly loves—"the lust of the flesh and the lust of the eyes and the ambition of the secular world [*ambitio saeculi* in Augustine's Vulgate]" (1 John 2:16)—Augustine the bishop confesses he is still prone to fall for the third temptation: The "wish to be feared or loved by people for no reason other than the joy derived from such power, which [he now realizes] is no joy at all. It is a wretched life." It is the sort of life that hollows you out, sucking every ounce of your energy to the surface to maintain the veneer that captures attention. Indeed, we're prone in this idolatry to make ourselves the idols: "It becomes our pleasure to be loved and feared not for your sake, but instead of you."[24] We make ourselves little gods even while falling prey to the lie that the attention of others will make us happy.

If the Christian is still prone to this, how much more the priest or pastor whose role demands a kind of publicity—a role that requires him or her to be seen and heard and to exercise influence? But Augustine isn't willing to give himself the easy out of simply excusing himself from leadership to avoid this temptation, as if the way to avoid the shadow side of ambition was to eschew excellence or the power that comes from public influence. "If we hold certain offices in human society it is necessary for us to be loved and feared by people." Abandoning the office to avoid the temptation is its own sin of irresponsibility, a Jonah-like evasion of the call on one's life. The trick, Augustine points out, is to aspire to one's office, and aspire to excellence in that office, without letting praise for your excellence be the overriding goal of your ambition. "Be our glory," he prays. "Let it be for your sake that we are loved." And if our excellence in the pursuit of God's call on our lives engenders the proverbial praise of men, let us learn to receive even that as a gift. "If admiration is the usual and proper accompaniment of a good life and good actions, we ought not to renounce it any more than the good life which it accompanies."[25]

Augustine's spiritual realism is enacted here: the esteemed bishop admits that he's still a sucker for praise and adoration. He can't always be confident that he's doing the right thing for the right reason. Or, to put it differently, he's quite confident that he's often doing things for both sorts of reasons at the same time. If you ask him, "Are you doing this for God or for your own vanity?" Augustine's answer is an honest "yes." Indeed, you can feel him constantly asking himself, "Just why am I writing these *Confessions*? What am I hoping for? Whose attention am I seeking?" If he were alive today, he'd admit all the time he spends posting on Instagram about his upcoming book on humility. But he'd risk it, confident not in his own purity but in the grace of a God who can use his best efforts in spite of his motives.

Resting in the love of God doesn't squelch ambition; it fuels it with a different fire. I don't have to strive to get God to love me; rather, because God loves me unconditionally, I'm free to take risks and launch out into the deep. I'm released to aspire to use my gifts in gratitude, caught up in God's mission for the sake of the world. When you've been found, you're free to fail.

SEX : *How to Connect*

What do I want when I crave intimacy?

Jacques Derrida, the famous (notorious?) French philosopher, is seated in his living room. Evening has settled on Ris-Orangis, the Parisian suburb Derrida called home. He looks tired, but remains patient and attentive. Amy Ziering Kofman, producer and director of the documentary *Derrida*, puts to him an open-ended question: "If you were to watch a documentary about a philosopher—Heidegger or Kant or Hegel—what would you like to see in it?"

After a long, pensive pause, Derrida names it briefly and decisively: "Their sex lives."

Kofman is obviously taken aback, so Derrida explains: "Because it's something they don't talk about. I'd love to hear about something they refuse to talk about. Why do philosophers present themselves asexually in their work? Why have they erased their private lives from their work?" His interest isn't prurient ("I'm not talking about making a porno film about Hegel or Heidegger," he clarifies). It's a matter of love. "There is nothing more important in one's private life than love. . . . I want them to speak about the part love plays in their lives."

Has any philosopher done this more baldly, more vulnerably, or more transparently than Augustine? He not only recounts his past escapades;

he's a bishop who admits his continued wet dreams.[1] And, confirming Derrida's hypothesis, Augustine concludes that what was going on in his sex life, even if disordered, really was about *love*: "The single desire that dominated my search for delight was simply to love and to be loved."[2] There are hints of euphemism here, and maybe a bit of sublimation (albeit some fifteen centuries before Freud)—a deft deflection that is the stuff of Woody Allen films. Though Derrida was looking for a philosopher willing to talk about his sex life, he might have complained that Augustine overdid it. He could have left more to the imagination.[3]

But what could we possibly learn about sex from the so-called "inventor" of original sin, this celibate scold and ancient misogynist?[4] What could we, liberated from repression, possibly learn from a monk?

Admittedly, to journey with Augustine on these matters is like an awkward road trip to your grandparents' cottage with a great uncle you hardly know. An hour into the long drive, you realize he holds opinions that seem unfathomable, even revolting, to you. He seems irrelevant to the world you inhabit. But about four hours into the trip, he lets slip an insight you've never considered, one that inexplicably sets your world atilt and has you almost hate the fact that you're rethinking things. There's something uncanny about his corny metaphors: they speak to your experience. You realize that he too was once young and that his world is not so different from yours. Six hours into the trip, after vociferously arguing with him, confident of all the things he gets wrong, you nonetheless hear in his counsel the hints of a soul who knows something about disappointment, and something about happiness because of that. By the time you reach the cottage, in the bliss of summer's late twilight, with your extended family bustling around the edge of the lake and guffawing on camp chairs, you thank your great uncle for more than the ride.

I have my own disagreements and frustrations with Augustine on this score. I can still recall the moment when our profound differences came to the fore—and why journeying with Augustine didn't always look like agreeing with him. While a doctoral student at Villanova University, investigating Heidegger's debts to Augustine, I had the opportunity to learn from Fr. Robert Dodaro, an Augustinian priest and scholar, then president of the Augustinianum in Rome. Father Dodaro taught summer institutes at Villanova, which were a critical part of my immersion in patristic scholarship on Augustine. It was Father Dodaro who taught me to read the sermons and letters, not just the treatises. So as I was preparing for my dissertation year, we came up with a plan for me to spend the year in Rome, with my family, studying at the Augustinianum. I had set about applying for funds and arranging logistics. I can recall a wide-eyed visit to the Italian embassy in South Philly, where every agent was encased in thick bulletproof glass, shades of Scorsese movies creeping into my imagination. The red tape was arduous and almost dissuaded me.

But another surprise is what would derail the plan. I can still remember the afternoon Deanna came home from work and told me, "I'm pregnant." This would be our fourth child, and we both immediately knew this meant Rome was out of the question. But we were both perfectly OK with that, grateful and excited for this rather unanticipated expansion of our burgeoning household.

That spring, Father Dodaro was back in Philadelphia for a conference at Villanova, so I was able to tell him the news in person. Apologetically, I told him that I wouldn't be able to enjoy the year at the Augustinianum because we had just gotten word that we were expecting our fourth child. I remember his eyes widening, albeit with a grin, but one that communicated its own assessment of the situation. Worlds were colliding: the celibate Augustinian scholar, the "fecund" young Protestant. It's like I was proving Augustine right: sex and marriage and the "affairs of the world" would distract from higher goods. My wife's and my fondness for bodily pleasure and for one another was stealing the opportunity to focus on matters of the mind.

I didn't regret a thing. I harbored no inferiority complex. I was answering a call, and it was Augustine who taught me to listen carefully to the unexpected cries of children.[5]

Sometimes learning from Augustine means deconstructing Augustine. We'd been on the road long enough that I'd mustered the courage to point out some of his missteps. But in the long road since then, I've continued to appreciate how much this celibate saint has to teach me about sex.

WHAT DO WE want when we want to have sex? More starkly: what are we hoping for when we imagine happiness looks like having as much sex as possible? What story are we buying into when we believe a dominant narrative that tells us fulfillment looks like the multiplication of orgasms? What does it feel like to live into that story?

Sexual hunger comes naturally and has its own complex of desires embedded in it. We crave an intimacy that blurs the boundary between lover and beloved. We want to give ourselves away, to lose ourselves in a tangle of limbs and folds, to speak our love in tongues, as it were.[6] At the same time, it is a hunger that craves satisfaction. Our self is its most self-interested as it seeks the titillation of nerve endings that lie dormant in our workaday lives. We yearn for the release, the exception, the explosion that we hope pours sparks on the mundane we inhabit the rest of the time. Sex is that paradoxical combination of vulnerability and assertion, giving ourselves up and wanting all the more.

When Augustine was a young student in Madauros, all of this was anticipated just over the horizon, as if he'd heard rumblings of possibilities that his body already knew. The lure of sex was haloed with the aura of the unknown, the mysterious, as it so often is in adolescence, causing us to pour into it all the more hope and expectation. Such hunger was in the water, so to speak, and he swam in it like everyone else. It was no wonder, then, that "the bubbling impulses of puberty" asserted themselves.[7] What he would later describe as a "lunatic lust" took over; it "had come to lord it over me, after I made a complete surrender."[8] Similarly, when his family finally saved up the funds to send him to university in Carthage, "all around me hissed a cauldron of illicit loves," and Augustine was more than happy to drink it up. "I was in love with love," he recalls.[9] Retroactively, he recognizes a hunger behind this, a hunger that stemmed from a certain kind of starvation. The soul's built-in hunger for the transcendent, the resplendent, the mysterious was deflected to the sensual, the bodily, the reverberating shudder of climax. The inherent desire to give himself away settled for giving up his body. Ignoring infinite Beauty, he pursued finite beauties all the more. He traded the cosmic for the orgasmic.

He could recognize what Leslie Jamison calls that "narrowing of repertoire" that nonetheless comes with widening expectations. This helped explain his disappointment and exhaustion. Because the satisfaction of sexual hunger was really a way of trying to stave off a more fundamental, transcendent hunger, it meant he was always expecting too much, asking sex to do something it could never do. And so, the aura of mystery and unparalleled delight that sex had as Augustine arrived on the shores of puberty began to look different a few years later when seen from the other side of disappointment, through the tired haze of a malaise that had hoped for more. Promiscuity didn't keep its promises.

This is not the conclusion of a detached square, the wishful thinking of a celibate who never got any, like the virginal geek telling the playboy that sex isn't all that important in some imaginary John Hughes movie. To the contrary, Augustine speaks "from experience," as we say. And his conclusion, while jarring in a libertine culture (like his own, we might add), is not unheard of from others who tried to find something more in sexual pursuit. Indeed, one might be struck by some remarkable parallels between Augustine and a contemporary like Russell Brand. Having leveraged his fame for a life of philandering, for which he became more famous, Brand looked at his sexual hunger anew when he broke free of other addictions in his life. In a podcast conversation with Joe Rogan, Brand offers his own introspective reading of what he was looking for in his promiscuity: "The great gift of promiscuity," he told Rogan, "is that you get to experience all of the intimacy with all of these strangers and it seems exciting. And the kind of sexuality that I've always had is more about worship than any kind of domination. I adore, I adore, you know?"[10] This recognition of an almost liturgical aspect to sexual desire would not surprise Augustine. But, as Brand goes on to ask, just who am I worshiping in this? What am I giving myself away to? Is this devotion, or is it a sacrifice?

Brand confesses to the isolation he experienced in this chase: you acquire "all of these wonderful experiences and encounters," he says, "but . . . within it, this kind of ongoing seam of loneliness, unignorable." When he can't ignore the unignorable any longer, he starts to be honest in his appraisal of just what he's getting out of this:

> And also—this is the thing—when you get the things your culture tells you you should be doing and you experience them now you know you can stop chasing the carrot 'cause you've had a bite out of it and it's like, "Hold on a minute: this is bull——." It's a hard one to learn because anything that's got an orgasm at the end of it, you know, there's a degree of pleasure to be had. But it takes a while to recognize the emotional cost on me, the spiritual cost on other people, the fact that it's preventing me from becoming a father, from becoming a husband, from settling, from becoming rooted, from becoming actually whole, from becoming a man, from becoming connected. It takes a while to spot that. I think a lot of people don't get the opportunity to break out of that pattern. I would never have spotted it had I not first been a heroin addict and gone, "Hold on a minute, you're doing that thing again." Same with fame and same with celebrity. . . . Because I had the template and experiences, "Ooooh, this is addiction; you're expecting this thing to make you feel better."

Like all of our addictions, promiscuity fails to deliver what we're asking of it.

PAIN IS HOW the body tells us to stop, to slow down, to attend to a problem. Frustration, sadness, and heartbreak are the pains of a life that's running against the grain. What's both sad and endlessly ingenious in a diabolical way is the extent to which we can deny the pain, paper over it with explanations and rationalizations, mute it with louder music and more partners. We are masters of dissimulation; we can construe almost anything as if it were pleasure in order to talk ourselves into being happy. We are great pretenders.

Those superpowers of self-deception are amplified when society tells us that pain is pleasure, that our disappointment is happiness, that we're living the dream. Getting the emperor out of his clothes is the new lie we're all complicit in, even if it's killing us, isolating us, and leaving us lonelier than ever. We don't just buy the spin; we purvey it.

This dynamic was illustrated in an episode of the HBO drama *Succession*. The story revolves around the Shakespearean family drama of a Murdoch-like media empire, presided over by the unforgiving, heartless patriarch, Logan Roy. One of the outsiders in the clan is Tom Wamsgans (played masterfully by Matthew Macfadyen). A midwesterner who has somehow fallen in love with Logan's daughter, Siobhan ("Shiv"), Tom is constantly marginalized, looking for approval, hoping to climb the ladder of the family business only to feel Shiv's brothers stomping on him each time he tries to grab the next rung. But he is devoted to Shiv and manages to convince her to marry him.

His bachelor party is the occasion for an episode that is sad and dark despite the glitz and glam of lights in the club. Roman Roy, who couldn't care less about Tom, has taken over arrangements, mostly as a means to a business deal. Their crew is whisked into the underworld of New York to an exclusive sex club with shades of the stories coming out of Silicon Valley of late.[11] Taking the ritual of the bachelor party to a new level, the club is a Disneyland of lust, where every man's dream can come true. You can tell that Tom is trying to talk himself into buying this story, making this dream his own. If this is what everybody dreams of, he assures himself, then look at me: I'm the luckiest guy in the world. But you don't believe him, and you know he doesn't believe it himself, despite how many times he keeps telling himself, out loud, over and over. Indeed, he can't stop calling Siobhan, assuring her, needing her, wanting to hear her voice, longing for her to tell him what he *can't* do because he doesn't actually want to anyway.[12] But Shiv only grants permission. The rites of the bachelor party are sacrosanct; the ritual calf must be slaughtered to the god of pleasure.

When he finally feels like he needs to cave into the debauch, he returns to his soon-to-be cousin, recounts the disgusting sex act he just engaged in, and keeps telling everyone, unconvincingly, "It was so hot." When he sees Shiv the next morning, he's embarrassed to kiss her with the mouth he used last night.

Augustine tells us that there was a pain that attended his pleasures, and for the longest time he ignored it. But "you were always with me," he says, looking back, "mercifully punishing me, touching with a bitter taste all my illicit pleasures."[13] Becoming attuned to that pain was like a first revelation, a nudge that gave him permission to say, like Brand, "Hold on a minute: this is bull——."

What Augustine offers us is a strange new lens to look askance at the story we've been suckered into. It's like Brand's account of addiction, but it dives even deeper into a spiritual diagnosis. It's not just that I'm hooked and need a fix, or that I'm overly dependent on external stimuli to try to achieve happiness (and hence doomed to disappointment because of the law of diminishing returns).[14] That can all be true yet still an inadequate diagnosis of what's really going on if it doesn't recognize that the insatiability of my hunger isn't a bug but a feature—a signal that I long for something infinite. Wanting more isn't the problem; it's where I keep looking for it.

Augustine invites us to look at our promiscuity through the lens of idolatry, not in order to induce shame, but in order to illuminate the depth of the hunger and the significance of its disorder. The problem isn't sex;

it's what I expect from sex. The problem with promiscuity isn't (just) that it transgresses the law or that it chews up other people and spits them out as leftovers; it's not simply the fact that it hollows me out and reduces me to my organs and glands all as a perverted way to feed a soul-hunger. The baseline problem with promiscuity is that it doesn't work and is doomed to fail. "You can't get there from here" is what Augustine finally heard Lady Continence telling him. And by that point, after telling himself for years that "this is so hot," Augustine is ready to listen. The incessant chatter of his loins and the constant inciting of his old habits "was now putting the question very half-heartedly." The volume of those passions had been turned down just enough that he could hear another voice: the voice of "the dignified and chaste Lady Continence, serene and cheerful without coquetry, enticing me in an honorable manner to come and not to hesitate."[15] Exhausted by his pursuits, Augustine was susceptible to the lure of a different direction for his loves. Restraint looked like release from the frantic chase he'd been on. If the soul-hunger that had been trying to feast on the ephemeral could finally be fed by the eternal, then his expectations wouldn't be constantly disappointed. He was being wooed by chastity.

BUT PROMISCUITY ISN'T synonymous with sex. Like anything, creaturely goods are gifts when they are enjoyed in the right way. When I stop looking to some facet of finite creation to feed a hunger for the infinite, I don't have to reject or detest creation. To the contrary, in a sense I get it back as a gift, as something to be (small-*e*) enjoyed as a way to (big-*E*) Enjoy the Creator who made it. It's when I stop overexpecting from creation that it becomes something I can hold with an open hand, lightly but gratefully.

If Augustine overcorrects, it's because his own demons propelled him to confuse promiscuity with sex. The result is a tendency to collapse his conversion into answering the call to celibacy. The existential struggle in the garden plays out as a question of whether he is willing and able to be celibate for the rest of his life. Lady Continence gets more lines than Jesus, you might say. The infusion of grace is the gift he needed in order to make the "leap."[16]

While he might have overcome his old carnal habits, his old habits of mind persisted. At times the vision of healthy sexuality that Augustine extols—prioritizing celibacy—simply looks like the inversion of promiscuity and suggests his failure to imagine a sexual hunger that runs with the grain of a good creation. (This privileging of celibacy would be a primary target of reform when a later Augustinian renewal movement called the Protestant Reformation would revisit the question.)[17]

The collapsing of the two—identifying sex with sin—is understandable, in a way. It stems partly from his own demons and partly from a lingering Platonic devaluing of the body in vogue at the time—what Kyle Harper describes as the "grand ascetic experiments that are such a stunning feature of late antiquity," a movement "that originated in the desert and then hurtled itself across the Mediterranean."[18] And, of course, this also stems from an honest wrestling with Scripture, with the exemplar of the unmarried Jesus and the counsels of the apostle Paul that privilege virginity and celibacy in 1 Corinthians 7. In his reading of Paul's epistle to the Corinthians, Augustine turned what was a strategic *eschatological* priority—"time is short" (1 Cor. 7:29)—into a metaphysical hierarchy laden with biological disdain. As a result, he backs himself into strange backstories about procreation in the garden of Eden—procreation without passion, intercourse without arousal, genitals copulating like shaking hands: body parts, he envisions, will simply obey the will without the messiness of desire.[19] But this ends up demonizing the creaturely per se. Even when Augustine defends the good of marriage in an early tract, the rhythms he recommends look like monastery lite. In fact, in a later debate he castigates Julian for encouraging couples to "jump into bed each time they are overcome with desire, sometimes not even waiting for night to come."[20] There's no afternoon delight in Augustine's vision of ordered sexual desire.

Because Augustine felt least in control in the face of his sexual urges, and because of his cold-turkey recovery, he ratifies an all-or-nothing approach that reflects an emerging orthodoxy at the time—a vision that would stay in place, mostly unquestioned, until the Protestant Reformation. But we can demur to this and still learn a lot from him. Don't let disagreement about celibacy shut down the opportunity to hear wisdom in Augustine's provocative account of chastity, which might be exactly the sort of peculiar take on sex that we need to hear.

What Augustine offers us is a slant of detachment—a recognition of the power of sexual desire with a resistance to letting it *define* anyone.[21] "Continence"—Augustine's technical Latin term that Sarah Ruden translates as "self-restraint"—isn't just for the celibate. Indeed, continence isn't even just about sex. Continence is a general principle of being held together rather than dispersed, having a center rather than dissolving oneself in a million hungry pursuits.[22] Sexual continence—chastity—outside of celibacy looks like a relationship to sex that doesn't idolize it, doesn't let it define us, doesn't let it become a hunger that eats us alive. In other words, the gift of chastity is that it trains us not to *need*; it grants us an integrity and independence and agency in the face of various drives and hungers.

While Augustine emphasizes procreation as the end of sex, he begrudgingly makes room for a kind of remedial sex life beyond the procreative, yet another aspect of his pastoral realism.[23] As he recognizes in *On the Good of Marriage*, couples will "have intercourse also beside the cause of begetting children." This, he says, "is not committed because of marriage, but is pardoned because of marriage"; it is "a mutual service of sustaining one another's weakness."[24] Although I might resist this way of framing it, I can see the counsel of wisdom embedded in Augustine's point: part of a healthy sexuality will be refusing to let it consume me. There is a freedom that comes from not being a slave to my libido. Indeed, it is also a gift to my partner to learn not to need, not imposing a disordered hunger on our relationship—a hunger that, even in the context of a marriage, can be (if we're honest) rapacious. As Joseph Clair comments, "By claiming that all conjugal acts not aimed toward the goal of offspring are venially sinful, Augustine intends to highlight how difficult it is to achieve sexual intimacy in marriage without fleeting moments of selfishness—whether in the form of self-satisfaction or domination."[25]

I've been thinking about this a lot as my wife and I have worked to navigate the realities of menopause. I can still remember the morning when Deanna tearfully explained to me her experience of this natural season in a woman's life—the way her body felt like it was a stranger, recalcitrant, behaving in ways she couldn't predict and didn't like; the way she resented this diminishment of desire, even as she grappled with its chemical reality; the way she worried this would frustrate me and erode the bonds between us. I was immediately ashamed of all my socialization as a male sexual being and admired her courage and transparency. I was humbled by her honesty and pained by her sadness as she mourned her own body and rhythms we'd come to cherish (which, I'll confess to Augustine, included its fair share of afternoon delight). And in that moment Augustine's counsels took on a new relevance for me as I realized that in this season of our marriage and in this stage on the road, the kind of detachment Augustine encouraged—the refusal to be dominated by the libido—was exactly the word I needed to hear.

It also strikes me as paradoxical, or at least surprising, that an ancient celibate bishop might have insight that speaks directly to our #MeToo moment, as the systemic monstrosities of male sexual desire are uncovered and named for what they are: domineering, predatory, heedless, abusive. The myth of sexual fulfillment and self-expression doesn't look like it has coherent resources to curb the habits of the lecherous men of late modernity (men we have *made*, it should be noted). Perhaps it will be the horrors of abuse that get us to consider the virtues of chastity, monogamy, and even marriage. As Augustine puts it at one point in *On the Good of Marriage*, "For this purpose they are married, that the lust being brought under a lawful bond should not float at large without form and loose; having of itself weakness of flesh that cannot be curbed, but of marriage fellowship of faith that cannot be dissolved."[26] This theme returns over and over again in Augustine's defense of the good of marriage: the centrality of friendship, the importance of covenant, both finding expression in exclusivity. What if consent isn't enough? What if what we're looking for is covenant? What if only marriage will protect us?[27]

IN FACT, AUGUSTINE experienced a kind of preamble to reordered love when he made a commitment to a concubine while living in Carthage. Concubinage is not what we tend to project back onto this relationship. Rather than a kind of sophisticated prostitution, as we might think, the arrangement reflects the class structure of the day, and the way ambition infiltrated sex. A concubine was a kind of temporary but exclusive partnership that would be made while someone was climbing the ladder on the way to status or wealth that could secure a more "appropriate" marriage. It's worth noting, in fact, that right around the time Augustine made a commitment to a concubinage, a church council ruled that unmarried men who made such commitments could receive the Eucharist.[28] (It should also be noted that Monica was generally happy with this arrangement for a while, since she harbored high hopes for her son's marital prospects.)[29] "In those years," Augustine recalls, "I had a woman. She was not my partner in what is called lawful marriage," he admits. "Nevertheless, she was the only girl for me, and I was faithful to her."[30]

In fact, they also had a son together. His name says something about their relationship: Adeodatus, a gift of God. She and Adeodatus would journey with Augustine across the Mediterranean to Rome, would follow him to Milan, faithfully trailing him in his ambitions. Surely Augustine learned something about friendship in this relationship, knew something of covenant. Indeed, the depth and intimacy of their relationship is attested in Augustine's heartbreak when ambitious Monica finally pressures Augustine into dismissing her for a more promising marital contract. She was "torn away from my side," as Augustine recalls: "My heart which was deeply attached was cut and wounded, and left a trail of blood."[31] But Adeodatus, the fruit of their union, the gift of God, remained. We see the precocious son participating in some of the early dialogues that emerged from a season in Cassiciacum after his conversion. And when Ambrose would baptize Augustine, he would also baptize his son.

Both his partner and son are effaced from the tradition. These companions that journeyed with him to Rome and Milan, alongside him in his anxieties and struggles, appear nowhere in the iconography of later centuries. They are conspicuously absent from those frescoes by Gozzoli in San Gimignano, nowhere to be seen in that ship braving the Mediterranean, not even in the frame as he departs Rome. Augustine's later arguments about celibacy end up retroactively rewriting history.

But who are we to spurn the gifts of God? Who is Augustine to do so, to efface the *datus deo*? What if following Augustine means disagreeing with him? Indeed, as Augustine himself would recognize, the central mystery of the Christian faith, the incarnation of God, says something surprising about sex: "For the same nature had to be taken on as needed to be set free. And lest either sex should imagine it was being ignored by its creator, he took to himself a male and was born of a female."[32] Every saint has been born of lovemaking. It's when we stop idolizing sex that we can finally sanctify it.

MOTHERS : *How to Be Dependent*

What do I want when I want to leave?

If ambition means leaving home, it often means spurning family. For many, like Gatsby, ambition requires the erasure of the family name and its claim on us. Finding and forging an identity means asserting our independence, breaking the bonds of dependence we're thrown into as children. Like the prodigal, we effectively say to our parents, "I wish you were dead," then gather up all they give us and strike out to make a life of "our own." In ancient, literary, and even Hollywood versions of this story, the assertion of our independence is usually a father-directed defiance, even violence: the father as competitor, controller, master is the obstacle to our autonomy, the enemy to be overcome.

Mothers, often caricatured, come off differently in such tropes. From *Portnoy's Complaint* to *Lady Bird*, from *Everybody Loves Raymond* to *Gilmore Girls*, the mother must be overcome because her suffocating embrace is the means of her manipulation. Her presence swells and overwhelms and inhales all the oxygen an independent self needs to breathe. She denies our autonomy with kisses; she steals our self-reliance with hugs. She manages to make us hate ourselves for resenting her, which makes us all the more resentful. A snippet of conversation in Jonathan Franzen's *The Corrections* is a subtle example of this maternal power. Enid Lambert, midwestern mother, eager to gather her grown chicks once again, poses a question to her daughter, Denise:

> "Anyway," she said, "I thought that if you and Chip were interested, we could all have one last Christmas in St. Jude. What do you think of that idea?"
>
> "I'll be wherever you and Dad want to be," Denise said.
>
> "No, I'm asking *you*, though. I want to know if it's something you're especially interested in doing. If you'd especially like to have one last Christmas in the house you grew up in. Does it sound like it might be fun for you?"
>
> "I can tell you right now," Denise said, "there's no way Caroline's leaving Philly. It's a fantasy to think otherwise. So if you want to see your grandkids, you'll have to come east."
>
> "Denise, I'm asking what *you* want. Gary says he and Caroline haven't ruled it out. I need to know if a Christmas in St. Jude is something that you really, really want for *yourself*."[1]

Fathers you can leave, but the reach of mothers transcends geography and chronology. Leaving home and growing up never seems to be enough. Independence is the affront mothers cannot countenance. We saw and saw and saw on this umbilical-cord-cum-tether, frantic to unhook, to achieve ourselves, our independence, only to feel the cord snap taut again, surprised to find it's reeling us in.

Mothers seem to cast a unique spell on philosophers from North Africa, haunting and hounding them long after they cross the Mediterranean. Albert Camus, author of *The Rebel*, rushed home to his mother in Algeria when she broke her leg, despite the literary furor in Paris surrounding his new book. On his writing desk he kept photos of Tolstoy, Nietzsche, and his mother.[2] His affection for his mother impinged on his political and philosophical positions in ways that made him anathema in postwar Paris. When in Stockholm to receive the Nobel Prize, Camus was shouted down by an Algerian protestor, who was castigating him for failing to champion Algeria's independence. When he finally had an opportunity to explain why he distanced himself from the National Liberation Front, Camus remarked: "I must condemn a terrorism that works blindly in the streets of Algiers and one day might strike at my mother and my family. I believe in justice, but I will defend my mother before justice."[3] And in the uproar of criticism that followed, Camus continued to choose his mother. When Camus died in a car accident southeast of Paris, inside his briefcase was found the unfinished manuscript of his last novel, *Le Premier homme* (*The First Man*). Handwritten on the first page was a dedication to his mother: "To you, who can never read this book."

When Jacques Derrida wrote his "Circumfession," he established his solidarity with fellow North African Augustine not in terms of geography or theology but in terms of their orienting relationship to their mothers. "What these two women had in common," Derrida noted, "is the fact that Santa Monica, the name of the place in California near to which I am writing, also ended her days, as my mother will too, on the other side of the Mediterranean, far from her land, in her case in the cemetery in Nice."[4] As he writes, his mother, Georgette, has already lost her memory, has lost language for the most part, has lost the ability to name what was so dear to Derrida. "I am writing here at the moment when my mother no longer recognizes me," he confesses, "and at which, though still capable of speaking or articulating, a little, she no longer calls me and for her and therefore for the rest of her life, I no longer have a name."[5] In one of her last semicoherent moments, his mother tells him, "I have a pain in my mother"—"as though she were speaking *for* me," he remembers, wondering if, in the end, "I am writing *for* my mother."[6]

"I have a pain in my mother." Augustine could identify. But that pain might be a symptom of a deeper issue—the challenge of negotiating an identity without effacing the dependence that makes us human. Mothers are a reminder of both, which is why they are so often a foil.

WHAT DID AUGUSTINE see in his mother? It depends on which Augustine you ask.

The young Augustine is ambivalent, resistant, perhaps even resentful. As a young man itching to make his mark and carve out his own territory of identity, his mother, Monica, was an omnipresent force who imposed her own life path on him, scripting events to conform to what she'd plotted. Augustine bristles at playing the role of a puppet in her schemes. Even if he comes to want the same things that she wants for him, he, like any emergent adult, wants to own the decisions as his own, to establish his agency in the face of the one who birthed him into being. Finding one's freedom is an odd dance: the very power to choose is *given*—"gifted," one might even say—but its realization requires a refusal of that status. The mother gives birth to the child who becomes an adult by living as if he materialized *ex nihilo*. And so the mother's designs grate against not so much his own goals as his sense of ownership of those goals. (We might recall that when Heidegger takes up these themes much later, "authenticity" is *Eigentlichkeit*, "ownmostness.") These are tendencies we develop early, as every parent of a two-year-old who insists, "I do it *myself*!" can attest.

Because almost everything we know about Monica comes from Augustine's haloed recollections of her, we need to read between the lines to see this drama playing itself out. If he were to follow the professional path she had predetermined for him, he would at least do it on his own terms. Hence the eagerness to throw off boyish innocence, which looked too much like the chastity his mother praised. When lack of parental funds means a hiatus from school, back at home he takes up with the local crew in acts of defiance and vandalism. Eventually, sick of her meddling (and perhaps the way she treated his unnamed concubine[7]), it gets to the point where he has to take drastic measures: deceiving his mother, he and his small family escape Africa under cover of night and the machinations of a lie. Even in his sanctified recollections, you can hear Augustine's lingering sense of her cloying presence: "As mothers do, she loved to have me with her, but much more than most mothers."[8]

Not even leaving the continent is enough. This mother—"strong in her devotion," Augustine coyly notes—will track him down all the way to Milan, "following me by land and sea."⁹ And perhaps what most sticks in his throat is that Augustine, to his own surprise, is starting to be the answer to her prayers. Nothing is more distasteful to the rebel child than realizing mom was right.

But there is another dynamic buried in these recollections: embarrassment. If the young Augustine in Africa couldn't imagine being a Christian, it's in no small part because he associated Christianity with the simple, "ethnic" expression of what he saw in Monica. Her own professional ambition for Augustine birthed in him a resistance, even revulsion, to the "Punic" faith he associated with his mother. The education she and Patrick funded would be precisely what made a biblical faith so implausible for Augustine. As Justo González aptly comments, "The form of religion that his mother, Monica, was calling him to accept had clearly African overtones, and this was partly the reason why Augustine, a man versed in Greco-Roman letters and traditions, could not accept it."¹⁰ The son has become a snob who prides himself on his "enlightenment," an intellectual and spiritual snobbery that only intensified when he joined the Manicheans who took themselves to be the "Brights" of their day—the rational, enlightened ones who saw through the myths that everyone around them had been suckered into believing.¹¹ It was the enlightened Manicheans who wove Augustine into the networks of power that got him his posts in Rome and Milan, not Monica's backward "brothers and sisters" in the church.

These worlds would collide in Milan. In Ambrose's preaching, Augustine heard a Christianity that he had never entertained, a faith with intellectual firepower that could stand toe-to-toe with philosophy. In Ambrose he saw a sophisticated, intelligent influencer who had relinquished power and privilege (and, ahem, reproduction) to follow One who had died on the despised Roman cross. Then, just as Augustine is starting to entertain the plausibility of Christianity once again, trying to get close to Ambrose, his mother shows up and gloms on to the bishop. Monica shows up with her "African" faith and backward customs that Ambrose had forbidden in his diocese. When she hears the bishop's admonishment, she respectfully obeys his exhortation and finds other channels for her devotion. So now when Augustine has the chance to run into Ambrose, hoping to talk about skepticism or the problem of evil, he can't get two words out of his mouth before Ambrose is praising Monica for her devotion, "congratulating me on having such a mother, unaware of what kind of son she had in me."[12]

THIS OVERLAP AND intersection between Ambrose and Monica, the convergence of his spiritual father and earthly mother, would birth in Augustine a new hermeneutic, and a completely different take on his mother and her "African" faith.[13] If Ambrose could praise his mother's Christianity, then it must be the same faith. He needed an Ambrose to make Christianity intellectually respectable enough to be plausible again, and once he stepped inside the faith he saw his mother's piety—and hence his mother—in a new light.

When Ambrose raises Augustine from the baptismal waters, Augustine's heritage is retroactively reframed. A child of God, he sees anew what it meant to be a son of Monica. What did Augustine see in his mother? Once he becomes her brother in Christ, almost everything about his relationship with her looks different. An epistemic empathy becomes possible; he can see what it was like to be his mother from the inside, as it were: the tenacity of her concern for his soul, her confidence in God's promises, her unflagging faithfulness to a wayward son, her pain as she watched him spin out of control. "She had tended to her sons, suffering birth pangs, so to speak, again every time she saw them leave the true path and move away from you."[14] He sees, now, that he was a son of tears, reborn, finding himself—of all places—in his mother's faith.

THE CULT OF Monica is as wide as the world, found wherever there are weeping mothers. Indeed, if you roam around Italy with your eyes peeled, looking for Augustine's legacy, Monica seems more ubiquitous. She represents the yearning of mothers everywhere, weeping over their children, hoping, praying, tenacious in their fierce love that the children confuse with control. It took a pilgrimage to Rome for me to finally grasp this—and watching Deanna, my wife and the mother of our four children, encounter Monica.

At Deanna's suggestion, we wound our way from the splendor of the Pantheon through a maze of narrow side streets in search of the Basilica di Sant'Agostino on the Piazza di Sant'Agostino. A busker in the piazza was strumming "Your Own Personal Jesus" (I kid you not) while a gaggle of young boys were playing with a beat-up soccer ball in the square. The church itself didn't seem worthy to house what was inside. The travertine façade felt fortresslike, with pockmarks in the stone that were reminiscent of bullet holes. Cardboard boxes littered the entrance. Someone was curled up under a soiled blanket on the stairs.

We creak our way tentatively inside. The back of the church is dark and silent, but a cacophony of marble almost overwhelms. The humble, beaten-down exterior explodes in pinks, persimmon, and gold when we pass through the diminutive door. A crossing ray of light feels suspended in the upper reaches of the transept.

We make our way past a few scattered worshipers in prayer and begin to wander independently. I'm struck by the chapel of St. Joseph, in which Joseph is hidden in darkness, a father not present. Noting the columns astride the altar, to the left I'm heartened to see Augustine paired with his lifelong friend Alypius. Across from them are Simplicianus and Ambrose.

Turning, I stop, caught by surprise: at the chapel to the left, Deanna is weeping and I don't know how to read these tears. As I inch closer, I realize she's found what she came looking for: Monica's tomb. On the outer wall is the original sarcophagus that held her remains in Ostia, transferred to this location in Rome in 1430. The relics of Monica now lie under the altar. The vault of the chapel is a series of frescoes by Ricci recounting Monica's life, culminating in her ecstatic vision with the son of her tears in Ostia just a few days before she died (see figure 5).

What has moved Deanna is a small prayer card. On one side is a detail of this fresco, Monica with hands raised in prayer and adoration. On the other side is a prayer that, even in its clunky English translation, is like a prayer that so many mothers know by heart:

> God, Holy Father,
> mercy for those who trust in You.
> You granted Your servant Monica
> the invaluable gift for reconciling
> the souls with you and one another.
> With her life, her prayers and her tears
> she took her husband Patrick
> and her son Augustine to You.
> In her we praise Your gifts;
> by her intercession
> give us Your Grace.
>
> O Saint Monica,
> who spiritually nourished your children
> giving them birth so many times
> as you saw them becoming estranged from God,
> pray for our families, for young people
> and for those who can't find the path of sanctity.
> Obtain for us the fidelity to God,

the perseverance in longing for Heaven
and the capacity to lead to the Lord
those he puts under our care. Amen.

In this hushed space, witnessing this encounter, I realize something I hadn't appreciated before, and probably can't ever fully understand: a solidarity that spans centuries, a sympathy that transcends geography, this bond between Monica and mothers who weep and pray and chase their children—misunderstood, unappreciated, resisted, resented. And yet none of that resentment could stop them, none of that resistance will deter them, no lack of gratitude could ever persuade them to give up. Like grace, Monica and her emissaries don't work on a logic of return.

For all the caricatures of mothers we're trying to escape, literature gives us glimpses of the Monicas all around us, who we so often fail to see. The Irish writer Rob Doyle has no investment in religion (quite the contrary, in fact), but in his short story "No Man's Land," Monica's presence is palpable, if unintended. A young man has just returned home from university in the wake of a mental health episode ("a severe nervous affliction," he tells us, in a kind of nineteenth-century euphemism). I thought it was a tick of my own Augustine-soaked imagination that called to mind the young Augustine's hiatus from school in Carthage that brought him back to Thagaste—until in the very next paragraph we meet a weeping mother who sounds like a latter-day Monica. The young man's mother leaves her job to care for her son in his depression. "On several occasions I walked in on her weeping in the kitchen, or in the cemented back garden that was hidden from the neighbours by high, grey-brick walls. Sometimes I heard her weeping in the bathroom. She always tried to hide her crying from me."[15] We've met a son of such tears before.

His mother enfolds the lethargy of his depression; she becomes to him (again) an amniotic sac of compassion, hoping against hope to birth him back into a life. He eases out of his lethargy with a ritual of daily walks in an abandoned industrial estate, wandering contemplatively amid the labyrinthine corridors of this rusted region of former industry. Here he regularly encounters a thirtysomething man who has gone mad, spouting proverbs of nonsense ("There is no therapy. There is no father."). The young man is jarred, disturbed, mostly because he sees in this raving wanderer a possible future for himself. After a chilling dream, a revelation of brokenness generates a new resolve.

> I woke up sobbing, drenching the pillow with tears that streamed out of me like never before or since, pierced with a desolation I knew to be incurable, a condition I would carry with me for ever. I rose from the bed, feeling my way through the dark. I found my way to my mother's bedroom and turned the handle on the door. I heard her gasp in the dark. "Don't worry," I said. "Go back to sleep. I'm sorry. Just let me lie here on the floor, just like this." I could hear her hesitating, waiting to get up and fix this, but it couldn't be fixed and she lay back down. I knew she was staring upwards into the dark, her face gaunt with worry. After a while she got up and draped some covers over me, then got back into bed. I closed my eyes and tried to hear her breathing.[16]

Rituals are not solutions. They don't "fix" things. They are how we live with what we can't fix, channels for facing up to our finitude, the way we try to navigate this vale of tears in the meantime. But precisely for that reason they can also be conduits of hope and rhythms of covenant. Mother/Monica didn't need to say anything; she needed to be there, present, breathing, placing the covers over her boy.

When he later wakes up, he tells his mother that he's going to call the university about returning. "Peering at me with widened eyes over the curve of her teacup, my mother nodded faintly. [There are unspeakable wells of restraint and fear in that "faintly."] She hesitated, fearful of crushed hopes. Then she said, 'I knew ye would. I never stopped prayin for ye.' Tears welled up, her voice was cracking. 'I never stop praying for ye. I mean it. I never will.'"[17] This is the ritual; it's just that someone else performs it. So be it: the mother as monastic, a quiet Benedictine of the everyday praying for the world that forgets her, keeping a fire alive for the future when the gleam of transgression is dulled and the hubris of our enlightenment wears out.

Perhaps it's not an accident that the arts best capture such mothers. Embedded in a longer poem called "The Burning Girl" by Mary Karr is a moving portrait of this unswerving, Monica-like devotion, with a mother's appreciation for its *power*:

> She was an almost ghost her mother saw
> Erasing the edges of herself each day
> Smudging the lines like charcoal while her parents
> Redrew her secretly into being over and
> Again each night and dawn and sleepless
> All years long. Having seen that mother's love,
> I testify: It was ocean endless. One drop could've
> Brought to life the deadest Christ.[18]

I know this mother. She sleeps beside me every night. She prays at a Pentecostal church in Lagos every Wednesday. She is awake in Rio, heart whirring, until the door clicks and the light goes out. She keeps prescriptions filled in Los Angeles like a sacramental fight against the darkness. . . . Her name is Monica. She is legion.

Not long after his conversion, in one of his early works, Augustine comments on an episode in which a grieving widow approaches Jesus because now she has also lost her only son (Luke 7:12–15). He had compassion on her, Luke tells us, and Jesus raises him from the dead. Augustine, from his own experience, knows the power of a mother's faith: "What benefit did the widow's son get from his faith, which he certainly did not have while he was dead? Yet his mother's faith was so beneficial to him that he was restored to life."[19]

SUCH MOTHERS ARE like sacramental echoes of the unfailing love of God, the Shepherd who goes looking for lost sheep, the Father who welcomes prodigals at the end of the lane because he's already been there looking for them. Such mothers are preambles to grace, a grace before grace, a primal, *natal* grace.

Indeed, years after Monica's death, Augustine, preaching a sermon in Carthage, considers the motherlike grace of God and the Godlike virtue of maternal devotion. He is meditating on Jesus's promise to "gather the chicks of Jerusalem under his wings [Matt. 23:37], like a hen that is weakened with her babies." He is struck by the power of maternal "weakness," the saving power of the one who humbled himself, a power that mothers exhibit every day. "This is maternal love, expressing itself as weakness," he tells his congregation. "All this is the mark of a mother's weakness, not of lost majesty." The mother, in other words, is an icon of the incarnation, that central mystery of the faith, in which the God of the universe would humble Godself, become human, and take on our sin and brokenness ("we confess that he participated in our weakness, but not in our iniquity, to the end that by sharing weakness with us he might destroy our iniquity").[20] That kind of "power" is often despised in a world that can only imagine power as domination, in a patriarchal world—let's be honest—where power is confused with testosterone-laden bravado. But Augustine is reminding us of that uniquely maternal power of God, echoed in the sacrifices that mothers make every day—the "weakness of God" that is stronger than men (1 Cor. 1:25).

That prayer card now hangs on the wall on Deanna's side of the bed, its own relic of that encounter at Monica's tomb. When I look across the bed, these two mothers are one—I see two Monicas, two dogged lovers of their children, steadfast. And on those mornings when tears spring from Deanna's eyes closed in prayer, brokenhearted but hoping, anxious but trusting, I commend her to Monica, and to the grace of God who, from stones, can raise up sons and daughters of Abraham.

ULTIMATELY, MONICA SHOWS Augustine how to go home, even though she'd never see Africa again. In his paean to Monica in book 9 of the *Confessions*, one of the most moving eulogies in Western literature, Augustine recounts their conversation that became an ascent to the divine they both craved—Augustine as a Neoplatonist, Monica as one who, quite apart from philosophy, had long looked for "another country." After a lengthy land journey from Milan, they withdrew from the bustling crowds of Ostia, busy in commerce and pagan devotion, to rest up for the voyage back to Africa. In this quietude, looking over the garden, they mused together, not nostalgically about Thagaste, but about what it would be like in that heavenly city, where the Son is the light. They found themselves transported, to the extent that Monica turned to her son and asked, "So what am I doing here?"[21] "I'm ready to go," she as much as said, not back home, across the Mediterranean once again, but to the home she sighed for, for which she was homesick, because she'd just caught a glimpse of it. Augustine's émigré spirituality is something he learned from Monica.

Augustine's brother was perplexed by Monica's nonchalance about her homeland as she approached death: "My brother," Augustine recalls, "said something about hoping she would pass away not in a foreign country but in her own native one." But "she scolded him with her eyes," as only mothers can do. "Soon afterward she said to both of us, 'Bury this body anywhere you like.'" She let go of the dream ("this frivolity," Augustine calls it) of being buried in the tomb alongside her husband. "Nothing is far from God," she told Augustine's friends. "And there's no reason to fear that when the world ends, he won't know the place from which to resurrect me," she joked.[22]

When Monica died, Augustine's son Adeodatus cried out in grief. For Augustine "the fresh wound from the sudden tearing asunder of our close day-by-day relationship" was especially searing, given the ways he had sought to evade his mother on the other side of the sea. "And yet, my God who made us, how could the respect I paid her possibly be compared to her servitude to me?" he cried out.[23] Having found himself in the One who made them both, Augustine had learned that being himself meant depending on others—a lesson his mother had been showing him his whole life. "I have a pain in my mother" is finitude's thorn in the flesh, an embodied reminder of the dependence that characterizes creaturehood.

FRIENDSHIP : *How to Belong*

What do I want when I want to belong?

Road movies are always buddy movies: the Blues Brothers, Thelma and Louise, Wendy and Lucy, Billy and Wyatt easy-riding across America, the entire family crammed into their VW van in *Little Miss Sunshine*. We hit the road to find ourselves but hardly ever do it alone. The paradox is that the voyage of discovery—the search for authenticity—is *mine*, and yet the search almost always seems to be shared. Becoming authentic is how we're alone together. Our individualism remains oddly communal. "I'm off to find myself," we exclaim. "Wanna come?"

This tension, even contradiction, is inscribed in our screenplays because it's baked into existentialism from the start. Take, for example, Dasein, that strange pilgrim character we meet in Heidegger's *Being and Time*—the character who is us, Heidegger claims.[1] My world is always shared, he emphasizes: "The world is always the one that I share with Others. The world of Dasein is a *with-world* [*Mitwelt*]." Indeed, "others" are not "out there," the swirling external mass of not-I; rather, they are "those from whom, for the most part, one does *not* distinguish oneself— those among whom one is too."[2] I *am* others; I live and move and have my being in the world *they* have made.

That's why Heidegger suggests that "proximally and for the most part"— his favorite phrase for naming our cultural defaults—our "everyday" existence is an unreflective absorption and immersion in the defaults "they" have set for me. I run in the grooves that everyone else is running in; the rutted paths worn by others become the easiest way to go. And so I go with the flow and live someone else's life—except it looks like the bland mass life that *all* of us are living. Who am "I" when I live absorbed in this shared world? I am "they," as Heidegger awkwardly puts it; I am *das Man*, the "they" we invoke when we defer to social defaults (as in "they say you shouldn't wear white after Labor Day" or "they say our love won't pay the rent").[3]

There is a working picture of intersubjectivity here: in this everyday version of "Being-with," Heidegger says, I live "in *subjection* to Others." Indeed, in a sense, I *am not*: my "Being has been taken away by Others."[4] "They" have taken over my identity; I am them. It's like we're all Manchurian selves. "When Dasein is absorbed in the world . . . it is not itself."[5] And this happens simply by the way I swim in my milieu, by going with the flow of an environment. Heidegger's 1920s illustrations can be easily extrapolated to the twenty-first century.

> In utilizing public means of transport and in making use of information services such as the newspaper, every Other is like the next. This Being-with-one-another dissolves one's own Dasein completely into the kind of Being of "the Others," in such a way, indeed, that the Others, as distinguishable and explicit, vanish more and more. In this inconspicuousness and unascertainability, the real dictatorship of the "they" is unfolded. We take pleasure and enjoy ourselves as *they* take pleasure; we read, see, and judge about literature and art as *they* see and judge; likewise we shrink back from the "great mass" as *they* shrink back; we find "shocking" what *they* find shocking.[6]

Heidegger's insights are at once dated and prescient. It doesn't take much imagination to project this into a digital world of mass consumer (de)formation. Even our nonconformity is mimicked: I refuse mass-marketed fast fashion by shopping at thrift stores *like "they" do*; I rail against the hegemony of the bourgeoisie with my tats and piercings *like "they" do*; I refuse the demure gentility of "political correctness" *like "they" do* by watching Fox News. "Every secret loses its force," Heidegger concludes: instead, what we get is an inauthentic "averageness," a "levelling down" of possibilities to what is shared. "In these modes," he observes, "one's way of Being is that of inauthenticity and failure to stand by one's Self."[7]

So what does authenticity look like, then? Singular, resolute, individual. For Heidegger, to be authentic is to answer a call that resounds above the din of "the they." And who is calling? *Myself.* The "call of conscience" is that appeal that snaps me out of my everyday absorption, my inauthentic they-self, and calls me to become Myself. The call of conscience is an appeal that rings like some existential cell phone and, when you pick it up, on the other end of the line is the Self you're supposed to be, exhorting you: "Be yourself!" "To what is one called when one is thus appealed to?" Heidegger asks. "To one's *own Self*."[8] Authenticity, then, is having the courage to take that call—the "anticipatory resoluteness" to live into what you alone can be, not what "they" have been offering and suggesting.[9] "When the call of conscience is understood, lostness in the 'they' is revealed."[10] I once was lost (in the "they") but now am found (by Myself). As Heidegger loves to put it, this is a matter of seizing my *ownmost* possibility.

Authenticity, then, always looks like an emergence from "them," a refusal of conformity, because inauthenticity is, by definition, a failure to resist the domination of Others, the tyranny of the "they." Others constitute an existential threat. Is it any wonder, then, that in his play *No Exit* Jean-Paul Sartre would put in the mouth of Joseph Garcin the jarring suggestion that "hell is other people"? This is not a bland misanthropy; rather, it stems from a picture of intersubjectivity not unlike Heidegger's, in which others are fundamentally competitors, threats, robbers of my peace and rest. If for Heidegger this finds expression in the dynamics of conformity, for Sartre Others represent a diminishment of my freedom—other people suck up the oxygen I need to realize the "absolute" independence that alone deserves to be called freedom. For Sartre, being is a zero-sum game: it's you *or* me. This cosmos isn't big enough for the two of us to be free. "Man cannot be at times free and at other times a slave: either he is always and entirely free or he is not free at all."[11] The Other is a scandal to my consciousness. Intersubjectivity, for Sartre, is an essential and ongoing contest of assimilation and objectification—of either devouring or being devoured. Even love, for Sartre, is a contest, a battle of wills for domination—to seduce is to entice the Other to give up their freedom to me.[12]

Behind Heidegger's account of authenticity and Sartre's notion of freedom—which have seeped into our collective popular consciousness in ways we still don't realize—is a take on intersubjectivity, on what it means for human beings to be alongside each other, sharing a world; it is a take on being-with. And that take is overwhelmingly negative. It construes our relationships with others as a threat to authenticity. Others are like dementors that threaten to suck out our very selfhood. Which is why authenticity is imagined as a matter of individual resolve, stand-alone resistance, an individuality that breaches defiantly above the sea of mass humanity.

These are *takes*, construals, interpretations that we have tacitly imbibed without realizing it, and therefore never challenged or questioned. We let them script not only our movies but our lives, and so we valorize "resolute" individuality even if it mostly keeps looking like some new conformity. More significantly, we tacitly adopt the construal of other people embedded in this vision of freedom and authenticity, even if we keep asking our friends to join us on the road trip to the Self-calling-itself that no one else can hear.

Gabriel Marcel, a contemporary of both Heidegger and Sartre, already saw this when existentialism was winning hearts and minds in the middle of the twentieth century. At the heart of Sartre's absolute freedom is an independence that has to refuse any and every gift. "For Sartre," Marcel observes, "to receive is incompatible with being free; indeed, a being who is free is bound to deny to himself that he has received anything."[13] Freedom is debt-free, which means living without attachments, connections, absolved of relation to others. "Is this not plainly contrary to experience?" Marcel asks. Is there any one of us who isn't indebted to a past that makes our choices possible, to relationships that have birthed and formed this "I" with agency?[14] Maybe freedom looks different from such a fabulous independence. Maybe others could be our friends.

And maybe Jean-Paul Sartre received more gifts than he realized. Marcel crystallizes his point: "I do not believe that in the whole history of human thought, grace, even in its most secularized forms, has ever been denied with such audacity or such impudence."[15] Indeed, Sartre's entire dialectic "rests upon the complete denial of *we* as a subject, that is to say upon the denial of communion."[16] To refuse the existentialist script for authenticity is not to embrace inauthenticity; it is to imagine why friends are gifts, how grace is communal, and how I find myself in communion. It would be a different kind of road movie that *has* to be a buddy movie.

IF HEIDEGGER CONSTRUED the influence of others in overwhelmingly negative terms, we should be honest that he learned this lesson from Augustine. In fact, we can now see that some of the crucial passages about *das Man* (the "they") in the 1927 *Being and Time* were reworked from his 1921 lecture notes on the *Confessions*. What becomes his analysis of "everydayness" and inauthenticity in *Being and Time* is forged in a reading of Augustine's account of temptation in book 10. When Augustine remarks that all of temporal life is a trial, Heidegger translates: "*Dasein*, the self, the being-real of life, is an absorption. The self is being lived by the world, all the more strongly so if it in fact thinks that it lives authentically."[17] When the self gives in to the temptation of ambition and "worldly praise," the self's "care" (*curare*) is taken over by others, and "the self is lost for itself in its ownmost way." I "fall into the communal world."[18]

Others, it is true, are characterized as the accomplices of Augustine's fall. In a key passage of the *Confessions* (in book 2), Augustine recounts the time that he and some of his crew of idle students were overcome by a kind of mob mentality that led them to steal fruit from a nearby pear tree only to toss it to some nearby swine (again echoing the parable of the prodigal son). Augustine emphasizes the way his own garden transgression—stealing fruit not even to enjoy it but to enjoy *enjoying* what ought to be used ("I loved my fall"[19])—was a communal endeavor. Indeed, others are not only companions in this fall; they are the *condition* for his fall: "Alone I would not have done it," Augustine repeatedly protests. Others appear in this drama as tempters, pulling me away from myself, drawing my loves from higher goods to lower things. "Friendship can be a dangerous enemy," Augustine remarks.[20] ("These people aren't your friends," as the Postal Service sings.[21]) Indeed, Augustine seems to withhold the honorific title of "friendship" from such collectives. Instead, they are a crew, a mob, a gang. "My love in that act was to be associated with the gang in whose company I did it," he recalls. What does he love when he loses himself to this gang? He loves the association, the belonging, the affirmation and recognition—distorted as it is. "My pleasure was not in the pears," he tells us. "It was in the crime itself, done in association with a sinful group." It makes no sense, Augustine concedes (this influence of others lies "beyond the reach of investigation"), and yet we all know its power. It's the collective power of transgressive association, a camaraderie in crime. "As soon as the words are spoken 'Let us go and do it,' one is ashamed not to be shameless."[22] I lose myself to others.

These self-sucking others show up again, in a different episode involving the young man who would become Augustine's lifelong and best friend, Alypius. Having struggled with an addiction to the gory, dehumanizing violence of the gladiatorial games, Alypius had achieved a new level of resolve to resist the temptation. But one evening on his way back from dinner, Alypius runs into a crew of fellow students—think roguish frat boys—who invite him to come along to the games with them. What starts as an invitation turns to razzing and then devolves to "friendly violence to take him into the amphitheatre during the days of the cruel and murderous games." The young but earnest Alypius overestimates his resolve and willpower—and simultaneously underestimates the power of spectacle on the body. When he finally caves to their insistent jostling, he remains (overly) confident: "If you drag my body to that place and sit me down there," he told them, "do not imagine you can turn my mind and my eyes to those spectacles. I shall be as one not there, and so I shall overcome both you and the games."[23] He was that young.

When they arrive, the coliseum "seethed with the most monstrous delight in the cruelty." In his resistant resolve, Alypius, like a choir boy at a strip bar, kept his eyes shut and intently thought about other things. In Augustine's play-by-play he wryly remarks: "Would that he had blocked his ears as well!" He then succinctly replays the drama, both external and internal:

> A man fell in combat. A great roar from the entire crowd struck him with such vehemence that he was overcome by curiosity. Supposing himself strong enough to despise whatever he saw and to conquer it, he opened his eyes. He was struck in the soul by a wound graver than the gladiator in his body, whose fall had caused the roar. The shouting entered by his ears and forced open his eyes. Thereby it was the means of wounding and striking to the ground a mind still more bold than strong, and the weaker for the reason that he presumed on himself when he ought to have relied on you.

There is an insight embedded here about freedom and agency, but at this juncture Augustine focuses again on the role that others play in this downfall. Alypius "was not now the person who had come in, but just one of the crowd which he had joined."[24] No longer himself but just part of the mob, Alypius was lost to the "they," his individual resolve melted.

He was now "a true confederate of those who'd brought him along."[25] And they were no friends.

You can trace here the genealogy of Heidegger's resolute "authentic" self, which then spawned Sartre's authentic "free" self, which then bequeathed to us the generic cultural version of authenticity we drink up with our Disney Channel subscriptions: resist the crowd, rise above the masses, be true to yourself, forge your own path. "You do you!" they tell us. Of course, you need to Instagram your trailblazing path to self-discovery so everyone can see, and constantly check your likes to confirm that your authenticity has been validated. But others are there for adulation; the only "we" is the we competing for attention.

Does this recipe for authenticity explain why we are so lonely?

RESEARCHERS CREATED A banal scenario in which a group of people would play a frivolous game of catch, tossing the ball to one another to pass the time and trying to keep it aloft. But the scientists set up the game with one condition: unbeknownst to her, one member of the group would never have the ball tossed her way. Try to put yourself in her shoes: you're in a group that starts a game of catch; the ball randomly popcorns around the group; giggling and frivolity ensue; you keep waiting for your chance to join in the fun, but the ball never comes your way. You're patient at first. You smile when others smile. You inch a little further into the circle to try to draw attention. Your smile is becoming more forced now. There's still a sliver of hope that your exclusion is random. Until eventually you conclude: the ball is never coming your way. This game isn't for you. You pretend you didn't want to play anyway. You stop trying.

But this isn't a game. As the researchers discover, that ostracized person will testify to an increased sense that life is meaningless and devoid of purpose.[26] The game is just a way to pull back the curtain on a fundamental human need.

Now imagine this isn't an experiment but the shape of a life: instead of waiting for a ball to come your way in a silly game of catch, you're waiting for anyone to call or drop by or speak your name. You can't even express it, but you're hungering for some sign that you are known. But no one calls. No one asks how you're doing. No one listens to your thoughts about the morning news. You are alone. Except there are hundreds of thousands of you. You're not alone in being lonely—not that that makes you any less lonely.

Loneliness—often a factor of social isolation—has become a societal epidemic in late capitalist societies. The Centre for Social Justice provides a succinct snapshot of loneliness in the UK, for example:

> As many as 800,000 people in England are chronically lonely and many more experience some degree of loneliness. 17 per cent of older people interact with family, friends or neighbours less than once a week, while 11 per cent do so less than once a month.
>
> It is linked to cardiovascular disease, dementia and depression and according to some researchers, its effect on mortality is similar to smoking and worse than obesity. One study revealed that it can increase the risk of an early death by as much as 30 percent.
>
> In addition to this there is a strong link between isolation and poverty: having two or more close friends reduces the likelihood of poverty by nearly 20 percent.[27]

The repercussions are felt in bodies, physical and social. It's not only the lonely who suffer because of this. It rends and destabilizes the commonweal. And there are costs. In response, the UK has now appointed a Minister for Loneliness to address the societal impact of this epidemic. The question is whether governments beholden to modernist narratives are willing to actually see the sources of the problem, such as family breakdown and even secularization itself. As the poet Franz Wright so powerfully captured in his poem "Flight," written to his absentee father,

"Since you left me at eight I have always been lonely / star-far from the person right next to me."[28] This is one of the reasons why, paradoxically, we can be lonely in a crowd.

But we have no one to blame but ourselves. We made this world. As Charles Taylor puts it, in modernity we remade the human person into a "buffered self," protected and autonomous and independent, free to determine our own good and pursue our own "authentic" path. We shut out incursions of the divine and demonic to carve out a privatized space to be free on our own terms. We didn't realize the extent to which we were shutting ourselves *in*. In liberating ourselves by locking out transcendence, the price we paid was sealing ourselves in a cell. We thought we were our own liberators; turns out we might be our own jailers.

Or, returning to Taylor, we might suggest that the construal of the self as buffered doesn't actually overwrite its nature as porous, as open and vulnerable, longing for connection. Indeed, the disastrous effects of social isolation put the lie to the modern spin on the self as autonomous and self-sufficient. Even when we believe that spin, the hunger of the soul proves otherwise. As Clay Routledge observes in the *National Review*, "Since social connections and love are so central to the human experience, we are vulnerable to great social suffering."[29] As even Heidegger recognized, loneliness is a mode of being-with.[30]

In her famous posthumous essay "The Opposite of Loneliness," Marina Keegan expressed this fundamental human longing and the fear of losing it. One might be tempted to dismiss this as privileged and coddled, except that it names a hunger (and fear) of every human heart.

> We don't have a word for the opposite of loneliness, but if we did, I could say that's what I want in life. What I'm grateful and thankful to have found at Yale, and what I'm scared of losing when we wake up tomorrow and leave this place. It's not quite love and it's not quite community; it's just this feeling that there are people, an abundance of people, who are in this together. Who are on your team. When the check is paid and you stay at the table.[31]

What if authenticity is the source of our loneliness? What if it's precisely this unquestioned, unrecognized construal of others as threats to my freedom and autonomy that has sequestered us? Is authenticity worth it? Or could we imagine authenticity otherwise?

Maybe the fact that every road movie is a buddy movie points to some other fundamental hunger of human nature, some ineffaceable impulse to communion. What if the opposite of loneliness is finding ourselves together? What if friends aren't threats or competitors but gifts? In the deepest corners of our hearts, we all want the person next to us to turn, with a smile, and shout: "Catch!"

HEIDEGGER MISSED THE rest of the story. He heard Augustine say, "Alone I would not have done it" but missed it when Augustine confessed, "I couldn't be happy without friends."[32] If friendship can be a dangerous enemy, for Augustine it is also the conduit of grace. The problem isn't other people but what they love, and how they love me.

Heidegger fixated on Augustine's portraits of inauthentic friendship, the camaraderie of the gang, the solidarity of the mob that, in the end, doesn't care about me and only loans me a sense of belonging as long as I perform, "join in," conform. This faux friendship provides thin gruel that pretends to feed what is a creaturely hunger: "to love and to be loved."[33] It's the infomercial form of friendship that feeds on my weakness and despair, with grand promises and big stories and people who have talked themselves into thinking they've discovered the good life. And because all Heidegger saw in Augustine was this disordered mode of fake friendship, to him it looked like others were always a distraction from myself, as if "friendship" was how you lose yourself. Authenticity, then, is a private project of individuation. Forget all the haters (and, for Heidegger, everybody else is a hater): you do you.

But that's inheriting a stunted Augustine, and it misses the end of the story. Augustine has his own rendition of what we might call "authenticity." Like Heidegger's version, it involves answering a call, hearkening to an appeal, responding to a summons to become who I'm made to be. But that call doesn't come from an echo chamber; it comes from the One who made me, a "friend who is closer than a brother," who laid his life down for his friends. And who calls to me *through* others, through friends.

Friends, in fact, are at the heart of Augustine's conversion narrative. Book 8 of the *Confessions* is a series of episodes where other people keep showing up in Augustine's life, refusing to let him remain where he is, prodding and prompting him to answer the call. This climax of the narrative is a kaleidoscope of friends and exemplars—friends who point to exemplars for Augustine to imitate. In this frame, others are not a threat to his authenticity; they're the lure drawing him toward it.

Book 8 opens with Augustine in a waffling despondency, "attracted to the way, the Savior himself, but . . . still reluctant."[34] So God makes a kind of divine suggestion to him: maybe go visit Simplicianus, an older Christian who circulated in Ambrose's orbit (and who, in fact, had baptized Ambrose). When Augustine shares his struggles, both intellectual and spiritual, mentioning his wrestling with Platonism, Simplicianus sees an opening to tell him a story about someone else, an exemplar. Marius Victorinus had been a learned, well-regarded orator in Rome. In many ways, Victorinus had achieved everything that Augustine would have hoped to achieve, even being honored with a statue in the Roman forum. And he was the translator of the "books of the Platonists" that had just transformed Augustine's philosophical imagination.

Simplicianus knew that Augustine could see something of himself in Victorinus: an orator, a scholar, a philosopher with political connections. Simplicianus was a friend to Augustine in the way that he pointed to Victorinus in order to press Augustine to become the self he was called to be and to imitate the courage of Victorinus, who had been willing to give up all his achievements to become a Christian. What made Simplicianus a friend was his willingness to be a conduit of the call to authenticity and to be wise enough to know that this was the perfect example to jar Augustine with a wake-up call. He was a "true" friend, Augustine would say, because he was spurring Augustine to become himself. Not every Other is the "they."

The encounter had its desired effect: "As soon as your servant Simplicianus told me this story about Victorinus, I was ardent to follow his example."[35] In this case, the influence of the Other is not diminishing but revivifying. The Other isn't stealing the oxygen of my individuality and authenticity; he's breathing new life into a self on the verge of resurrection.

The road to conversion for Augustine—the road to finding himself—is lined with these sorts of friends. Shortly after his visit with Simplicianus, Augustine has another "chance" encounter. As already noted in our discussion of ambition, Simplicianus proves himself a friend to Augustine by stoking an ambition for better things. And he does so by pointing him toward *exemplars* who answered such a call in their own encounter with *The Life of Antony*, a book that extols the example of someone who gave up worldly ambition to pursue the kingdom of God. Again, the example of another makes it possible for them to imagine themselves answering a similar call. Resolved to follow, the first turns to his friend and tells him of his decision. And now the friend will be an example for his friend. "If it costs you too much to follow my example, do not turn against me," he pleads.[36] But his friend is ready to follow. They set upon this new path together, friends and exemplars motivated and moved by friends and exemplars. Rather than the leveling effect of the "they," this drama unfolds through a cast of solicitous friends who are prompting Augustine to become who he's meant to be.

The result is a Dorian Gray–like encounter with himself. These examples are like portraits of who Augustine is called to be, which then show him himself in negative. The exemplars held up by Simplicianus and Ponticianus become a kind of carnival mirror for Augustine to see himself from a new angle. "While he was speaking, Lord, you turned my attention back to myself. You took me up from behind my own back where I had placed myself because I did not wish to observe myself, and you set me before my face so that I should see how vile I was, how twisted and filthy, covered in sores and ulcers. And I looked and was appalled, but there was no way of escaping from myself."[37] These friends are friends to Augustine, not because they come with affirming praise, but because they love Augustine enough to bring him face-to-face with himself, with who he is *not*, and unapologetically hold up a substantive vision of who he is called to be. A friend is not an enabler; love doesn't always look like agreement.

I'm reminded of a scene near the end of *Good Will Hunting*, the break-out hit for Matt Damon and Ben Affleck, featuring Robin Williams in one of his first dramatic roles. Will Hunting, you may recall, is a math prodigy with the bad luck of being born in the bombed-out, working-class wasteland of south Boston, a place where ambition is a sin. Despite being courted by Harvard academics and think tanks, Will has decided that it would be more true to himself to stay put and slug it out in dirty, backbreaking jobs, whiling away his life in dilapidated bars.

One afternoon when their shift at a demolition site is over, Will and his friend Chuckie are slurping cheap beer, leaning on a pickup. Chuckie asks whether Will is going to take one of the lucrative job offers on the table.

"Yeah, sit in some office doin' long division," he replies with disdain.

"Make some bank though," Chuckie reminds him. "Better'n this s——. It's a way outta here."

"What do I want a way outta here for?" Will replies, hoping Chuckie sees and values his loyalty. "I'm gonna f—— live here the rest of my life. You know, be neighbors, we'll have little kids, take 'em to Little League together."

Chuckie is incredulous but will have none of it. "Look, you're my best friend, so don't take this the wrong way. But in twenty years, if you're still livin' here, comin' over to my house watchin' Patriots games, still working construction, I'll f—— kill you."

Will is surprised and defends himself, telling Chuckie he's spouting psychobabble about "being true to yourself" that he's heard from all the pricks at Harvard.

"You don't owe it to yourself," Chuckie retorts. "You owe it to *me*. Because tomorrow I'll wake up and I'll be fifty and still doin' this s——. You're sitting on a winning lottery ticket and [not willing] to cash it in."

"Ah, what do you know!" Will responds, the retort of someone without a reply.

"Let me tell you what I know," says Chuckie. "Every day I come by your house and I pick you up. You know what the best part of my day is? For about ten seconds, when I pull up to the curb and when I get up to your door, because I think maybe I'll get there and I'll knock on the door and you won't be there."

The true friend is the other who hopes you'll answer the call, who's willing to challenge you and upset you in order to get you to look at yourself and ask yourself: What am I doing? What do I love? Who am I? The true friend is the other who has the courage to impose a conviction, who paints a substantive picture of the good, who prods and prompts you to change course and chase it—and promises to join you on the way.

THERE'S AN INTRIGUING passage in Heidegger's *Being and Time* where he entertains two very different modes of intersubjectivity, two different ways that others might influence me, two different forms of what he calls "solicitude." The first is an inauthentic relation he calls "leaping in." When others leap in to my life, they relate to me in a way that takes over. It's an influence from others that robs me of agency, makes my decisions for me, turns me into a kind of puppet of the "they." Often this will look like making things easier for me, alleviating me of the burden, "protecting" me from having to face up to existential anxiety. "This kind of solicitude takes over for the Other that with which he is to concern himself," Heidegger says. "In such solicitude the Other can become one who is dominated and dependent, even if this domination is a tacit one and remains hidden from him."[38] Friends who leap in imagine they're helping by preventing you from facing the question: Who am I?

Heidegger contrasts this with a mode of other-regarding concern he describes as "leaping ahead." The friend who leaps ahead isn't trying to fix things, or alleviate the burden, or disburden me of the choice I need to make. Such a friend leaps ahead "not in order to take away his 'care' but rather to give it back to him authentically as such for the first time." This, says Heidegger, is "authentic care." "It helps the Other to become transparent to himself *in* his care and to become *free for* it."[39] The friend who leaps ahead is one who's glimpsed what you're called to be and is willing to let you be uncomfortable as you wrestle with the call, who loves you enough to let you struggle for your soul but is standing by with a bandage and a map.

It's hard for me to imagine that Heidegger wasn't thinking about Augustine and Alypius when he came up with this distinction. The climax of the drama of the *Confessions*, and book 8 in particular, builds to Augustine's decision in the garden—but Alypius is there the whole time. There is no lone-wolf, individuated resolve in this picture of authenticity. When Augustine answers the call, finds himself, he is finding himself *in relation* to the One who made him, and he is finding himself alongside a friend who loves him.

In a fit of anxiety, his old self duking it out with the self he knows he's called to be, he steps into the garden to get some fresh air and elbow room. "Alypius followed me step after step," he points out. "Although he was present, I felt no intrusion on my solitude. How could he abandon me in such a state?"[40] Alypius doesn't leap in, but neither does he step aside. He is both present and absent, a comfort without being an intrusion, a co-pilgrim without pretending to take over the reins of the journey Augustine has to take. "This debate in my heart was a struggle of myself against myself," Augustine recalls. "Alypius stood quite still at my side, and waited in silence for the outcome of my unprecedented state of agitation."[41] It can be a horrible thing to watch someone in such an existential struggle. But alleviating the burden is not a way to love them. Friendship is staying close enough to put a hand on their shoulder while giving them enough room to feel the weight.

In a way, Alypius is an icon of the community of friendship that is the church. The church will fail at this in a million ways. And yet the church is still one of those places, in spite of itself, where you can count on people to be an Alypius for you: present, listening, leaving you room but not leaving you.

One of my favorite pictures of this ho-hum, mundane-yet-miraculous friendship that is the church is a quiet scene in the remarkable film *Lars and the Real Girl*. While the narrative is driven by drama surrounding a sex doll, don't miss the fact that it is probably the most powerful portrayal of the church in recent cinema. I want to zoom in on just one scene later in the film, where Lars (played by Ryan Gosling) is sadly awaiting the death of his "friend," Bianca, the sex doll he has imagined is his missionary girlfriend. He awakes once more during this vigil and emerges bleary-eyed from the house, standing on the porch to consider the day. When he turns around, he finally notices that the porch is awash in flowers and candles and prayer cards for Bianca.

Stepping back inside, he finally notices several older ladies knitting on the couch. "We brought casseroles," one of them points out. The quiet clicking of their knitting needles is the soundtrack of compassion.

Lars sits quietly, moving his food around the plate. "Is there something I should be doing right now?"

"No, dear. You eat," one of them encourages him.

"We came over to sit," another says.

"That's what people do when tragedy strikes," a third offers. "They come over and sit."

Alypius is the model for the community of friendship the church is trying to be: a people who are called to come and sit with the world. To be present with it in its tragedy. You might not have imagined it, but sometimes the good life looks like casseroles in the quiet sadness of a mournful home—a table prepared in the wilderness by a people who are hoping for a feast to come.

I realize that there are many places that call themselves "churches" that don't feel like this, that seem anything but hospitable. You won't find any defense of them from me. But I might encourage a second look. Let your eyes skate past the megachurch industrial complex and take note of the almost invisible church in your neighborhood that you've driven past a thousand times without noticing. Check on it some Tuesday night, and see if there aren't lights on in the basement. Maybe the food pantry is open. Or the congregation is offering financial management classes or marital counseling for couples who are struggling. It might just be the choir practicing, giving some souls an appointment to look forward to each week that pulls them out of their loneliness.

Or it could, quite likely, be an AA meeting, which are themselves echoes of a very different take on authenticity, a radically different construal of "others." As Leslie Jamison notes, at the heart of recovery is *meeting*, communion. "The meeting itself," she recalls, "was just a bunch of strangers gathered around a huge wooden table, past a kitchen tracked with footprints, old linoleum curling upward at the edges of the room. People smiled like they were glad to see me, almost like they'd been expecting me to come."[42] You don't go to the meeting to get information, to figure something out. The point of the meeting is *meeting*, the solidarity forged in shared struggles. While she hems and haws about whether to go in, she realizes that in there is a community of strangers who know her and are waiting for her. Maybe they're friends? "No matter how long you sit in the car, somebody is waiting in that wooden building."[43] Maybe it's not an accident that building is a church.

The church you've probably never seen is the invisible community of friendship in your neighborhood. The church isn't a group of holier-than-thou saints who've formed a club; it's a remarkable, otherwise impossible communion of people who, by the grace of God, stick alongside one another. I remember a jarring but touching example of this in a conversation between Lena Dunham and poet Mary Karr. Dunham, as you might guess, is not much given to religious impulses, but she is quietly fascinated by Karr's faith, her association with this guy "Jesus." So Dunham asks: "What's it like to be a person who thinks and cares about Jesus and has religion in your life but hangs out with the New York literati?" Karr tries to defuse some mistaken impressions of Christianity, but then tells a simple story about church.

> I had this amazing thing happen to me in Mass a couple of weeks ago. A guy came up to me. I had my iPad, and there's a thing that lets you follow the readings, the Church readings. I'm looking at that. I'm not reading my email, I'm looking at that. This guy comes up from the back of the church, dressed up in a coat and tie like Uncle Assistant Principal or something. He says, "Could you turn that off?" I said, "Excuse me?" He said, "The light is bothering me." I thought for a minute, *I'm trying to be a Christian*, and I said, "OK, yeah, sure. I can. Yeah, no problem." Then I sat there and wished him dead during the entire Mass. Then when I was walking out of the church, he came up to me and said, "I'm so sorry. I know there's something wrong with me."

"No he did not," Dunham retorts. "He did," Karr assures her. She reflects on the experience: "I was so glad that I had turned it off. I got to help him to feel a little better or whatever, feel like he had some agency in the world. What did that cost me? Do you know what I mean? For me, a lot of times I walk into Mass and I look at people and I think, *These are not my people*. Invariably, by the end of Mass, I walk out and people look different to me."[44]

People look different through the lens of grace: instead of being competitors or threats, they're gifts. Some are even friends.

It's no surprise that after Augustine's breakthrough, when grace has finally made the choice possible, when he embraces and becomes the version of himself he'd been haunted by, Augustine immediately turns to his friend Alypius. Turning to the next passage of Scripture after Augustine flipped open the Bible to Romans 13, "Alypius applied this to himself," and "without any agony of hesitation he joined me."[45] But of course, he'd been there all along.

And would be for the rest of his life. Alypius would be one of the most constant presences in Augustine's life, even if they didn't get to enjoy living in proximity. Baptized together, Alypius too would go on to become a priest and then bishop in Thagaste. They are nearly inseparable, and if Augustine's life is a road movie, Alypius is the faithful sidekick who, in the end, proves to be the most faithful friend.

In one of his earliest dialogues, the *Soliloquies*, Augustine testifies to the depth of their friendship in a sort of backhanded way. The *Soliloquies* are a kind of internal dialogue that Augustine has, arguing with "Reason." "What do you want to know?" Reason asks. "God and the soul," Augustine replies. "Nothing more?" Reason asks. "Nothing whatever."[46] But this raises questions about the very possibility of knowledge. *Can* we know God with any sort of intimacy and confidence?

Well, asks Reason, "if anyone promised to give you a knowledge of God like the knowledge you have of Alypius, would you not be grateful and say it was enough?" The knowledge of Alypius is as intimate as Augustine could imagine. "Indeed I should be grateful," Augustine replies, "but I should not say it was enough." Why? "I do not know God as I know Alypius," Augustine admits, "but even Alypius I do not know sufficiently well." This isn't an indicator that Alypius isn't close; to the contrary, the point is that even when it comes to those who are closest to us, who are kindred souls, our "better halves," even they retain a secret, an "inside" that eludes us. "Do you dare to say that your most familiar friend is unknown to you?" chides Reason. "There is no daring about it," Augustine responds. "I think that law of friendship is most just which lays down that a man shall love his friend as himself, neither less nor more. So, seeing that I do not know myself, how can I be reproached for saying that I do not know him?"[47] I know Alypius better than anyone, and Alypius knows me better than anyone, Augustine is saying. And yet we remain mysteries to ourselves. The vision of friendship here is also haunted by a realism—namely, that we see (ourselves and others) through a glass darkly. There are secrets we don't know about ourselves. Why should we be surprised that even our closest friends have a kind of transcendence that eludes us, a depth we cannot plumb? Friendship makes room for the mystery of communion and the mystery behind our communion.

And none of that undermines or weakens a friendship. It certainly didn't for Alypius and Augustine, who would remain the closest of friends until the end. More than forty years later, in 428, Augustine still longs to see Alypius: "For I desire also to see Your Fraternity as soon as possible now that the hope for your return, which you indicated to me by letter, draws near."[48] As they approach the end of life, both of them near to knowing as they are known, Augustine still can't wait to see the friend who has been there since the beginning.

AUGUSTINE WAS, IN fact, rarely alone. He lived in community his entire life. When he was pressed into his role as bishop, one of the conditions he stipulated was that he be permitted to found a monastic community of clergy who would live with him in the bishop's residence. The *Rule of Augustine*—the oldest monastic rule in the Western church—was originally written for this intimate community around Augustine himself, later taken up as the rule of life for Augustinian monastic communities around the world. The *Rule* is another example of Augustine's spiritual realism: it is an honest, unsentimental guide for the challenges of living in community, well acquainted with the heart's crooked bent toward selfishness, snobbery, greed, and exclusion. The *Rule* confronts the realities of class condescension as well as the perverted sanctimoniousness of those who see themselves as "slumming it" with the hoi polloi. Thus the *Rule* admonishes: "Nor should they put their nose in the air because they associate with people they did not dare approach in the world. Instead they should lift up their heart, and not pursue hollow worldly concerns." Many of the guidelines of the *Rule* can be summed up in one of its asides: "Pride lurks even in good works."[49]

The Augustinian embrace of community and friendship is not utopian or idealistic. It is unstintingly clear-eyed about the realities of being-with, identifying the sorts of grievances and annoyances that still infect even our best friendships. Affirming the good of community, the *Rule* is a set of guidelines that provides a script for real-world friendships where every friend is still prone to egoism and selfishness, where jealousy is a struggle even for the saints among us. "I couldn't be happy without friends," Augustine testified. The community he lived in for the rest of his life was testament to that. We find ourselves in community; we need friends on the road. In the *Rule*, what looks like advice for travel turns out to be advice for the cosmic journey we're on: "Whenever you go out, walk together, and when you reach your destination, stay together."

ENLIGHTENMENT : *How to Believe*

What do I want when I want to be rational?

For the aspiring provincial, the university looks like a ladder. An education is a tool for climbing. Sadly, we live in an age in which the university has adopted this picture of itself. Colleges are credential factories, and the Ivy League is a ridiculously expensive employment agency connecting the new meritocracy with hedge funds and Supreme Court clerkships that function as escalators to wealth and power.

In other words, not much has changed since a young Augustine made his way to Carthage. Study was almost a distraction from the extracurricular activities of playing games and getting laid. And learning itself was instrumentalized as a means to achieve some other good: "My studies which were deemed respectable had the objective of leading me to distinction as an advocate in the lawcourts, where one's reputation is high in proportion to one's success in deceiving people."[1] The liberal arts, in Augustine's experience, were something to be weaponized rather than a curriculum for cultivating the soul. The notion that his university education might touch on matters of wisdom was almost laughable.

But even broken clocks are right twice a day, and even a bastardized curriculum can be a portal to another world. In a university that revolves around the quest for profit and prestige, a lingering liberal arts curriculum is like a distant echo that keeps calling. You never know when the still, small voice of Plato can pierce through all the noise in a marauding frat boy's life and resound as a wake-up call for a soul—that his taut, frantic, voracious body *has* a soul, that the soul is made for a quest and not just sexual conquests, and that there is a kind of learning that doesn't just position you but transforms you.

This is what happened to Augustine. In the seething carnal cauldron of Carthage, where students took vandalism more seriously than they took learning, where everyone was on the make and only there to find a way up and out, Augustine was assigned to read Cicero, and in that reading we witness his first conversion. Cicero's *Hortensius*, an exhortation to pursue wisdom, caught Augustine off guard and set him off-kilter. It plucked strings in his soul he didn't even know he had. "The book changed my feelings," he recalls. "It altered my prayers, Lord, to be towards you yourself. It gave me different values and priorities. Suddenly every vain hope became empty to me, and I longed for the immortality of wisdom with an incredible ardour in my heart."[2] Philosophy had lodged an existential thorn in his heart and he couldn't shake it.

For the next decade, Augustine would live what Charles Taylor might call a "cross-pressured" existence, tugged and pulled in various directions, a playboy who's caught the philosophy bug.[3] A new interest and curiosity has been kindled, but old habits and hungers remain alive and well. Philosophy became something he *added* to his life, not a way of life. And in fact, it's remarkable how philosophy—the alleged love of wisdom—can be domesticated by those other lingering habits of the heart, such that philosophy actually becomes just one more lust, one more game of domination and conquest (something I've seen in a thousand sophomore philosophy majors and, sadly, much of "professional" philosophy). The encounter with Cicero's *Hortensius* birthed something new in Augustine, but his infant interest in wisdom became the child that served other masters still ruling his heart.

Augustine would give a name to this kind of disordered relationship to wisdom and learning: *curiositas*. Curiosity for Augustine is not the spirit of inquiry we prize and encourage; rather, it is a kind of quest for knowledge that doesn't know what it's for—a knowing for knowing's sake, we might say, or perhaps more to the point, knowing for the sake of being known as someone who knows.[4] For Augustine, the *reason* I want to know is an indicator of the sort of love that motivates my learning. Am I learning in order to grow, learning in order to know who and how to love? Or am I learning in order to wield power, get noticed, be seen as smart, be "in the know"? The disordered love of learning makes you a mere technician of information for some end other than wisdom, and the irony is that philosophy could devolve into just another way of idolizing. Indeed, Augustine could still see this in himself by the time he was a teacher: "I was seeking to use my education to please other people—not to teach them, but just to please them."[5]

Curiosity is characterized by a fetishization of something *as* "truth" in order to serve my own interests and ends. When learning is reduced to *curiositas*, actual truth and wisdom are disdained as an affront to *my* interests, *my* authority, *my* autonomy, and I become a so-called philosopher (lover of wisdom), Augustine says, for whom actual truth "engenders hatred." Augustine's diagnosis of what is going on here is timely:

> Their love for truth takes the form that they love something else and want this object of their love to be the truth; and because they do not wish to be deceived, they do not wish to be persuaded that they are mistaken. And so they hate the truth for the sake of the object which they love instead of the truth. They love the truth for the light it sheds, but hate it when it shows them up as being wrong.[6]

What masquerades as the pursuit of truth becomes an agenda for confirming my biases and making me comfortable, for justifying my enjoyment of what I ought to be using. If the actual truth disrupts my enjoyment, I resent the truth all the more. What I love in this case is *my* truth, not *the* truth. "What is loved at the moment," Heidegger comments, "a loving into which one grows through tradition, fashion, convenience, the anxiety of disquiet, the anxiety of suddenly standing in vacuity; precisely *this* becomes the 'truth' itself."[7] This Augustinian diagnosis, taken up by Heidegger in the 1920s, seems ever more true in a culture of clicks and likes:

> They love [the truth] when it encounters them as glitzy, in order to enjoy it aesthetically, in all convenience, just as they enjoy every glamour that, in captivating, relaxes them. But they hate it when it presses them forcefully. When it concerns them themselves, and when it shakes them up and questions their own facticity and existence, then it is better to close one's eyes just in time, in order to be enthused by the choir's litanies which one has staged before oneself.[8]

Curiositas generates its own frenetic anxiety, because now I have to "keep up" and stay in the know, striving to be the person who knows *before* everybody else (Google "Portlandia OVER"). It's the exhaustion of being perpetually "in the know." Which explains why *this* sort of pursuit of "truth" doesn't ever feel like the *beata vita*, the happy life. As Heidegger puts it, "The bustling activity in which they are absorbed, the cheap tricks to which they abandon themselves, rather makes them even more miserable."[9] To be among "the enlightened ones" comes with its own anxiety—of being found out, of *not* knowing, of being in the out-group of the ignorant rather than the inner sanctum of winks and nods and inside jokes. *Curiositas* is the anxious burden of having to always be clever.

IF THE ENCOUNTER with Cicero's *Hortensius* woke up something in Augustine, it wasn't true *philosophia*, love of wisdom, but rather a lust for knowledge that served other cravings—for advancement and access to an inner circle.[10] He wasn't really interested in wisdom; he simply wanted to be part of the enlightened crowd. This was still a craving to *belong*. Which perfectly explains why, not long after this wake-up call, Augustine fell in with the Manicheans.

This detour in Augustine's journey—and his lifelong wrangling with them—will seem hopelessly irrelevant to twenty-first-century seekers if we merely consider what the Manicheans, these devotees of Mani, believed. The teachings of Mani are so foreign and fantastical that they don't seem to have any contemporary analogue; it's not like Manichean-ism is a live option today. As Robin Lane Fox comments in his succinct but fulsome account, "Mani's cosmology strikes what he would call 'semi-Christians' as a teeming myth, more like *Star Wars* than their own Chris-tianity."[11] Indeed, its radical dualism, with eternal forces of Darkness and Light inscribed into the very fabric of the cosmos, feels like something we'd encounter only in *Game of Thrones*. (That its rites seemed to include a cabal of the elect consuming bread baked from flour "fertilized" by sex rituals is, sadly, not entirely outlandish today.)

We need to look past the content of the Manichean's doctrine and see what actually drew Augustine in: the *way* they claimed to know. What's instructive about Augustine's attraction to Manicheanism is less what they taught and more how they held to that teaching. In this respect, we will notice something shockingly contemporary about the Manicheans' epistemic posture: they were the "rationalists" of their day. While their worldview seems fantastical to us, the Manicheans prided themselves on having escaped superstition and the embarrassments of believing, instead arriving at the shore of enlightened *knowledge*. Indeed, it's not a stretch to say the Manicheans considered themselves the scientists of significance: instead of trusting the testimony of prophets, their knowledge was rooted in the course of the sun, moon, and stars. These purveyors of Light and of secret enlightenment were the "Brights" of their day; they prided them-selves on refusing authority and instead *knowing* how things worked.[12]

The attraction, then, was less to explanatory power and more to as-sociation with people who confidently imagined they had an explanation for everything—and were well connected in high places, to boot. (It was Manichean connections that landed Augustine his appointments in both Rome and Milan.) The attractiveness of the Manicheans was an inter-twined set of benefits that spoke directly to an aspiring provincial, run-ning from his mother's backwater faith, newly interested in being "in the know," and still clambering for positions of power and influence.

In 392, not long after he was ordained to the priesthood, Augustine wrote to an old friend, Honoratus, who was still associated with the Manicheans. Augustine felt a special burden for Honoratus since he was to blame for Honoratus falling in with them. If he writes passionately and pastorally to a friend led astray, it's because Augustine is also writing to his younger self, as if he owes this to Honoratus as an act of penance. But it also means Augustine knows something of the psychology of attraction here *from the inside*. "There is nothing easier, dear friend, than to say one has discovered the truth," Augustine writes, "and even to think it, but from what I write here I am sure you will appreciate how difficult it really is."[13] Imagine Augustine, a newly ordained priest, writing to Honoratus, who's busy reading the new atheists.

The attraction to Manicheanism was about association with people who confidently offered a *posture* as much as a doctrine. "We fell in with them," Augustine reminds his friend, "because they declared with awe-some authority, quite removed from pure and simple reasoning, that if any persons chose to listen to them they would lead them to God and free them from all error." They promised a way to rise above those "held in fear by superstition." "Who would not be enticed by promises like that?" Augustine asks. "What was it that attracted you, I wonder? Was it not, I beg you to remember, a certain grand assumption and promise of proofs?" The Manicheans found us at an opportune time, Augustine reminds him: "scornful of the 'old wives tales' [told by mothers?] and keen to have and to imbibe the open, uncontaminated truth that they promised."[14]

This is a familiar recipe for recruitment, trotted out today by ratio-nalist purveyors of scient*ism* who promise to unlock all the mysteries of the universe by a "science" that shows there are none. From Richard Dawkins to Steven Pinker, the priests of enlightenment are prophets of overreach, promising a status more than an adequate explanation. And we buy in, less because the "system" works intellectually (we often don't even expend the energy to confirm the evidence, and we suppress lingering questions), and more because it comes with an allure of illumination and sophistication, with the added benefit of throwing off the naivete of our parents' simplistic faith. What their "knowledge" offers is a shortcut to respectability.

Just don't ask too many questions when you make it inside. That was Augustine's problem: ultimately, he wasn't satisfied with association; he actually wanted to understand. And when he kept pressing the Manicheans with questions, they kept telling him: Wait til Faustus gets here; he'll explain everything.[15] Except he didn't. In such circles of enlightenment, there are always questions you're not allowed to ask, as Augustine discovered.

In writing to Honoratus, Augustine doesn't offer a counterpoint to the specific doctrines of the Manicheans (he does that abundantly elsewhere). Instead, his critique is more "radical," we might say, getting to the "radix"—the root—of their epistemic posture, of what they claim to stand on. The Manichean rationalists "boast that they do not impose a yoke of belief but open up a fountain of doctrine"; they "attract numbers in the name of reason."[16] In other words, the Manicheans prided themselves on their refusal to submit to any authority outside of their own reason, which was not so different from the rallying cry of Immanuel Kant's essay "Answering the Question: What Is Enlightenment?" fourteen centuries later: *Sapere aude*! Have the courage to use your own reason! It's the same watchword used today by those who like to imagine themselves "free thinkers."

But Augustine pulls the rug out from under the feigned stance of rational self-sufficiency. Everyone believes. Everyone submits to some authority. And all these people priding themselves on enlightenment have decided to simply trade belief in one set of authorities for belief in another. "Credulity," Augustine points out, is not a defect; it is inherent to being human. Tongue-in-cheek, Augustine points out the number of times Honoratus expects his interlocutor to trust him, to *believe* him, so that he can show him the path to enlightenment.[17] Trust is the oxygen of human society, Augustine says, and believing the testimony of others is at the very heart of the scientific enterprise. Understanding doesn't transcend belief; it *relies* on belief. If someone says believing is wrong, Augustine wryly notes, "I do not think he can have any friends. If it is wrong to believe anything, then either one does wrong by believing a friend, or one never believes a friend, and then I do not see how one can call either oneself or the friend a friend."[18] Augustine is striking at the very heart of what the Manicheans offered: not just enlightenment, but *belonging*, a circle of those "in the know," a friendship of light. Indeed, why would we have ever been drawn to the Manicheans if we hadn't believed what they promised? "I would not come to someone who forbids me to believe unless I did believe something. Could there be any greater insanity than this: they blame me only because I have belief that is not supported by knowledge, although it is only that which brought me to them?"[19]

Augustine is not promising a different version of self-sufficient enlightenment to counter what the Manicheans are offering. He's calling into question the very myth of such a stance. The question isn't *whether* you're going to believe, but *who*; it's not merely about what to believe, but who to *entrust* yourself to. Do you really want to trust yourself? Do we really think humanity is our best bet? Do we really think *we* are the answer to our problems, we who've generated all of them? The problem with everything from Enlightenment scientism to mushy *Eat-Pray-Love*-ism is us. If anything looks irrational, it's the notion that we are our own best hope. So Augustine invites Honoratus to consider what's at the heart of Christianity, which is not a teaching per se, but an event, an unthinkable event from a Manichean perspective, and yet one that speaks to humanity's deepest hungers and fears. "Since, therefore, we had to model ourselves on a human being but not set our hopes on a human being, could God have done anything kinder or more generous than for the real, eternal, unchanging wisdom of God itself, to which we must cling, to condescend to take on human form? . . . By his miraculous birth and his deeds he won our love, but by his death and resurrection he drove out fear."[20] Many years later, in 417, still confronting the challenge of the Manicheans' rationalism, Augustine pleads with his congregation in a sermon: "You cannot be your own light; you can't, you simply can't. . . . We are in need of enlightenment, we are not the light."[21] You're going to entrust yourself to somebody. Would you entrust yourself to the One who gave himself for you?

THERE'S NO RUSH. It took Augustine a long time before he'd consider this. His disenchantment with the false promises of the Manicheans did not translate into an immediate embrace of Christianity. In fact, the result was a long period of destabilizing skepticism, a sympathy for the "Academics," skeptics who despaired of ever arriving at the truth.[22] While he was still happy to leverage the Manicheans' connections to land his post in Milan, by the time he arrived, he bordered on cynicism.

Our cerebral struggles are often intertwined with other anxieties. What we identify as intellectual barriers are sometimes manifestations of emotional blocks. We pride ourselves on being rational but then miss the biases and blind spots that constitute our rationality (a feature of the human condition confirmed by recent developments in behavioral economics). We decide that something "doesn't make any sense" when we no longer want to be associated with the people who believe it, or a "light goes on" and we "see" something after we've spent time hanging around people who believe it. Rationality turns out to be more malleable than we'd guess.

Sometimes plausibility is pegged to a person. The turning point for Augustine was not an argument; it was Ambrose. What Ambrose said, what he taught and preached, was not insignificant. But what made a dent on

Augustine's imagination was Ambrose's very being—what he represented in his way of life. Ambrose was a living icon of someone who integrated assiduous learning with ardent Christian faith. If to that point, based on his childhood experience, Augustine had concluded that Christians were simple, backward, and naive, the encounter with Ambrose was the destabilizing experience of meeting someone with intellectual firepower who was also following Jesus. Even more than that, it was Ambrose's hospitality that prompted Augustine to reconsider the faith he'd rejected as unenlightened. What ultimately shifted Augustine's plausibility structures? *Love.* His recollection is warm and speaks to a hunger even more fundamental than the intellectual: "That man of God took me up as a father takes a newborn baby in his arms, and in the best tradition of bishops, he prized me as a foreign sojourner."[23] More than arguments or proofs, Ambrose offered the seeker Augustine something he'd been hungering for: a home, sanctuary, rest. For this refugee in a new city, arriving with questions and with so much unsettled in his life, the cathedral in Milan became an outpost of the home this spiritual émigré had been seeking. And there was a father there waiting to welcome him.

This was the point he'd later make in *The Advantage of Believing*: there is a *relationality* to plausibility. Illumination depends on trust; enlightenment is communal. It's not that Augustine immediately comes to affirm the catholic faith; rather, Ambrose's kindness and hospitality to a precocious outsider was the affective condition for him to reconsider the faith he'd spurned. "I fell in love with him, as it were, not at first as a teacher of the truth—as I had no hope for that whatsoever in your church—but simply as a person who was kind to me."[24] You can feel in this encounter something of the gratitude of the African outsider not being marginalized by an intellectual at the center of power. It's not that he immediately comes to believe but that Christianity becomes more and more believable (and Manicheanism less and less so). "Though now I hadn't yet verified that the church was teaching the truth," he admits, "it was plainly not teaching what I'd so obnoxiously accused it of teaching."[25]

From Ambrose, Augustine would realize that the Christianity he'd rejected was not Christianity. But it was Ambrose's love and welcome that created the intellectual space for him to even consider that.

This relationship between love and knowing, affection and intellection, would become a hallmark of Augustine's thought for the rest of his life. By constantly emphasizing, "I believe in order to understand," Augustine's more subterranean point was, "I love in order to know." He crystallized this in one of his earliest works after his conversion, *Soliloquies*. Adopting a visual metaphor for knowing—as in "the mind's eye"—Augustine picks up the Platonic metaphor of knowing by means of illumination. But there's an important difference: "it is God himself who illumines all." Reason, Augustine's interlocutor, then continues: "I, Reason, am in the minds as the power of looking is in the eyes. Having eyes is not the same thing as looking, and looking is not the same as seeing. The soul therefore needs three things; eyes which it can use aright, looking, and seeing."[26] But only healthy eyes can see, and faith restores the health of the eyes.

"If the mind does not believe that only thus will it attain vision, it will not seek healing." In other words, if skepticism leaves us despairing of ever attaining the truth, we'll never go looking. "So to faith must be added hope." But reason will only be motivated to set out on the quest if it is also animated by a desire, if it longs for the promised light. "Therefore a third thing is necessary: *love*."[27] If this remains abstract in the Platonic dialogues of his early career, in the *Confessions* we see this point embodied. It's not just that reason needs love in order to know; I need to be loved into such knowing, welcomed into such believing, embraced for such hoping. If the arguments are going to change your mind, it's only because an Ambrose welcomes you home.

THE EMBRACE OF Ambrose didn't smother the questions. There was no dichotomy, only a priority: not love instead of understanding, but loving in order to understand. If Ambrose engendered a shift in plausibility structures for Augustine, it meant that he could consider anew whether Christianity had resources to answer some of his oldest, most lingering questions—about evil, the nature of God, free will, and other intellectual questions that continued to dog him. The relationship to Ambrose nudged him to find an intellectual well in Christianity he didn't know was there, as if tapping into an artesian aquifer that had been right under his feet all the way back home in Africa.

Augustine slowly started to realize how stunted his philosophical imagination was. While the Manicheans had promised him enlightenment, he was coming to see that they had furnished his imagination with a limited array of blunt instruments that were inadequate tools for the complex questions he was asking. His conceptual muscles had a limited range of motion. For example, he was unable to imagine a kind of substance that wasn't somehow material—anything that existed had to be physical.[28] This limited his ability to conceive of a God who transcended time and creation, as well as his ability to understand his own mental powers, the nature of the soul. Similarly, because of the habits of mind he'd acquired from the Manicheans, when he sought to understand the origin of evil, he says, "I searched in a flawed way and did not see the flaw in my very search."[29] It was slowly dawning on him: the cabal that had promised him enlightenment turned out to be remarkably parochial. The enlightened ones who prided themselves on being rational were working with a limited intellectual toolkit but had never told him (likely because they didn't realize).

The intellectual breakthrough Augustine needed came, once again, from philosophy. But not from Cicero this time. Instead, it would be "the books of the Platonists" that would refurnish Augustine's theoretical imagination—or, to change the metaphor, that would serve as an intellectual gymnasium where he could work to increase the range of motion in his conceptual muscles. He could reach conclusions that weren't available to him before, stretching his mind around ideas that had been conceptually out of reach, affording new possibilities to both settle some questions and live into a coherent way of life. He wouldn't have to choose between faith and reason; philosophy would be the preamble to his embrace of Christianity.

But this gearing together of Platonism and Christianity would generate its own tensions and cause Augustine to have to make a choice. Much has been made of Augustine's Platonism, and it's beyond question that Platonism—or, more specifically, the Neoplatonism of Plotinus—provided a crucial intellectual scaffolding at the time of his conversion and through the rest of his life. In *Of True Religion*, one of his earliest works, Augustine paints Christianity as the completion of Platonism—that if Plato were alive in the Christian era, he too would be a follower of Jesus.[30]

Yet to overstate the continuity is to miss what Augustine sees as a fundamental distinction of Christianity that makes all the difference: humility. Platonism lifted his attention from the temporal and material to the eternal and invisible. Platonism helped him conceive of an *ascent* to higher things, to the purity and eternity of the Good. But what Platonism could never have imagined was that the Good would *descend* to us; that the eternal God would condescend to inhabit time and a body; that the divine would humble itself and swing low to carry humanity home.

The books of the Platonists, Augustine says, helped him grasp half the gospel: "In the beginning was the Word and the Word was with God and the Word was God," as the prologue to John's Gospel puts it. "But that 'he came to his own and his own did not receive him; but as many as received him, to them he gave the power to become sons of God by believing in his name,' that I did not read there."[31] That the Son could be equal to God is something the books of the Platonists effectively helped him to understand. "But that 'he took on himself the form of a servant and emptied himself' [Phil. 2:7] . . . that these books do not have."[32] Philosophies of ascent would confirm his worst vices: the pride and arrogance of the climber, the self-sufficiency of the intellectual who would think his way to salvation and congratulate himself upon arrival. But here was the scandal of Christianity: You can't get here from there, God says, so I'll come get you.

For someone who had been drawn to the elitism of enlightenment, who had tried to make it into the exclusive Manichean club of the elect who had risen above the masses and made it to the top, perhaps what was most scandalous about Christianity was its utter democratization of enlightenment—the way the gospel held out the grace of illumination to any and all. You can feel this in a snobby remark Augustine made right before his conversion in the garden. After hearing story after story of people finding their way to the Way, he says, "I turned on Alypius and cried out: 'What is wrong with us? What is this that you have heard? Uneducated people are rising up and capturing heaven, and we with our high culture without any heart—see where we roll in the mud of flesh and blood. Is it because they are ahead of us that we are ashamed to follow?'"[33]

Platonism made some crooked places straight in Augustine's imagination, enabling him to find his way to the Way in Jesus—in God's condescending to become human, and more so in humbling himself to the point of death, even death on a despised cross. Augustine saw a humility that was unparalleled in the ancient world and unthinkable to philosophers. That humility spilled over into an offer of grace and epistemic mercy that transgressed all boundaries of class and tribe. The affront to philosophy was that "you have hidden these things from the wise and revealed them to babes, that toiling and burdened they should come to him to be restored."[34] Augustine kicks out the pretentious stilts of intellectual striving: "Those who are raised high in the air, as if by the stage boots of a loftier teaching, the platform boots of actors supposed to represent divinities, don't hear Jesus saying, 'Learn from me, since I am gentle and humble at heart, and you will find rest for your souls.'"[35] Platonism offered a ladder to (re)connect God and humanity; in Christianity, God climbs down.

Albert Camus, in fact, is someone who appreciated this crucial difference—that at stake in the confrontation between philosophy and Christianity, between Platonism and the gospel, was the reality of epistemic *grace*. "In Christianity, it is not reasoning that bridges this gap," Camus rightly observes, "but a fact: Jesus is come."[36] This, inevitably, is how many earnest seekers end up shipwrecked. They insist on paddling their own boat, and they refuse the raft that is a cross.

Gnosticism, on Camus's reading, was "one of the first attempts at Greco-Christian collaboration," but one in which the Greek trumped the Christian precisely because, in the end, Gnosticism refuses the scandal of grace: "The spiritual are saved only by gnosis or knowledge of God. . . . Salvation is *learned*."[37] The result is an epistemic Pelagianism akin to the hubris of the addict: I'll figure this out, I'll find a way, I've got this covered, to which those in recovery reply: "Your best thinking got you here."

At its heart, Neoplatonism is another version of the same pretension, confident in its own ingenuity. Salvation is contemplation, and only epistemic elites have the wherewithal (and luxury) of achieving such a state. "Here God allows only his admirers to live," as Camus put it.[38] Which is why the Neoplatonist is revolted by Christianity's "anarchy," its refusal of an epistemic meritocracy and the spiritual aristocracy of the "wise." "The theory of unmerited and irrational Salvation is at bottom the object of all the attacks" in Plotinus's *Enneads*, Camus points out.[39] And what we get in Augustine, he concludes, is "opposing Incarnation to Contemplation." It is Camus, haunted by but still refusing the Augustinian option, who provides one of the clearest insights into what was at stake:

> Greek in his need for coherence, Christian in the anxieties of his sensitivity, for a long time he remained on the periphery of Christianity. It was both the allegorical method of Saint Ambrose and Neoplatonic thought that convinced Saint Augustine. But at the same time they did not persuade him. The conversion was delayed. From this it appeared to him that above all the solution was not in knowledge, that the way out of his doubts and his disgust for the flesh was not through intellectual escapism, but through a full awareness of his depravity and his misery. To love these possessions that carried him so low: grace would raise him high above them.[40]

If Camus himself ultimately opted for the Greek, he knew it was because he was refusing grace.

Sadly, this may have stemmed from his own misreading. At the opening of his dissertation, when he is summarizing what he calls "evangelical" Christianity—a fabled "primal" Christianity of the New Testament—he encapsulates it as a dichotomy. "One must choose between the world and God."[41] Camus himself accepted the dichotomy, then chose the world. What if he had read Augustine a little more closely and had seen that Christianity imploded the dichotomy—that in the incarnation, God chose the world?

AUGUSTINE'S CONFESSION, HIS intellectual stand on this mystery, did not preclude humility. Conviction is not synonymous with dogmatism. Augustine was more than willing to admit: "I do not know."[42] Indeed, one of his last acts as an author was a remarkable project: he became his own critic. Augustine's (unfinished) *Retractations*—a personal, critical survey of the vast corpus of his writings (he made it through ninety-three of his works)—is a remarkable testament to intellectual humility. It is an ancient version of "how my mind has changed" in which he entreats his readers to cheer his progress rather than denounce the change as intellectual compromise. Augustine hopes for readers not to take glee in his mistakes but to appreciate the honesty of his admissions ("only an ignorant man will have the hardihood to criticize me for criticizing my own errors").[43] It is an intellectual virtue, for Augustine, to follow illumination where it leads, even if it means admitting one was wrong.

We see him make the same appeal to those who are so confident that Christianity is wrong or that it is intellectually feeble and thus something to be abandoned, outgrown. He encourages caution about hastily considering the matter settled: "If you are not sure what I am saying and have doubts about whether it is true, at least be sure that you have no doubt about your having doubts about this."[44] Sometimes doubting your doubts is the beginning of wisdom.

STORY : *How to Be a Character*

What do I want when I want an identity?

One of the obstacles that novelist Leslie Jamison had to overcome on the road out of addiction was the peculiar way stories function in recovery groups. For the novelist, of course, the burden is to be original: to tell the story that's never been told, the one that makes a new world, discloses something we've never seen before. It's why the anxiety of influence hangs over the artist's aspiration: to make something new *as if* you had no influences, no debts, no history.

But in Alcoholics Anonymous, she noticed that the "addiction stories" traded back and forth as the oxygen of the group all made you think, "I've heard this before" because "addiction is always a story that has already been told."[1] It's why every book on addiction and recovery seemed like the same book (*I've already read that book*, the glazed eyes of others told her). So why write another?

It took Jamison a while to realize that stories function differently for such a community. The point of a story isn't originality or ingenuity; that would make the story really about the storyteller. "Look at me" is the secret desire of originality. But the stories that circulated in a recovery meeting served a different end: they were weaving a web of solidarity. The point wasn't to draw attention to the storyteller; the hope was to give a gift to the listeners, to create a world in which listeners could see themselves, orient themselves, and maybe even see a way forward, a way out. "In recovery," she recalls, "I found a community that resisted what I'd always been told about stories—that they had to be unique—suggesting instead that a story was most useful when it wasn't unique at all, when it understood itself as something that had been lived before and would be lived again. Our stories were valuable because of this redundancy, not despite it."[2] What is meant to be damning in the review of a book (*just another addiction memoir*) "gets turned on its head by recovery—where a story's sameness is precisely why it should be told. Your story is only useful because others have lived it and will live it again."[3]

But why would I listen to the stories of this motley crew in a church basement who've never seen me before and know nothing of my own story? What makes their stories matter?

A therapist gave Jamison a concept to name how these stories function: *witness authority*. This is the authority you accord to someone who knows the trouble you've seen, who garners authorial attention from you because they've walked in your shoes. And when they tell *their* story, it's like they've been reading your mail. Addiction stories work because of this solidarity of experience. Jamison recalls what her friend Dana whispered at her first meeting, upon hearing someone else's story: "'That's me,' as if her whole life had been spent listening to the wrong radio station."[4]

To find ourselves in someone's story—to feel known by the witness of another—is not unique to addicts, surely. Rather, the brokenness of addiction only distills what is a *human* hunger: to be known, to find a place, to be given a story that gives us bearings, a sense of identity that comes from solidarity. "I've found my people," we say when we discover a community that shares with us what we thought was a solitary passion or alienating affliction. Despite all the ways we've been schooled in expressive individualism, we are all the more aware of the dynamics of *identity*, of finding ourselves in relation to some group that gives us meaning, significance, a cause. Identity is a characterization to which we accede because the group comes with a story that makes us a character, gives us a role to play. Someone bears witness to what it means to be them, and we whisper, "That's *me*." Identity is our name for being found by a story someone else told.

WHY SHOULD WE care about Augustine's story? Why listen? This is a question he wrestled with explicitly. And his only appeal—his only claim to authority—is witness authority. Augustine recognizes that he can't prove anything: "I can't prove to them that what I confess is the truth."[5] He's not offering a demonstration that marshals evidence to prove a conclusion. He's not trying to argue anyone into his story. Instead, he shares a story that he invites his readers to "try on" and see if it might perhaps fit their own experience. Why write these confessions to God "in such a way that other people can hear?" he muses. If I'm just confessing to God, why not keep a journal, work all of this out in private? Well, for the same reason that addicts share their story at a meeting: maybe someone will see themselves in my story, Augustine says. Maybe someone will hear this prodigal tale, with all its dead ends and heartbreak, and whisper, "That's *me*." And maybe if they can see themselves in my story, they might be able to imagine finding themselves in God's story as the one making their way home, being gathered up by a father who runs out to meet them and throws a feast. Augustine's story is only of interest if it is *un*original, a story that's been told a million times, one that rehearses the prodigal adventures of the human condition.

He pleads with God: "Make clear to me what the advantage is of my testimony." Why risk satisfying all the haters who will chalk this up to my vanity? Why give fodder to the ancient African TMZ station so eager to get its hands on dirt about the bishop of Hippo? His response: "When the confessions of my past wrongdoings—which you forgave and hid so that you could make me happy in yourself, changing my soul with faith and your rite of baptism—are read and heard, they arouse the heart out of its sleep of despair, in which it says 'I can't.'"[6] It's all worth it, Augustine says, if someone despairing might find herself in my story and imagines she could be otherwise—imagines that grace could irrupt in her life too. Someone might hear my story, Augustine hopes, and see in my past a familiar stretch of road. They might hear me describing my misadventures and anxiety and be able to say, "I've been down *that* road"—which means they might also be able to see a way out, a way forward, a way home. I write for others, he says, as "partners in my joy and sharers in my mortality, my fellow citizens and sojourners abroad with me"—so they might find compatriots of a *patria* they didn't know they were longing for. If in my past they can see themselves ("That's me"), perhaps in my present they might be able to imagine: "That *could be* me." The despair of "I can't" is invited into the story Augustine shares: "You can."

This is why the *Confessions* should never be confused with a memoir or an autobiography. If Augustine shares his story, it's not to disclose something about himself. To the contrary, there's a sense in which his own particularity is diminished, his biography eclipsed. The point is to share a story that is "generic" enough for any and all to be able to imagine themselves in it. In that sense, his story is not unlike the addicts' stories in recovery: Dave and Arlene aren't sharing their stories so you can get to know them; they're sharing their stories so you can get to know yourself. Their story discloses something about you. It's meant to help you face up to yourself. What the *Confessions* ask of a reader is not, "What do you think of Augustine?" but rather, "Who do you think you are?" Augustine is writing to get readers to respond not to him but to God. Jean-Luc Marion, in his philosophical study of Augustine, discerns this better than anyone: "The readers do not have to respond to the author about their literary enjoyment, nor about their psychological sympathy, but to God about their own confessing *affectus*," their own desire. "The response asked for by the author does not ask of the reader that he or she respond to the author (for example, to pity him, to approve him, to acquit him, to admire him, etc.) but to respond directly to what God asks." The *Confessions*, Marion suggests, are really "a machine to make a confession made by each of its readers by inciting in them the human *intellectus* and *affectus* for God."[7] Augustine's story is a tool, a machine, that—like everything else in creation—is to be *used* in order to enjoy God.

This is not a stern demand, as if God were standing there, arms crossed, scowling, waiting for an answer. Rather, the story is meant as an invitation to see oneself in a new frame, as a "character" in a very different story—"to see oneself as God alone sees us: as *lovable*, however deformed we might have let ourselves become."[8] The *Confessions*, far from being an egocentric memoir or autobiography (like those penned by Montaigne and Rousseau),[9] are "a *hetero-biography*," as Marion puts it, "my life told by me and especially to me from the point of view of an other [*hetero*], from a privileged other, God."[10] Augustine's story is the story that was given to him by the grace of God, an identity in which he found himself, and he tells his story for others with the same hope: that they might find themselves in the story God has to tell about them as his children, his friends, his beloved—as those for whom he is willing to lay down his life.

In the *Confessions*, but also in the preaching that would occupy the rest of his life, Augustine constantly invites fellow sojourners, sisters and brothers in the human condition, to try on a story they might not have considered, the story that they are made for more than the mundane, that they have hungers no *thing* can satisfy, that they are loved by the One who made them, that there is a home that's already been made for them, that the God of the universe knows everything about them and still loves them and is waiting to welcome them home with scars on his outstretched hands. "That can't be me," we might at first protest. It's too fantastical, too unbelievable. It might even offend our need to earn God's love or prove ourselves. "I know what you mean," we can almost hear Augustine saying. "I've been there. What if I told you that you can be released even from that? Would that be the secret you've been hoping is true? Welcome to a story you've imagined. I'm here to tell you it's true."

OUR LONGING FOR an identity is bound up with finding a story. That story might be covert and submerged. Its plot may never be diagrammed. But we nonetheless find ourselves adopting a role, playing out a script that has been given to us by some narrative. That's not inauthentic or some version of bad faith. To find a role is to find yourself ("I was made for this"). It can be freeing to effectively live as the understudy of some exemplar who gives us an orientation to the world, something to live for and a way to live. To be without a story is to live without any sort of script that might help us know who we are and what we're about. We flail and meander. We frantically try on roles and identities to see if they fit. To be character-ized by a story is to have a name, a backstory, a project—all of which serve as rails to run on, something stable and given that we count on. We can be known because there's someone to know. Jonathan Franzen captures the anxiety that stems from being un-storied in a passage in *Freedom*, documenting an episode where the protagonist, Walter, feels like his world is melting because he keeps flitting from narrative to narrative.

> He let the phone slip from his hand and lay crying for a while, silently, shaking the cheap bed. He didn't know what to do, he didn't know how to live. Each new thing he encountered in life impelled him in a direction that fully convinced him of its rightness, but then the next new thing loomed up and impelled him in the opposite direction, which also felt right. There was no controlling narrative: he seemed to himself a purely reactive pinball in a game whose only object was to stay alive for staying alive's sake. . . . How to live?[11]

It's the hunger for an orienting narrative that our culture industries tap into. Whether it's Disney or HBO, HGTV or Instagram, they're all myth-making, which is just to say they are offering scripts we can live into. The danger, of course, is that so many scripts today invite us to become not characters but models—people who are seen but have no story, whose generic stares seem to have no identity behind them. Instead, we know only the clothes they wear, the façade they've assumed, which will be stripped and replaced in an instant. They are not selves but machines for displaying products.

An actor, unlike a model, at least has the potential to show us a character we can adopt. It might be an aspirational call to justice in the Mr. Smith who goes to Washington, or crusading for the same in the character of Atticus Finch. It might be black empowerment in *Black Panther* or female empowerment in *Wonder Woman*. It might be journalistic communities chasing the truth in *Spotlight* or *The Post*. In response to any of these a young person might say, "That's me," and then spend a life following their lead. Our fictions often hold out better characters to emulate than the dead-end desire to be merely "famous" (and "famous for being famous") that plays out in "reality" TV.

It was books that used to play this role (and still do, to some extent): we see ourselves in characters of mythology and fiction. Sometimes we see our own vices and resolve *not* to play out that character trajectory. In other cases, the allure of a character's heroism or sacrifice or compassion becomes an aspiration: "I want to be like that," we say in our hearts, and live a life that steals from the character's script. Books, as the arks of such stories, are not just technologies for information transfer; they become incubators of life, enshrining icons of who we want to be.

Thomas Wright captures this dynamic in an interesting case study: the life of Oscar Wilde. We might call Wright's *Built of Books* a "bibliobiography," a telling of Wilde's complex, tragic life in which books are the spine of the narrative. That we can do this is itself part of the tragedy: while Wilde was in prison awaiting the trial that would lead to his demise, the entire contents of his house in Chelsea had to be auctioned off to cover the legal costs of his rash—and ultimately unsuccessful—libel case against the Marquess of Queensbury. Thanks to a surviving copy of the sale catalogue, we know that Wilde's library, which he had been building since he was an adolescent, contained around two thousand volumes, including French novels, a large library of classics, first editions of his own books, sumptuous *éditions de luxe*, and volumes of poetry inscribed by the authors. The entire collection was sold off for a song (some friends and acquaintances tried to reacquire some of them once they hit booksellers' shelves in London).[12]

It was hard to imagine a more invasive revenge on Wilde, whose library was not just a collection of artifacts but the personally curated archaeological strata of his life. As is true for many, to look at his shelves was to see the person, the spines speaking to the unique shape of a life. "Wilde's library was far more than a museum of personal mementoes," Wright argues. "It was the source of so much that was vital in his life. . . . Books were the single greatest influence on Wilde's life and writings. He sometimes referred to the volumes that most affected and charmed him as his 'golden books.'" Indeed, he made the same true of his characters: it was the infamous "yellow book" that would lure Dorian Gray into the life that would destroy him. Live by the book, die by the book. Books, for Wilde, were ersatz friends, conduits of personality: "these readerly encounters were as significant as his first meetings with friends and lovers."[13]

Wilde is not unique in being "built of books," but our possession of the catalogue does give us a unique opportunity to peek into the secret script that generated a life. Wright notes a tension on this point. On the one hand, Wilde builds a life out of what he reads. It is an act of self-creation fueled by fiction and mythology. On the other hand, that means even this virtuoso of self-invention—who would decry "influence" in his essay "The Critic as Artist"—was *receiving* roles to play. "Wilde did not so much discover as create himself through his reading," Wright suggests. "He was a man who built himself out of books. . . . He always came to life via books, literally seeing reality through them." But then again Wright sees in Wilde someone who was emulating what he had read. "He was essentially a pre-modern author who adapted and conflated the books he read, rather than a Romantic writer concerned with originality and self-expression."[14]

It explains why, "when the prison doors were closed upon him, books were the first things he asked for."[15] And which volumes did he request from the doldrums of Pentonville prison? The first two on Wilde's list were Augustine's *Confessions* and *City of God*.

The notion that we are built of books, that we live into stories, is as old as the novel itself. At the heart of Miguel de Cervantes's *Don Quixote* is the errant knight for whom chivalrous romances are not an escape but a how-to manual. He reads them not as fantasy but as a rule for living. This insight is one that we find inscribed in Augustine's ancient *Confessions*. If Augustine writes a hetero-biography, he also offers us a bibliobiography, his life in books. Different books offered different maps of the world, charting different courses, each a different encapsulation of the world. Virgil's *Aeneid*, Cicero's *Hortensius*, Mani's *Letter of Foundation* and *Book of Treasures*, the *Enneads* of Plotinus, the epistles of Paul, the parable of the prodigal son: all are stories that Augustine "tried on," as it were, stepping into their narrative, assuming a role, playing the part of someone who assumed their take on the world. They are books he treated like compasses at various points in his life, until he found one that was finally calibrated to true North.

It's no surprise, then, that books function like characters in his own book's rehearsal of his conversion. In book 8 of the *Confessions*, the drama unfolds as a call-and-response litany of friends with books, including Simplicianus—who points Augustine to Victorinus, the translator of the Neoplatonic books Augustine has been reading and who was himself transformed by reading the Bible—and Ponticianus, who drops in and, when he spies the book of Paul's letters on the gaming table, shares the story of his friends' discovery of *The Life of Antony* (itself the story of a life revolutionized by hearing the Gospels), which then turns out to be a bookish encounter that changes everything. All of these books are like literary stained glass, holding up images of exemplars to imitate, trailblazers to follow. And so the culmination of Augustine's conversion is picking up a book in which he finds himself. In Gozzoli's portrayal of the scene in San Gimignano, Augustine's conversion is depicted almost as a kind of studiousness (see figure 6). But perhaps we might imagine him poring over the book as an atlas, as if the world were finally coming into focus—like he'd spent his life trying to drive in Los Angeles with a map of San Francisco, but now someone has given him the sacred *Thomas Guide*, and all of a sudden he knows where he is, and where he wants to go, and how to get there. He realizes he's holding a map given to him by the One who made the cosmos. Spying the arrow that reads, "You Are Here," Augustine says to his friend, "That's *me*." And in Gozzoli's image, Alypius is eager to get his hands on such a book.

Books will be the wallpaper of all ensuing iconography. Just like Wilde always posed for pictures in his library, or with book in hand, the bishop of Hippo will always appear with books: reading them, writing them, studying them, stomping on them, surrounded by them, inhaling them (see figures 2 and 8). It's also not surprising that someone so shaped by books gave his life to writing them ("ninety-three works in two hundred and thirty-two books," plus letters and sermons).[16] He would die writing, in fact. Hounded in his old age by Quodvultdeus to write a critical catalogue of heresies (which Augustine promised), he would fail to finish his *Answer to Julian*. Also unfinished would be his *Retractations*, the book in which he reviewed all of his own books. He found himself in a story that had once been unbelievable to him. He would spend the rest of his life inviting others to find themselves in that story.

THE BOOK THAT would finally arrest this search for a story was the Bible. The script that would finally guide his way was the Scriptures. As Brian Stock notes in his magisterial study *Augustine the Reader*, Augustine realized that identity was storied, and that meant finding your story in the story revealed by your Creator. "What distinguishes him from other philosophical thinkers on this issue," Stock comments, "is the link that he perceives between self-knowledge and an appreciation of God's word, in which the reading of scripture plays a privileged role. Throughout the lengthy period of his intellectual development after 386–387, his main guide was scripture."[17] What was it about the biblical story that "fit"? Why was it that this particular story became the governing narrative for the rest of his life?

The very notion will scandalize us, we who've been encouraged to live "our" truth, to come up with our own story, for whom authenticity is the burden of writing our own *de novo* script. The notion of a governing narrative that is not your own feels like signing over the rights to your life—which it is! But for Augustine, being enfolded in God's story in Scripture was not an imposition but a liberation. When you've realized that you don't even know yourself, that you're an enigma to yourself, and when you keep looking inward only to find an unplumbable depth of mystery and secrets and parts of yourself that are loathsome, then Scripture isn't received as a list of commands: instead, it breaks into your life as a light from outside that shows you the infinite God who loves you at the bottom of the abyss. God's Word for Augustine wasn't experienced as burden or buzzkill but as autobiography written by the God who made him. Scripture irrupted in Augustine's life as *revelation*, the story about himself told by another, and as *illumination*, shining a light that helped him finally understand his hungers and faults and hopes.

To spend any time in Augustine's corpus, but perhaps especially the letters and sermons, is to hear a voice that has been soaked by the language of Scripture. The Bible—especially the psalms—was Augustine's gift of tongues. Augustine's speech is so suffused with the Scriptures that the contemporary translator is almost at a loss to know where the Bible stops and Augustine begins. For the rest of his life, Augustine, like a hip-hop bricoleur, "samples" Scripture in everything he says. The psalms, especially, are always on the tip of his tongue, a storehouse of metaphors and comfort.

It's incredible how quickly the Scriptures became Augustine's first language, so to speak. The Scriptures are the heart of Augustine's lexicon because the cosmic story of redemption is his governing story. This was the language of the homeland he'd never been to. Like glossolalia, he quickly found himself able to speak a language that wasn't his but also wasn't foreign. It's less a language he owns and more a language that owns him and comes naturally. Jacques Derrida, his fellow North African, would say something similar much later: "I said that the only language I speak is *not mine*, I did not say it was foreign to me."[18] This is the lexicon of an émigré spirituality, when a foreign tongue finds you and becomes your first language. You become who you are because this Word gives you the words to finally say who you are.[19] "To hear you speaking about oneself is to know oneself."[20]

When, in the garden, Augustine scrambles back to pick up the book of Paul's epistles and lights on Romans 13, there is an infusion of more than information—this Word will be the conduit of the grace that transforms him. "I didn't want to read further, and there was no need. The instant I finished this sentence, my heart was virtually flooded with a light of relief and certitude, and all the darkness of my hesitation scattered away."[21] The Word is a sacrament—it is a means of God's *action*, not just God's disclosure. When Augustine explains why he would bother sharing his own story with others, "my fellow citizens and sojourners abroad with me," he situates his words in relation to the Word, but more important, he situates his act in relation to God's action. "And this, your Word to me, would not have been enough as a mere precept spoken by you; it had to precede with action by you. And I myself carry out that Word with both actions and words; I carry it out under your wings; the danger would be too great unless my soul were under your wings," echoing (you guessed it) the psalms.[22]

After that garden transformation, Augustine, Alypius, Adeodatus, and several others retreated north of Milan to Cassiciacum, between the city and Lake Como. While this would be a season of philosophical reflection that would generate some of Augustine's earliest works, preceding his baptism, in the *Confessions* he notes that this was really an opportunity for intensive language learning, giving himself over to the psalms. The episode illustrates how this language was a gift that he could also make his own. In the psalms, God gave him words that he could speak back to God. These songs, he says, were a school for his passions: "The words I poured out to you, my God, when I read the Psalms of David, those faithful songs, the sounds of godliness that shut out the spirit that's full of itself! I was then unschooled in true passion for you."[23] The Cassiciacum curriculum of psalm-singing was like a Berlitz program for the soul, training his affections by giving him new words, a new cadence of aspiration, a new story to live out. But this wasn't instantaneous. As he notes, when he wrote to Ambrose from Cassiciacum and asked where he should begin reading in the Scriptures, Ambrose recommended the book of Isaiah (perhaps wanting to challenge any lingering Manicheanism in Augustine's imagination that would have dismissed the Old Testament). "But I didn't understand the first part I read," Augustine admits, "and thinking it was all like that, I put off taking the book up again until I was more practiced in the Master's way of speaking."[24]

The Master's way of speaking. If Scripture became Augustine's governing narrative, then *story*, we might say, became the bass note of his rhetorical method. As Stock notes, Augustine ultimately landed on a different understanding of identity that was tied to Scripture in a way the philosophers would never have entertained, and his rhetoric would reflect this conviction. Augustine spent his life inviting others into this story, in his *Confessions* and then in a lifetime of preaching, by a performance of the truth rather than an argument. To side with performance over proof was, in a sense, to stand with the imagination as prior to reason—to take sides in the longstanding battle between philosophy and poetry.

From its beginning, philosophy banished poetry. When Plato imagined the ideal republic, governed by philosopher-kings trained in logic and mathematics, he wanted the mushy poets exiled outside its walls. The republic would be governed by *ratio*, not rhetoric; the city would traffic in syllogisms, not stories. You're welcome in this city as long as you leave your imagination at the door. Otherwise, the philosopher-kings and thinking things will see you out.

Riffing on Philip Rieff, we might call this "the triumph of the didactic." It is a construal of the world that treats us as brains-on-a-stick, reducing what matters to what we think, what we can analyze, what we can quantify and process in server farms owned by Google and Amazon. Our so-called information age is still an outpost of this city.

And it is surely an irony that Christianity has been prone to a similar kind of rationalization and privileging of the didactic (especially in Protestantism). We reduce the wonder and mystery of grace to teachable bullet points and statements of faith. We prefer the didactic environs of the epistles to the action and metaphor of the Gospels. We reduce the dramatic narrative of Scripture to a doctrinal system. We say we love Jesus, but we prefer to *learn* from Paul, who gives us God straight, without the meandering meaning of parables.

I confess that this is how I came to Christianity, or how I learned to be a Christian very early on. The gospel quickly became something to know, to analyze, to systematize, to *wield*. The nineteenth-century Princeton theologian Charles Hodge taught me that the Bible was a "storehouse of facts," and Christian philosophers taught me the logic that would chop it up into digestible bits for cognitive processing. In fact, as a young man I used to be proud of the fact that I didn't read novels or poetry—why would I waste time on such sentimental stuff when there was all this *knowledge* to acquire? Why would I wallow in the lies of made-up fictional worlds when I was interested in the Truth? I had effectively re-created the kingdom of God as if it were Plato's republic: Poetry prohibited. Imagination excluded.

I can't remember exactly how I began to break out of this. I do remember reading Frank McCourt's memoir *Angela's Ashes* and coming to understand something about the broken beauty of God's world that I couldn't have understood any other way. And I remember an English professor at the University of Waterloo, John North, who introduced me to the enchanted wonder of Gerard Manley Hopkins. And I remember Cardinal Ratzinger, long before he was Pope Benedict XVI—in fact, when he was head of the Congregation for the Doctrine of the Faith, the doctrine police of the church—challenging this triumph of the didactic when he said: "Christianity is not an intellectual system, a collection of dogmas, or moralism. Christianity is instead an encounter, a love story."[25]

But perhaps it has been my decades of wrestling with St. Augustine that have most challenged the rationalization of faith. If you know Augustine only from a distance, as one of the great "doctors" of the church, or someone anthologized in theology textbooks, you might imagine that he too falls prey to the triumph of the didactic, just another scholastic who flattens the gospel to the measure of the intellect. But then you've probably never read his *Confessions*, which are infused with the grace of God from beginning to end and could never be confused with the sterile skeletons of systematic theology. The *Confessions* is a book that breathes, a book with a beating heart. Augustine isn't just trying to convince you; he's trying to *move* you. He is trying to "stir up" his fellow travelers.[26]

Augustine had to work through some of his own early "didacticism." It's worth remembering that Augustine was trained in rhetoric, in the flourishes of speech meant to elicit the affect. He had always wanted to put this at the service of the emperor (and his own ambition), so when he finally scored a post in the imperial court in Milan, he had realized that goal. But when he became a Christian there, significantly influenced by Platonism, one of the first things he did was abandon his post as a rhetor and retreat to a philosophical monastery of sorts north of town. For the young Augustine, conversion seemed to require privileging logic over rhetoric. He assumed that becoming a Christian meant converting to didacticism.

By the time he writes the *Confessions*, though, we can already see him reconsidering this assumption. In many ways, the *Confessions* represent the redemption of rhetoric for Augustine. He doesn't give us a philosophical dialogue or a collection of syllogisms: he invites us into a story. But that means deploying the dynamics of drama. The *Confessions* are more art than science, more aesthetic than logic. In the *Confessions*, Augustine doesn't just analyze his thoughts; he paints a picture of the adventures (and misadventures) of his loves. The parallel isn't Descartes's *Meditations*, populated with "thinking things"; the parallel is more like Kerouac's *On the Road*, filled with characters who hunger and thirst, strive and fail, and yes, bump and grind.

Near the end of the drama, in book 10, Augustine owns this. He openly worries about his motives in writing the book: "Why then should I be concerned for human readers to hear my confessions?" he asks.[27] (Augustine the bishop is still haunted by ambition, by a heart that drinks up the "praise of men." In a sense, Augustine probes a dynamic that many artists grapple with.)[28] The point of the *Confessions* isn't to parade himself or to write a treatise trying to argue people into the kingdom of God. Instead, Augustine is writing to *move hearts*. The "good" he hopes will result from this undertaking, he says, is that God would "stir up the heart when people read and hear the confessions of my past . . . which you have forgiven and covered up to grant me happiness in yourself."[29] Augustine is writing to the imagination, appealing to the affections, to *move* people into a different story—just as Augustine's heart burned when he heard the stories of St. Antony of Egypt, Victorinus, and others.[30]

Why does Augustine give us the drama of this narrative instead of the arguments of a treatise? Because his apologetic is aesthetic. Augustine knows that the heart traffics in stories, that the lingua franca of love is more like poetry than logic. It's a song that takes you home. And so he pens his *Confessions* to "prevent their heart[s] from sinking into the sleep of despair and saying, 'It is beyond my power.'" Don't despair, Augustine pleads; listen to my story. If even someone like me can find grace, you can too.

If Augustine is a cartographer of the human heart, it's because the Scriptures are the God-breathed map that orients his understanding of the human condition. He suggests exactly this years later in *City of God* when he returns, once again, to his favorite metaphor: the journey. The problem is that we can't *think* our way home. "The mind of man, the natural seat of his reason and understanding, is itself weakened by long-standing faults which darken it." Our eyes are too weak even for the light. So "in order to give man's mind greater confidence on its journey towards the truth along the way of faith, God the Son of God, who is himself the Truth, took manhood without abandoning his godhead, and thus established and found this faith, so that man might have a path to man's God through the man who was God." Christ is the Way, the road, the bridge who, as God-become-human, makes it possible for humanity to reach God.

> For there is hope to attain a journey's end when there is a path which stretches between the traveler and his goal. But if there is no path, or if a man does not know which way to go, there is little use in knowing the destination. As it is, there is one road, and one only, well secured against all possibility of going astray; and this road is provided by one who is himself both God and man. As God, he is the goal; as man, he is the way.[31]

Augustine then immediately points to the Scriptures, which function as a map given to us by the Mediator. The one who is the road has given us a map. "This Mediator spoke in former times through the prophets and later through his own mouth, and after that through the apostles, telling man all that he decided was enough for man. He also instituted the Scriptures, those which we call canonical. These are the writings of outstanding authority in which we put our trust concerning those things which we need to know for our good, and yet are incapable of discovering by ourselves."[32]

Here Augustine suggests a different test for why you might consider the Bible as a guide: Does it provide guidance you couldn't get elsewhere? Even if the way it delineates is difficult, does it look like a way out, a way home? If every other map has left you lost, what's to lose trying out this one? In Augustine's experience, the Word was like an enchanted map. It not only told him, "You Are Here" and pointed him toward home; it also gave him legs to run.

THE FIRST TIME I visited the Seattle Art Museum (SAM) was also my first encounter with the arresting work of Kehinde Wiley. Now a presidential portraitist, over a decade ago Wiley was making a name for himself in the New York art scene but hadn't become a household name. A rainy day in Seattle seemed like a good excuse to hide out in the SAM for a while, so I wandered rather indiscriminately into the European Baroque gallery only to be gobsmacked by a large canvas (six feet by five feet) in almost-neon fuchsia and blues, featuring the confident gaze of a young black man in contemporary attire—a military jacket, teal pants, a funky octopus necklace hanging around his chest (see figure 7). His garb said "Brooklyn," but his pose and demeanor said "Renaissance."

What was this doing in the European Baroque gallery, alongside Italian and Spanish paintings from the 1600s? As I inched closer and saw the title, there was a clue. The artist, Kehinde Wiley, called the painting *Anthony of Padua*. This young man that Wiley had encountered on the street was given a new name, a new identity carried in his very pose. And not just any identity: Wiley invoked a saint, Anthony of Padua. As a young man, the Portuguese Fernando Martins had left his home to become a novice at an Augustinian abbey just outside Lisbon. But when he heard the story of Franciscans who had been martyred in Morocco, Fernando, who would become Anthony of Padua, was granted permission to leave the abbey and join the Franciscans.

Anthony was known for his immersion in the Scriptures and his power as a preacher and orator—which is why in later iconography he would be pictured with a book, sometimes with the Christ child resting upon it (as in El Greco's portrayal). His tongue is displayed for veneration in a large reliquary, along with his jaw and vocal cords, relics of his proclamation of this story. In popular piety, St. Anthony is the patron saint of lost things ("Tony, Tony, look around. Something's lost and must be found!"), a charism that seems to trace back to an episode in which Anthony lost his psalter and, after much prayer, found it.

What's happening, then, when Wiley titles this work *Anthony of Padua*? As critics have pointed out, the painting is a contemporary example of the "swagger portrait"—a style of portraiture that signals social status and communicates power and bravado.[33] Wiley is bringing together two worlds of swagger, the European and the African American, the portrait and fashion, Rembrandt meets Kanye.

But Wiley is also giving this man a story and hence an identity, which has echoes—of one who served the poor, who was studiously devoted to the Word, who was looking for the lost. An identity comes with its own sort of swagger, the confidence of knowing who one is, and whose one is. Anthony the exemplar gives orientation for aspiration.

So I had to grin when I turned to the opposite wall and saw a painting I recognized from prints: Bartolomé Esteban Murillo's *Saint Augustine in Ecstasy*, a Spanish painting from the late 1600s (see figure 8). Augustine is again surrounded with books. But his arms are outstretched. The weight of his bishop's mitre is resting on a table, the staff leaning in a corner. He is alone before God, face turned upward, pleadingly. A light illumines his face. And inscribed in the upper left corner are Augustine's own words: "My heart is restless until it rests in you."

Everyone is looking for rest, which is just another way of saying we're looking for an identity, a story that gives us the kind of gifted swagger of being known, named, and offered a map home.

JUSTICE : *How to Protest*

What do I want when I want to change the world?

There is an atheism that is entirely understandable. It is not the comfortable disbelief of the new atheists, for whom atheism is the overreach of their epistemic hubris, the blinkered conclusion of a reductionistic scientism that closes its eyes to all the facets of human mystery it can't explain, settling for just-so stories as if they were explanations. The atheism of the Brights is a dim shadow of the atheism I have in mind.

The hard-won atheism I have in mind, the atheism that is understandable and for which I have much sympathy, is an atheism forged in suffering. Rather than an arrogance that imagines it has outgrown belief, such an atheism is an inability to believe born of an empathy for those trod underfoot by the machinations of an inexplicable menace. This is not an atheism of comfort but of agony. It is the begrudging conclusion of cosmic loneliness arising from the experience of injustice.

"I would like to believe in God," Ta-Nehisi Coates admits. "I simply can't." This isn't a defiance; it is the despair of "can't," not the confidence of "won't." It is an atheism that wishes things could be different. Coates goes on to share the reasons for the hope that is not in him.

> The reasons are physical. When I was nine, some kid beat me up for amusement, and when I came home crying to my father, his answer—*Fight that boy or fight me*—was godless, because it told me that there was no justice

in the world, save the justice we dish out with our own hands. When I was twelve, six boys jumped off the number 28 bus headed to Mondawin Mall, threw me to the ground, and stomped on my head. But what struck me most that afternoon was not those boys but the godless, heathen adults walking by. Down there on the ground, my head literally being kicked in, I understood: No one, not my father, not the cops, and certainly not anyone's God, was coming to save me.[1]

This is not the sherry-sipping philosophical conclusion of a Bertrand Russell who has coolly assessed the evidence and lack thereof. This is protest that emerges from trenches. When Coates slips into his own overreach ("nothing in the record of human history argues for divine morality"), it would be grotesque to criticize the unsustainability of that categorical claim and better to admit his follow-up: "and a great deal argues against it."[2] To which even the believer can—and should—only nod in assent.

This was the atheism of Albert Camus. We might even call it an Augustinian atheism, a regrettable conclusion reached after a long journey through what Camus called "the blood-stained face of history."[3] As he told the priests at the Dominican monastery on the Boulevard de Latour-Maubourg in 1948, "I shall never start from the supposition that Christian truth is illusory, but merely from the fact that I could not accept it."[4] He would not haughtily dismiss Christianity, but neither would he pretend to be one. Instead, Camus evinces a sincerity that is disarming ("the world needs real dialogue") and emphasizes a point of solidarity: "I share with you the same revulsion from evil. But I do not share your hope, and I continue to struggle against this universe in which children suffer and die."[5] In fact, this is Camus's solidarity with St. Augustine: "We are faced with evil," he concludes. We hear anew a line we've encountered before: "And, as for me, I feel rather as Augustine did before becoming a Christian when he said: 'I tried to find the source of evil and I got nowhere.'"[6]

After his talk at the monastery, a priest who was an ex-revolutionary stood during a time of discussion and confronted Camus: "I have found

FIGURE 1

"The Death of Monica" (top)   "St. Augustine Departing for Milan" (bottom)

fresco by Benozzo Gozzoli (Chiostro di Sant'Agostino, San Gimignano, Italy)

FIGURE 2

Philippe de Champaigne, *Saint Augustine*

France, ca. 1645–50, at Los Angeles County Museum of Art

FIGURE 3

Ferdinand Hodler, *The Disillusioned One*

Switzerland, 1892, at Los Angeles County Museum of Art

FIGURE 4

Chrismon of St. Ambrose, Milan Cathedral

FIGURE 5

"Life of Monica" (1585)

ceiling fresco by Giovanni Battista Ricci (Chiesa di Sant'Agostino, chapel of St. Monica)

FIGURE 6

"St. Augustine Reading the Epistle of St. Paul"

fresco by Benozzo Gozzoli (Chiostro di Sant'Agostino, San Gimignano, Italy)

FIGURE 7
Anthony of Padua
2013 by Kehinde Wiley (Seattle Art Museum)

FIGURE 8

Saint Augustine in Ecstasy (1665–75)

by Bartolomé Esteban Murillo (Seattle Art Museum)

grace, and you, Mr. Camus, I'm telling you in all modesty that you have not." Olivier Todd, his biographer, recounts: "Camus's only response was to smile. . . . But he said a little later, 'I am your Augustine before his conversion. I am debating the problem of evil, and I am not getting past it.'"[7] Albert Camus: Augustine sans grace.

IT IS THE irruption of evil, its inexplicability, the madness of suffering, that plagues Camus. It is the weight that hangs over *The Stranger*, the peculiar story in which Mersault inexplicably shoots an unnamed Arab man on the shores of Algiers. Why did Mersault do it? There is no answer, no explanation, no chain of causality that grants the crime a place in the world. Not even Mersault can answer the question. The crime, like evil, is a surd, its own perverted *ex nihilo*. Mersault tries to stop asking "whence?" and instead finds happiness in "the gentle indifference of the world."[8]

And yet the whence keeps finding us, keeps asking itself in and through us, a guttural discomfort coughed up like a bark. At other moments the question is asked in quiet dejection that borders on awe before an inscrutable mystery. We keep asking it because this evil still feels like a cosmic affront to placid joys that sneak up on us: a warm rain in summer twilight that leaves us laughing as we run home with friends; the furtive, fierce grasp of a newborn around her father's finger; the way sunlight dapples the sand in a dune forest on the Michigan shore; the way your partner of thirty years still reaches for your hand.

This incongruity is pictured in Terrence Malick's masterpiece *The Thin Red Line*, where the horrors of war play out in the theater of Guadalcanal's stunning beauty. Sometimes the canopy of palms is like the vault of a cathedral, and Hans Zimmer's score sends us soaring as, with Private Witt, we catch glimpses of another world. But then the scream of a bomb pierces the quiet, and the blood and fire of our war-making erupts again.

In a scene of terror, as a village massacre unfolds, staging the fear and fearsomeness of these human animals, Malick puts "whence?" on the lips of a minor character named Private Edward Train, whose voice-over surveys the scene.

> This great evil. Where does it come from? How'd it steal into the world? What seed, what root did it grow from? Who's doin' this? Who's killin' us? Robbing us of life and light. Mocking us with the sight of what we might've known. Does our ruin benefit the earth? Does it help the grass to grow, the sun to shine? Is this darkness in you, too? Have you passed through this night?[9]

This is almost exactly Augustine's question—in fact, it's hard to imagine Malick, a former Heidegger scholar, *not* having the *Confessions* in mind. Augustine was dogged by this question of evil since his youth. It was what first drove him to the Manicheans, and ultimately why he left them disappointed. His sojourn in skepticism was an attempt to stave off the question. But in Milan, as his defenses were breaking down, the question burbled up again: "Where and whence is evil? How did it creep in? What is its root and what is its seed?"[10]

In a way that's harder to find in Coates, yet still present in Camus, Augustine's question turns inward like Private Train's haunted wondering: "Is this darkness in you, too?" It is not only the atrocities others commit that are inexplicable; there is a dark mystery to the evil that drives his own behavior. Evil is out there, other, *and* it is in here, all too close. Yet it is still unfathomable. His own heart is an abyss, and when he looks at the atrocities he commits, only a dark mystery stares back at him: "I became evil for no reason."[11] Mersault would look familiar to Augustine. "Is this darkness in you, too?"

AUGUSTINE SPENT THE rest of his life grappling with this surd without cause. From his early work *On the Free Choice of the Will* to the mature reflections in *City of God*, Augustine keeps tackling the problem of evil. But the point isn't to identify the cause as much as it is to fight for an intellectual coherence that will allow him to hold two convictions in tension with integrity: the corrosive nature of evil that eats away at the world and the goodness of the God who made such a world.

You can feel Augustine's angst in Evodius's question that opens *Free Choice*: "Tell me whether God is not the author of evil."[12] It is the plea of one who is looking for rest from intellectual anxiety, unwilling to deny the reality of evil but equally terrified if God is not the Good. This isn't the same as looking for a solution, hoping for some gnostic insight that grants intellectual safe harbor to then live placidly "in the know" and effectively act as if evil isn't real. To the contrary, Augustine looks for some kind of anchor in the midst of the storm, or a lighthouse that holds out hope as the waves of evil continue to roll. If he points to free choice—to the misuse of the good will God created us with—that isn't so much an answer or a solution or an explanatory cause as it is a plausible halfway house with room to hold these things in tension. The "answer" is an account of the mystery that gives us handles to hold on to without denying what we wish wasn't true. To say evil has its source in the choice of free wills still leaves a black box in the middle of our experience that we can't peer into. But we all live with black boxes of explanation—the things we don't want to hear questions about, that we've decided to take for granted because we've built so much of our lives upon them, the "whereofs" of which we cannot speak and about which we therefore remain silent (as Wittgenstein put it).[13]

Augustine is not trying to "make sense" of evil. To make sense of it, to have an explanation for it, to be able to identify the cause would mean that it has a place in the world. But then it isn't evil. Evil is what ought not to be, the *dis*order of creation, the violation we protest. Evil has no place, no room to fit, no home here in a good creation. When Evodius tries to understand Augustine's attribution of evil to the rogue choice of the will, it's understandable that he wonders whether this is something that "comes naturally," so to speak. Because if the will is just prone to this, if "this movement" of the will is "something natural," then that means it becomes absorbed by lower goods as a matter of necessity. If I'm naturally compelled to disorder, how can I be blamed for it?[14]

Exactly! replies Augustine. Which is precisely why this choice is *not* natural. It is voluntary, and thereby inexplicable.[15] Free will is an answer to this question only if you're also willing to live with the mystery. When Evodius tries to plumb beneath this and figure out what causes the will, Augustine cautions him: you can't really have what you want. You're going to get sucked into an infinite regress, so you're going to have to settle for recognizing a certain mystery of the will here—"the wanton will," as Augustine describes it, "is the cause of all evils."[16] Which is just to say: it is the sort of cause that can't be explained, only witnessed. Augustine takes us back to Private Train's questions about roots and seeds: "We may conclude that the root of all evils is *not being in accordance with nature.* . . . But if you ask again about the cause of this root, how will it be the *root* of all evils?" The cause of the root is the seed, one could say, but what causes the seed to grow into the root? There lies dark mystery. "Hence either the will is the first cause of sinning, or no sin is the first cause of sinning."[17] Here we confront the will's disordered, almost godlike power: it operates *ex nihilo*, without a why.

Twenty-five years later, in *City of God*, Augustine reemphasizes this point: "If you try to find the efficient cause for this evil choice, there is none to be found."[18] Instead, Augustine sees darkness. "One should not try to find an efficient cause for a wrong choice," he cautions. "It is not a matter of efficiency, but of deficiency. . . . To try to discover the causes of such defection—deficient, not efficient causes—is like trying to see darkness or to hear silence. Yet we are familiar with darkness and silence, and we can only be aware of them by means of eyes and ears, but this is not by perception but by absence of perception."[19]

What's the alternative, after all? If you could discern a cause and hence provide an explanation, then evil makes sense. You might even say evil is "natural." But if you say evil is natural, then it's no longer evil. It's the way things are, the way things are supposed to be. You can't protest what is natural; you can't lament what is meant to be. The price to pay for explaining evil is to give up naming and opposing it. As soon as you "explain" evil, it vanishes. Augustine considers the Devil as a limit case in this regard. If God created everything, and everything God creates is good, then where did the Devil come from? Not even the Devil is "naturally" evil. His fall, like mine, is inexplicable. "The Manichees do not realize," Augustine points out, "that if the Devil is a sinner *by nature*, there can really be no question of sin in his case."[20] The very face of evil, in that case, just *is*. You can't complain otherwise.

When we fall prey to the hubristic need for intellectual mastery, the need to *comprehend* everything and hence *explain* everything, we end up naturalizing evil and thus eviscerating it, undercutting the ability to protest against it. Such explanation takes us beyond good and evil. The quest for the root, the seed of evil—to identify the cause of how it stole into the world—undercuts the tortured perplexity that generated the question in the first place. The question arises from our experience of dissonance ("This can't be right! This isn't the way it's supposed to be!"). Our answers too often squelch that dissonance and thus make the question moot.

We also devalue or deny our intuitions of what *ought* to be—what is good and beautiful, what gratitude is for. When we try to extinguish the dark mystery of evil with the light of explanation, we simultaneously dim the radiance of beauty that befalls us unbidden. We forfeit the impulse to say "thank you"; we rule out the joy that attends those moments when we think, "This is how it's meant to be." We explain evil only to explain away love.

This is the bookend to Private Train's query in *The Thin Red Line*. While the diabolical machinations of humans understandingly raise the question of where evil comes from, there is a corresponding mystery that lurks throughout the film in epiphanies of sky and light and play. Private Bell, in a letter to his wife at home, asks the question this mystery engenders:

> My dear wife. You get something twisted out of your insides by all this blood, filth, and noise. I want to stay changeless for you. I want to come back to you the man I was before. How do we get to those other shores? To those blue hills? Love—where does it come from? Who lit this flame in us? No war can put it out, conquer it. I was a prisoner. You set me free.[21]

Is that flame in you too? Have you passed through this light?

THAT SAID, I wish there was more lament in Augustine.

While in principle Augustine refuses to give evil the comfort of an explanation, he constantly fends off intellectual options that would either make evil an illusion or make God blameworthy. As a result, he is sometimes given to painting schemes that, even if he refuses to name a cause, almost give evil a place—either as a tendency that stems from our creatureliness[22] or as the shadow of creation's tapestry that makes the whole all the more beautiful.[23] As a result, evil becomes something of an abstraction for Augustine, a generic, vague challenge that lacks concretion. But when he turns to *inward* evil—the darkness in himself—Augustine is a Proustian observer of all the specific ways his will is twisted and perverted and monstrous. The *Confessions* are a long lament of the devil inside.

But something of the Stoic remains in Augustine. Confronted by the tragic brokenness of the world, he looks more like the placid Socrates than the Jesus groaning in the garden of Gethsemane or weeping at the death of Lazarus. All of the psalmists' laments he spiritualizes inward, which leads him to weep over his own sin yet still feel an impulse to account for the invasive reality of violence and heartbreak. This seems oddly un-Augustinian. An Augustine who laments his own evil will should just as loudly and publicly lament the injustices that leave children hungry and women abused and creation exploited. He is sometimes so keen to defend the just punishment of mortality that he leaves himself no room to protest the tyranny of death.

Perhaps no episode is more jarring in this respect than his almost casual remembrance of the premature death of his son, Adeodatus. In book 9 of the *Confessions*, Augustine happily recounts the gift of his departed boy. He brags on his son's brilliance, displayed in *The Teacher*, one of his early dialogues. Augustine glows like any father who sees his son become a young man with an independence that surprises him. Adeodatus was a "partner in the conversation" and possessed a philosophical acuity that left Augustine (not so secretly) thrilled. "He was 16 at the time. I learnt many other remarkable things about him. His intelligence left me awestruck. Who but you could be the Maker of such wonders?" He remembers their baptism: Adeodatus, together with himself and Alypius. And then the cursory recall: "Early on you took him away from life on earth."[24]

Perhaps a lingering guilt prevented Augustine from being more demonstrative in his grief. His biographer Peter Brown describes this as "one of the most significant blanks in Augustine's life." There is so much he leaves unsaid. But perhaps an unspoken wound remained. "In the last book he ever wrote," Brown reminds us, "Augustine will quote a passage from Cicero that, perhaps, betrays the hurt of this loss: 'Surely what Cicero says comes straight from the heart of all fathers, when he wrote: *You are the only man of all men whom I would wish to surpass me in all things.*'"[25] An aged father musing on the untimely death of a child is not the way it's supposed to be.

It is in his preaching that we get beyond the Neoplatonic frames and greater-good schemes. In sermons, what is offered is not an "answer" to evil, as if it were merely a problem or a question; instead, what is offered is a vision of the gracious action of God, who *takes on* evil. The cross of

Christ—the incarnate God—is the site of a cosmic inversion where all that is not supposed to be is absorbed by the Son, taken to the depths of hell, and vanquished by the resurrection. Evil isn't answered; it is overcome. As Augustine would put it in a sermon in 404, "He took flesh from the lump of our mortality, yes, and he too took to himself the death which was the penalty for sin, but didn't take the sin; instead with the merciful intention of delivering us from sin, he handed over that flesh of his to death."[26] God doesn't abstractly solve a "problem"; God condescends to inhabit and absorb the mess we've made of the world. God "has not abandoned humanity in its mortal condition."[27] This, Augustine encourages his listeners, should serve as a source of hope in the face of fears and sorrows.

> So he handed over this flesh to be slain, so that you wouldn't be afraid of anything that could happen to your flesh. He showed you, in his resurrection after three days, what you ought to be hoping for at the end of this age. So he is leading you along, because he has become your hope. You are now walking toward the hope of the resurrection; but unless our head had first risen, the other members of the body would not find anything to hope for.[28]

The appeal here is not to the greater good or the free choice of the will or constitutive nothingness of creation that corrodes the good. Augustine the pastor and preacher avoids such abstractions and instead appeals to the mystery at the heart of the Christian faith: a humble God who endured evil in order to overcome. The point isn't that God has a plan; the point is that God wins. We shall overcome because of what the Son has undergone in our stead. This isn't an answer to evil; it is a response. Hope is found not in intellectual mastery but in divine solidarity.

Sometimes his body, the church, will display the same compassionate solidarity in the face of evil, a cruciform being-with that is not an intellectual dodge but rather an embodied epiphany. I have seen this close up. Several years ago, our niece died suddenly and tragically of an unexplained illness. She was seventeen months old. This is surely not the way it's supposed to be. Her parents had drifted from any connection to a faith community back in our hometown. But our own faith family back there wanted to reach out and minister to them. So we called our pastor, a dear friend and a model of Christ's servant love.

When Pastor Charlie arrived at the house, the grieving mother was rightly inconsolable. In fact, she was sprawled on the floor of her daughter's bedroom, tangled in her blankets and stuffed animals, variously sobbing and numb, not willing to emerge from the room. After waiting for a time, Pastor Charlie went into the room. She didn't even acknowledge his presence. And so Charlie did the only thing he could think of: he laid down on the floor beside her. He cried out *for* her and *with* her and longed with Spirit-filled groanings. He was Christ to her simply by being present to her in her lament.

The Minneapolis band Romantica offers an image that has lodged in my imagination. In their song "Drink the Night Away," they recount the playful joys of some Irish boys headed to a rival school for a cricket match ("Tell my little brother to look after my mother, I won't be coming home today"). They are boisterous and eager, looking forward to meeting girls from another school, with mischievous plans for some post-match libations:

> Oh it's gonna be cool, all the boys from school, and the girls from down the way.
> Gonna dance round the fire until we get tired and then we'll drink the night away.

They're dreaming about winning and filling the tournament cup with chardonnay: "then we'll drink the night away," the refrain repeats.

But tragedy disrupts everything, upending their plans and turning their world upside down. "Hear your momma crying when you lay there dying, somewhere in Donegall." The song turns to lament: "What was

Jesus thinking," they plead, "when he let you sink into the arms of the Lord?" This is not the way it's supposed to be. As the song continues to voice this question, there is a decisive turn at the end: a different cup, a different drink.

What was Jesus thinking, when he let you sink into the arms of the Lord?
Then he took the cup, lifted it up, and drank the night away.[29]

The cup Jesus drinks is the cup of our suffering, filled with a wine-dark sea of anguish. This is not some cosmic cost-benefit analysis in which God calculates "the greater good." This is the historical scandal of God-become-flesh, taking the evil and injustice of the world—*our* evil and injustice—onto himself and then bursting forth from the grave to announce, as the Puritan John Owen put it, "the death of death."[30] God doesn't give us an answer; he gives us himself.

THERE ISN'T REALLY an "answer" for evil, according to Augustine; there is a response, a divine action-plan rooted in solidarity and compassion. That action, first and fundamentally, is *grace*. When the aged Augustine is reading back through his corpus to write his *Retractations*, he is jarred by what is so glaringly absent in his account of evil in *On the Free Choice of the Will*: grace. Grace is the light that floods the darkness in me, too. Grace is what flows from God's response to our evil, the spillover effect of Jesus drinking up the cup of suffering and vanquishing evil.

That spills over into our own response such that Augustine doesn't just parse evil in a philosophical system; he battles it as a bishop and an activist. He undertakes the work of protection and protest on behalf of the wronged, and even wrongdoers. Augustine's life as a bishop in North Africa could be described as an activism campaign against evil on the ground.

Augustine knew himself well enough to appreciate that the injustices of his world were concatenations of bad actors and diabolical systems—that injustices could be generated by good intentions as well as evil conspiracies. So Augustine wasn't content just to have an account of evil; he had an agenda for addressing it, countering it, and mitigating its effects. And Augustine undertakes such advocacy not only for the just and deserving but even for the unrepentant and recidivist.

Macedonius, the vicar of Africa (a governor of sorts) and the sort of official to whom Augustine often presented entreaties for mercy and leniency, sent a letter to Augustine in 413 or 414 expressing his confusion. Why would Augustine undertake to advocate for mercy and leniency for the unrepentant, who haven't promised correction? "It is easy and natural to hate evil persons because they are evil," Augustine replies, "but it is rare and holy to love those same persons because they are human beings." A just and merciful punishment, he argues, can be a means of unleashing their humanity. "He, therefore, who punishes the crime in order to set free the human being is bound to another person as a companion not in injustice but in humanity. There is no other place for correcting our conduct save in this life. . . . And so, out of love for the human race we are compelled to intercede on behalf of the guilty lest they end this life through punishment."[31] Better to risk leniency and create room for reform than to stand for law and order and end up crushing any opening for transformation. Augustine would constantly plead for authorities to not exercise the death penalty. He would plead for leniency and sometimes clemency in criminal cases, recognizing the principalities and powers that compel and constrain both criminals and victims.

Augustine's advocacy for penal reform was complemented by his interventions in the particular injustices of the Roman institution of slavery. As Robert Dodaro recalls, "Augustine frequently drew from his church's treasury in order to purchase the freedom of slaves. Moreover, on one occasion, while he was absent from Hippo, some members of his congregation stormed a ship and freed over 100 slaves held captive there."[32] He was also an active supporter of the right of sanctuary in the late Roman Empire, which was to stand with debtors and take the side of those ground under by economic inequality. Augustine's church was a sanctuary for economic migrants, and he would appeal to imperial authorities on behalf of those displaced and in jeopardy.[33] In all of these ways and more, Augustine responded to on-the-ground evils and injustice as an ally and advocate—imitating the Advocate who gave himself for his enemies (Rom. 5:10).

THIS IS WHY Augustine could commend politics as a calling worthy of the Christian. The hard, good work of politics is a way to love your neighbor in a tragic, fallen world. If politics is the art of the possible, it can also be a prudential way to secure justice, beat back evil, and mitigate the effects of the Fall. Nevertheless, when Augustine counsels political actors like Boniface and Macedonius, he does so with wide-eyed realism. He is at once trying to roll back the effects of the curse while at the same time recognizing the enduring reality of evil and original sin. He's under no illusions about human nature triumphing over selfishness or escaping its proclivity for disordered love. He has no expectation of legislating our way to the kingdom; to the contrary, it's a matter of legislating in a world where we have to keep praying, "Thy kingdom come."

So Augustine never overexpects from politics. If he is an advocate, an activist of sorts, intervening in unjust systems, he will never be prone to what we might call activism*ism*—a kind of Pelagian overconfidence in our abilities to overcome evil with our political prowess. That is the danger that besets Coates's (understandable) atheism. Human action and sincerity and ingenuity are deified. "Ideas like cosmic justice, collective hope, and national redemption had no meaning for me," Coates admits. "The truth was in the everything that came after atheism, after the amorality of the universe is taken not as a problem but as a given." Coates sees this as liberating: "Life was short, and death undefeated. So I loved hard, since I would not love for long. . . . I found, in this fixed and godless love, something cosmic and spiritual nonetheless."[34] The logic of that "so" eludes me, I confess. I'm not at all sure how it follows.

It does, however, explain the ensuing investment of politics with a sense of urgency and ultimacy: "The need for purpose and community, for mission, is human," Coates later notes. Agreed. But then this move: "It's embedded in our politics, which are not simply fights over health coverage, tax credits, and farm subsidies but parcel to the search for meaning. It is that search that bedeviled the eight years of power."[35] If we're all we've got, then any hope for justice is on us, and politics is as close as we'll get to an engine for bringing about the naturalized kingdom of god. Pelagian activism—resigned to, yet confident in, human power and ingenuity—is prone to being blinded by innocence. Indeed, as a later Augustinian, Reinhold Niebuhr, would put it, our atheistic confidence makes us "incapable of recognizing all the corruptions of ambition and power which would creep inevitably into its paradise of innocency."[36]

Augustine has no illusions about innocence. But his activism does not bear the burden of bringing about the kingdom. His clear-eyed recognition of the perdurance of evil—in his own heart as much as anywhere—generates a politics of hope rather than Pelagian revolution. The naturalization—and idolization—of politics generates its own injustices. For Augustine, citizenship in the city of God means laboring as an ambassador of the way things ought to be, hoping to bend the way things are to follow the arc of justice, of *shalom*. Politics is one of the ways we respond to the reality of evil, so long as we recognize that only resurrection can overcome it. Evil is not a puzzle to be solved but an incursion to be beaten back.

DOES THIS MAKE belief in God more believable? I don't know. But I know that one arresting mystery in the midst of horror stopped us short: the inexplicable forgiveness extended by the saints of Emanuel AME Church in Charleston, South Carolina, after the heinous massacre carried out by a young white supremacist. The evil itself is enough to make anyone question the existence and goodness of God. Which is why the forgiveness is even more mysterious, especially since this upsurge of grace and mercy was nourished by their faith in the crucified God who rose from the dead—the same faith that made them the sort of people who would welcome the unsettled young man to their Wednesday night Bible study, the outcast who would become their executioner. Such hospitality and forgiveness—such light in the midst of darkness—is generated by a trust that, to some, will look mad, or even irresponsible. Such irruptions of grace are a sign that jars us into considering whether the ball of fire at the heart of the cosmos isn't, after all, in spite of everything, the fire of love.

FATHERS : *How to Be Broken*

What do I want when I want to be embraced?

If a trope is perennial, does that make it cliché? Or is it simply a reality that needs to be relived in the first person? If a hunger is replayed over and over again, generation upon generation, does that make it tired and stale—or does it signal something enduring within us, a palimpsest of human nature that refuses to be effaced? If I spend a lifetime searching for what a million ancestors before me have hunted, does that make my longing derivative—or *cosmic*, a hunger planted in the human chest? Even if Freud would reduce it to an archetype, can heartbreak be "typical"?

Such is our longing for absent fathers—the fathers who left, opening up black holes in the fabric of a child's universe, along with the fathers who stayed but whose mercurial distance made them absent even when present. So many people on the road are looking for their fathers.

The quest is epic, as old as Homer, whose *Odyssey* opens with a son who goes in search of his absent father and ends with that father returning to find his own father, his son in tow.[1] Fathers and homes blur and blend: the taciturn father makes us born to run, "exiles at home and strangers wherever we go."[2] Bruce Springsteen sees this trope as the heart of rock and roll: "T-Bone Burnett said that rock and roll is all about 'Daaaaddy!' It's one embarrassing scream of 'Daaaaddy!' It's just fathers and sons, and you're out there proving something to somebody in the most intense way possible. It's, like, 'Hey, I was worth a little more attention than I got! You blew that one, big guy!'"[3] Even when it looks like we've given up the search and couldn't care less, we act in ways that keep saying, "Look at me, Dad. Do you see me now?" We can't stop wanting to be seen, known, loved.

"You do not stop hungering for your father's love," Paul Auster observes, "even after you are grown up."[4] His memoir, *The Invention of Solitude*, is a long meditation on this hungering: "From the very beginning, it seems, I was looking for my father, looking frantically for anyone who resembled him." He would hungrily eat up any scraps of attention or some faint echo of affection. "It was not that I felt he disliked me. It was just that he seemed distracted, unable to look in my direction. And more than anything else, I wanted him to take notice of me." Auster recalls a trivial moment suffused with significance in this respect:

> When the family once went to a crowded restaurant on a Sunday and we had to wait for our table, my father took me outside, produced a tennis ball (from where?), put a penny on the sidewalk, and proceeded to play a game with me: hit the penny with the tennis ball. . . . In retrospect, nothing could have been more trivial. And yet the fact that I had been included, that my father had casually asked me to share his boredom with him, nearly crushed me with happiness.[5]

To be invited into such boredom is the height of intimacy, a rest that need not be covered with nervous chatter. Auster would spend the rest of his life looking for this again.

So many people on the road are looking for their fathers. In fact, the quest courses through Kerouac's *On the Road*, which ends with an ecstatic paragraph in which Sal Paradise is imagining the energy rippling across the country they have traversed. "So in America when the sun goes down," he muses from New Jersey, "the evening star must be drooping and shedding her sparkler dims on the prairie, which is just before the coming of complete night that blesses the earth, darkens all rivers, cups the peaks and folds the final shore in, and nobody, nobody knows what's going to happen to anybody besides the forlorn rags of growing old, I think of Dean Moriarty, I even think of old Dean Moriarty the father we never found, I think of Dean Moriarty."[6] The road is life where you never find your father. It's a familiar path.

Some have suggested this is the oldest story, the baseline narrative of the human condition. Thomas Wolfe, whose *Look Homeward, Angel* is a bald instance of the genre, later reflected on the impetus for the story. His answer appeals to the epic:

> From the beginning—and this was one fact that in all my times of hopelessness returned to fortify my faith in my conviction—the idea, the central legend that I wished my book to express had not changed. And this central idea was this: the deepest search in life, it seemed to me, the thing that in one way or another was central to all living was man's search to find a father, not merely the father of his flesh, not merely the lost father of his youth, but the image of a strength and wisdom external to his need and superior to his hunger, to which the belief and power of his own life could be united.[7]

And it's not only sons who go looking. The search is human. Margo Maine, for example, invented the term "father hunger" to help diagnose the cause of eating disorders in daughters, young women for whom the experience of father absence deflected their father hunger into unhealthy relationships toward hunger and food.[8] Who of us isn't an heir to the dreams of our fathers?

LATE CAPITALISM IS the age in which everyone has a computer in their pocket and a gaping hole where a father should be. It's part of what has drawn something of a cult following to filmmaker Wes Anderson, particularly from a generation (my generation, I should admit) whose parents reveled in the amorphous freedoms of the 1970s and found the permission to dissolve their marriages in the 1980s. While they comforted themselves with tales of enlightened divorces and intentional custodial practices, they rarely asked us or gave us permission to offer counterevidence. So we absorbed and internalized their stories that this was "better for everyone" and repeated the script. It was our way of trying to talk ourselves into believing it was true, with the added benefit of giving comfort to those who had rent our world in two.[9]

Anderson's body of work can be read as an aesthetic protest against this official narrative. At the heart of almost every Anderson film is a child on a quest born of absence and disappointment and failure, a quest that bears the imprints of a hunger for a father. From *Bottle Rocket* and *Rushmore*, through *The Royal Tenenbaums* and *Life Aquatic*, to *Moonrise Kingdom* and *Isle of Dogs*, the drama of these stories is propelled by an absence—the absence of what *ought* to be in the relationship between a father and his children, or our enduring sense of what ought to be, even if we've never experienced it. Many of Anderson's characters hit the road looking for fathers and find only substitutes.

The father figures in Anderson's movies are not without charm. They are never angry cartoonish villains we'd be only too happy to leave. They are instead broken vessels who give us tiny glimpses of their humanity, of *wanting* to be otherwise, which only deepens our disappointment because it teases us with the possibility. So when, after a horrible accident, the scheming Royal Tenenbaum approaches his son Chas with a Dalmatian, a replacement for the dog Chas and his sons have just lost, we are touched by his confession: "I'm sorry I let you down, Chas. All of you. I've been trying to make it up to you."

"Thank you," Chas replies. "We've had a rough year, Dad."

"I know you have, Chassy." Every once in a while, Royal's narcissism stutters, and he sees his children, and they know what it's like to be seen by a father.

But often this becomes just another occasion for the child to console the father's failure to be one, the parent demanding to be seen for his brief flash of virtue. "Do you still consider me your father?" Royal asks his other son, Richie.

"Sure I do," Richie assures him.

"I wish I had more to offer in that department," he admits, looking for sympathy.

"I know you do, Pop," pleasing and appeasing his fragile failure of a father.

The fragility of Wes Anderson's fathers is why we can't quit them, why we keep getting suckered into hoping they might actually be the fathers we need. Our empathy stems from sensing that maybe these fathers still haven't found what they're looking for. This crisscrossing of quests is seen in *Life Aquatic*. Oceanographer Steve Zissou is chasing his white whale, a mythical jaguar shark that killed his partner. But since only Steve saw it, many are questioning whether it really exists, and perhaps even Steve's role in the death of his partner. At the same time, a Ned Plimpton has arrived on ship, suggesting he may be Steve's son. While Ned is looking for his father, we get hints that Steve is looking for more than a fish.

In a culminating scene, the entire zany cast of the film is crammed into a steampunk submarine. Having finally tracked the shark, the crew is preparing to encounter it in this campy submersible. (Do yourself a favor and Google "Life Aquatic and Sigur Rós" to see the scene with its ethereal soundtrack.) The luminous Leviathan swims at and over them, confirming its existence as everyone sits mesmerized in silence, jostled by its indifferent, hulking presence.

"It's beautiful, Steve," his ex-wife comments.

"Yeah, it's pretty nice, isn't it?" But then Steve pauses, almost tremulous.

"I wonder if it remembers me."

His face scrunches to a grimace; his eyes well up with tears; a sob grabs at his throat. The entire crew extend their arms and lay hands on him, like some underwater altar call, a Pentecost of self-realization.

AUGUSTINE'S FATHER, PATRICK, died when Augustine was seventeen. Patrick would know nothing of what his son would go on to become. The son's recollections of the father in the *Confessions* are mostly a litany of disappointments. Early on his father is like an icon in negative, the poster boy for disordered love: "His delight was that of the intoxication which makes the world oblivious of you, its Creator, and to love your creation instead of you. He was drunk with the invisible wine of his perverse will directed downwards to inferior things."[10] And when, much later, he recalls all that his mother had to endure being married to this man, it's clear the metaphors here are intentional: Augustine recalls alcoholism, infidelity, and abuse.[11] Augustine the grown man is both embarrassed and resentful when he recalls his father's failure to channel his passion with the gift of discipline. Instead, Patrick enthuses over the son's new possibilities for concupiscence, almost cheering him to join the father in adventures of lust. His failure as a father reflects a certain failure at being human. Even when Augustine recalls his father's end-of-life conversion, it is an occasion to praise his mother for "gaining him" for God.[12]

The same year his father died, Augustine became a father. His son, Adeodatus ("gift of God"), was unexpected but welcome. If my own experience, millennia later, is any indicator, it's not hard to imagine Augustine's realization of his father's failures becoming clearer with the arrival of his own son. Trying to answer the call of fatherhood without a net can be a new occasion to feel an absence you had learned to live with, a reason to question the stories you'd been told. It can also unleash an anger and resentment no one had let you express before because it disrupted your parents' peace with their decisions.

Augustine left us so many words, shelves and shelves of articulated thought, that we almost never have time to ask: What did he leave unsaid? About his father? His son?[13] His hopes? How much was Augustine existentially working through the emotional distance from his own father, or his own failures as a father? In what way is his search for home really a search for a father? Does he embrace the role of the prodigal because he knows there's a father at the end of it?

EVERY CHILD LOOKING for an absent, distant father is on the road to cover up a deeper desire: that such a father would come looking for them—that the arrow of hunger would be reversed and the father would return. Because then we would know he was thinking about us, looking for us, loving us. What to make of this father hunger other than a deep longing to be seen and known by the One who made us?

Paul Auster recalls something close to this in *Invention of Solitude*—in a scene, much later in his life, of fatherly attention, an instance when his father went looking for him.

> Once, while I was still living in Paris, he wrote to tell me he had gone to the public library to read some of my poems that had appeared in a recent issue of *Poetry*. I imagined him in a large, deserted room, early in the morning before going to work: sitting at one of those long tables with his overcoat still on, hunched over words that must have been incomprehensible to him. I have tried to keep this image in mind, along with all the others that will not leave it.[14]

This, of course, is exactly the dream come true at the climax of the parable of the prodigal son. The son looking for home realizes that his father has been looking for him: "But while he was still a long way off," Jesus says, "his father saw him and was filled with compassion for him; he ran to his son, threw his arms around him and kissed him" (Luke 15:20). The son slinking home in shame is gathered up in compassion; the child who's been lost is found by a father who runs out to meet him. The air is charged with celebration: "Let's have a feast and celebrate," the father cries. "For this son of mine was dead and is alive again; he was lost and is found" (vv. 23–24). If Augustine will later be known as the doctor of grace, it's because Jesus introduced him to a father who came looking for him. In his search, he was found.

Augustine would have occasion to return to this parable later in a series of reflections on the Gospels. Reading Luke 15, Augustine sees the loving arms of this father as a picture of God's embrace of humanity made possible by the incarnation of his Son. But the intimacy is not lost in his cosmic account. "To be comforted by the word of God's grace unto the hope of pardon of our sins," Augustine comments, "is to return after a long journey to obtain from a father the kiss of love."[15]

Maybe this is what has drawn me to Augustine on an unconscious level: a shared longing for a father I've never known. I suspect I'm not alone in this. I know I'm not the only one whose father has left, whose stepfather left, who's been left bereft of fathers despite their multiplication in a world of serial marriages. I was almost thirty before an Everclear song (of all things!) dislodged an anger and sadness within me like an anthem of absence:

> Father of mine
> tell me where have you been
> I just closed my eyes
> and the world disappeared.[16]

My father left us when I was eleven. I've not seen or heard from him since I was twenty-one, the year I became a father. (I've been a father longer than I had a father.) My stepfather disappeared when I was thirty-three, and I haven't heard a word from him or laid eyes on him since. I don't know where either of them lives, nor do they know a thing about me. As a father, this is unfathomable to me: I can't imagine my children making their way somewhere in this cold, hard world without knowing we're at home for them. I can't imagine my children as a blank space vaguely "somewhere." Suffice it to say, neither my father nor my stepfather has come looking for me.

But a Father did. At the heart of the madness of the gospel is an almost unbelievable mystery that speaks to a deep human hunger only intensified by a generation of broken homes: to be seen and known and loved by a father. Maybe navigating the tragedy and heartbreak of this fallen world is realizing this hunger might not be met by the ones we expect or hope will come looking for us, but then meeting a Father who adopts you, who chooses you, who sees you a long way off and comes running and says, "I've been waiting for you."

It's no accident, then, that Augustine finds his way home because he is found by a father figure. We have already met Ambrose and hailed him as a decisive figure in making the Christian faith intellectually plausible for Augustine. But that is not the whole of the story, and it may not even be the most important part. Ultimately, what Augustine found in Ambrose is a father he never had. "That man of God," Augustine recalls, "took me up as a father takes a newborn baby in his arms, and in the best tradition of bishops, he prized me as a foreign sojourner."[17] Ambrose is the anti-Patrick (which explains why Monica's relationship to him is so intimate). What won Augustine's attention was first and foremost Ambrose's kindness. He helped Augustine over some intellectual hurdles by first loving him like a father.

If Christianity is ultimately the proclamation of a gracious Father who runs to the end of the road to gather up his prodigals, it is decidedly *not* an ethereal appeal to yet another absent but heavenly Father. To the contrary, Augustine's encounter with Ambrose is testimony to the incarnational nature of the grace of God, who gives us surrogates like sacramental echoes of his own love. Indeed, to be adopted by this Father is to be enfolded in a new household where family is redefined and bloodlines transcended by the genealogy of grace. In the household of God's grace, you find sisters and brothers you never knew you had, and father figures where you didn't expect to find them. God's grace has been tangible for me, as it was with Augustine, in no small part because God has lavished me with Ambroses in my life. There are wounds and scars from the fathers that left, but they have healed because of the fathers I've found in the body of Christ—who chose me without obligation, loved me without reservation, were present when others were absent—who *know* me and yet still love me. Like Augustine, I think they deserve to be named: Gary Currie, Gary Dix, Jim Olthuis, Ron Bentley, Tim Hibma, and Norris Aalsma have joined the mothers I've also found in the church—like Sue Johnson, Karen Bentley, and Lois Aalsma—as icons of the Father I met through the Son, signs that "a man can be kind and a father could *stay*."[18] They are reminders to me that the gospel speaks to that most human of hungers: for a father who sees me and knows me.

A RECURRING THREAD in Leslie Jamison's *The Recovering* is John Berryman's ongoing struggle with addiction and his hopes for recovery, trying to claw his way toward a new life. In a particularly poignant episode, we learn of Berryman's estranged son, Paul, who sometimes writes to his father with news about school and grades, signing off each one with his full name—Paul Berryman—"as if writing to a stranger."[19] We have one of Berryman's replies to his son. Jamison, I think mistakenly, reads it as still self-absorbed, as a note primarily about the father rather than reaching into the life of the son. But I think she misses one of the ways fathers want to love their sons—by sharing wisdom, giving some guidance, owning fatherhood by offering insight for living. If one appreciates that, the note is a veritable sacrament of extended love from the midst of brokenness.

> FOR MY SON: On the eve of my 56th birthday, after struggles, I think I
> have learned this: To give an honest (sincere) account of anything is the
> second hardest task man can set for himself. . . . The only harder task, in
> my opinion at the moment, is to try to love and know the Lord, in impen-
> etrable silence.[20]

Even broken fathers can be reborn, and honesty is its own sort of love. From the fog of his recovery, Berryman's missive reads like the best life raft he could throw to a son who felt distant, a word of wisdom pointing not to himself but beyond, not to himself as father but to God the Father. Indeed, the best way to be a father is to point your children beyond you, to a Father who never fails.

One of my favorite images in all of Augustine's life is the picture he paints of his baptism. After a philosophical retreat with his friends in Cassiciacum, having tried their hand at writing their own Platonic dialogues, they return to the bustle of the city and the bosom of the bishop of Milan to present themselves for baptism. In recalling the scene, Augustine adds this touching detail: "We made the boy Adeodatus our partner in baptism as well." Like Berryman, Augustine realizes one of the things he can do is be a father who points his son to a Father beyond. "We included him in your gift of baptism," Augustine testifies, "so that being born again with us, he was the same spiritual age, to be raised in *your* training."[21] Augustine could best be a father by learning to be an icon that his son sees *through* rather than an idol he worships. And before that Father, they are brothers—"the same age," as Augustine puts it.

I thought about this when we visited Milan and climbed down the narrow stairs to the archaeological area beneath the Duomo to see the baptismal font where Augustine, Adeodatus, and his friend Alypius were all baptized together. I didn't think of all the fathers who had left me. I thought about the Father who had found me—the Father who had gifted me with Deanna, *my* Alypius, still alongside me after all these years. And then I cast a sideward glance at my children, exploring nooks and crannies of the ancient cathedral's ruins, and I noticed they were watching me, and wanted to be there, making this pilgrimage with me. I recalled that one of the most persistent mercies in my life was their constant forgiveness of my faults as a father. And I realized that the most revolutionary grace in my life was the gift of a heavenly Father who, against all odds, graced me with the power to stay.

DEATH : *How to Hope*

What do I want when I want to live?

Who really wants to live forever? We scoff at the idea as a recipe for ceaseless boredom. We don't worry about what happens to us after we die because we're assured of nonexistence. This is less the fruit of some considered naturalism and more the default of a culture that's made a god out of present pleasures. "Do you really want to live forever?" the eighties band Alphaville asked under the threat of nuclear holocaust. No, we want to be forever young. We'll settle for temporal happiness, or at least incessant distraction, as a trade for some vague promise of immortality. "Why would anyone want to live forever?" asks Ernie on the AMC series *Lodge 49*. "I just want to live for real, for a little while, right here." He then surveys his lonely situation and ruefully adds: "What's the use of living forever if you're all alone on a Sunday?"

We've made peace with death. We'll settle for notoriety and memory. Even our funerals are elaborate exercises of denial, transposed into "celebrations of life."[1] Our hope is not life eternal but a legacy that survives us. And our confidence that we can achieve such immortality seems odd when you consider the myriad of forgotten ones who've preceded us.

Nobody really wants to live forever, but nobody wants to die either. Nobody wants to watch people dying, so we have created entire industries to sequester them or rid ourselves of them, or we cleverly convince them to excuse themselves from our attention by exercising their autonomy. Perhaps even more pointedly, we don't want to be seen dying, so the padded and privileged expend their energy and reserves on the creeping harbinger of death we call "aging." Thus emerges another market, the wellness industrial complex, which at once capitalizes on our fear of dying and leverages what physician Raymond Barfield calls our "desire to be desirable." "The fear of death, with no grasp of what makes a life truly good, is the stupendously irrational desire for mere duration."[2]

Nobody wants to live forever, and nobody wants to die, so our hope settles for extension, a posthuman future *we* will achieve, triumphing over mortality, at least for a while. Since we can only imagine this as more of the same, it starts to look like lingering too long at a party. These Silicon Valley dreams of technology mastering mortality have been explored (and satirized) in prescient novels like Gary Shteyngart's *Super Sad True Love Story* and Don DeLillo's *Zero K*. They capture both the longing and the sadness, the hope and the lingering futility. In *Super Sad True Love Story*, for instance, we witness an encounter between Lenny Abramov, the benighted protagonist, and Joshie Goldman, the owner of Post-Human Resources, a startup firm devoted to the technological achievement of immortality, a company where they use "a special hypoallergenic organic air freshener . . . because the scent of immortality is complex."[3] Lenny, at thirty, is already an embarrassing elder in the company, showing signs that he's not long for this world. He asks Joshie, the CEO, if he could maybe get some special access to "dechronification treatments" at a reduced rate. "That's only for clients," Joshie replies. "You know that." But Joshie assures him: "Stick with the diet and exercise. Use stevia instead of sugar. You've still got a lot of life left in you." But we feel Lenny's response:

> My sadness filled the room, took over its square, simple contours, crowding out even Joshie's spontaneous rose-petal odor. "I didn't mean that," Joshie said. "Not just *a lot* of life. Maybe forever. But you can't fool yourself into thinking that's a certainty."

"You'll see me die someday," I said, and immediately felt bad for saying it. I tried, as I had done since childhood, to feel nonexistence. I forced coldness to run through the natural humidity of my hungry second-generation-immigrant body. I thought of my parents. We would all be dead together. Nothing would remain of our tired, broken race. My mother had bought three adjoining plots at a Long Island Jewish cemetery. "Now we can be together forever," she had told me, and I had nearly broken down in tears at her misplaced optimism, at the notion that she would want to spend her idea of eternity—and what could her eternity *possibly* comprise?—with her failure of a son.[4]

What's the use of living forever if you're all alone on a Sunday?

But what if forever weren't just an extension of a sad, solitary present but instead meant being welcomed home—to the place that made up for all those lonely Sundays that you hoped could be otherwise? What if it's not just that *I* live forever but that *we* live forever? What if forever was meeting your mother, who could finally convince you that she doesn't see a failure but only a son, whom she loves?

THIS MODERN ALLERGY to death is a stark contrast to Christianity's almost morbid comfort with mortal remains. The hope of resurrection and eternal life doesn't generate an evasion of death but rather a raw, sometimes creepy honesty about it. You can sense this today at a site that is like a time slice back to Augustine's own age, offering an opportunity to step into a world that Augustine himself saw.

The Basilica di Sant'Ambrogio in Milan, near the university, was not always so named. Its first designation was the Basilica Martyrum, the Basilica of the Martyrs. Built by Ambrose when he was bishop of Milan, the church was consecrated with the relics of Protasius and Gervasius, martyred by an earlier Roman emperor.[5] On the day we visited, a warm spring sun seemed to deepen the blue of the sky between the two towers of the basilica as we walked through the portico toward the sanctuary. We passed a twentieth-century baptistry that commemorated Ambrose's baptism of Augustine and made our way toward the altar, then descended into the crypt.

The scene is jarring to modern sensibilities. Through a compressed entrance you descend into a squat space, like a gothic cave. At first you see a few rows of small pews, but once you're inside you see it: the pews are facing what looks like a macabre aquarium, a glass wall behind which are three skeletons with ghoulish grins. They are the remains of Protasius and Gervasius, and now Ambrose. But they are adorned in robes, awaiting their resurrection. Ambrose is still wearing his bishop's mitre.

To descend into this crypt is to be transported to a different world. It is like a time capsule, not just because it houses ancient remains, but because it is designed for an encounter that runs counter to modern sensibilities.[6] I saw this play itself out while there. The day we visited, a rambunctious class of elementary school students was visiting the basilica on a field trip. I had noticed them in the sanctuary—energetic, slightly irreverent, a few being mischievous. We were already in the crypt when a gaggle of them barreled down the narrow stairs, bustling and bumping one another, then almost screeching to a halt when they saw it. Their irreverence was hushed by a fascination, perhaps itself slightly grim. These children came from another world above—a world of plasticized youth and botoxed grasping at longevity; this crypt was a descent into a world where they came face-to-face with memento mori.

The schoolchildren's jarred surprise stood in contrast to two other visitors we saw that day. When my daughter, Madison, and I had first made our way down the stairs, we were behind an older couple, shuffling slowly, the wife leading her aged husband by the arm. Once we were in the crypt together, it became clear that the husband was suffering from dementia. But they settled into the pews quietly, one might even say expectantly, the old man's body finding a habit that came easily to him. Heads bowed in prayer, this wasn't a foreign world for them. It was something like home, or an outpost of the home they were longing for.

In his marvelous book *Letters to a Young Catholic*, George Weigel unpacks the unique way Catholic devotion to relics works—not as a morbid fascination or as superstitious magic, but as a tangible, tactile connection to hope. Commenting on a memorial to martyrs like this one, Weigel observes that, while such memorials of persecution "are a powerful and sobering reminder of the depravity to which hatred and evil can and do lead," still,

> the Memorial is ultimately a place of comfort and a place of joy: comfort, because we are reminded here that ordinary men and women, people just like us, are capable of heroic virtue under extreme circumstances; joy, because . . . this great multitude of witnesses and heroes, who have "washed their robes in the blood of the Lamb" [Rev. 7:14], now live in the radiant presence of the Thrice-Holy Trinity, their every tear wiped away and their every longing satisfied, interceding for us that we might remain faithful to the gift of Baptism and to friendship with the Lord Jesus Christ.[7]

My visit to this crypt made a special impression because I shared the journey with my daughter. Both mesmerized, we sat quietly together on one of the pews, not exactly sure what to do, but held there somehow by a weight that was not sad yet was tinged with an eerie eternity. It can be a somber experience, parent and child facing death together. Worries and fears well up unbidden. A future we try to forget about—of departure and rupture, loss and being left behind—roars into the present. But these fears were swallowed up by something bigger, by an uncanny sense of connection with these bones, these brothers. We were no longer parent and child; we were sister and brother on the field leveled by death but also haunted by the resurrection. Though we had descended to get here, we were being invited by these brothers to some place higher, some place else, into a time beyond time where they were already alive in God, praying for us. And all of us, even we in our still-breathing bodies, we are all waiting with the same hope of resurrection. So when I glanced and saw the tears in Madison's eyes, I knew they weren't tears lamenting a loss but the tears of one overwhelmed to be part of such a cosmic fellowship that faces the fear of death with eyes wide open.

To THEIR CREDIT, the existentialists did not shy from talking about death. For Camus, suicide is the "one truly serious philosophical problem," the problem that occupied his *Myth of Sisyphus*. And for Heidegger before him, being-towards-death is a definitive feature of human existence that holds the key to discovering authenticity. As Heidegger points out, one of the ways we actually evade the sting of death is by conceding its certainty as a vague abstraction—we push it to the background of "death and taxes," and thereby neutralize it by according it a *mere* certainty, a kind of biological fact that doesn't impinge on us. What this does, in fact, is grant me the comfort of not having to face up to *my* death. Death is deferred—to others, to "later." When it comes to death *in general*, we are certain that everyone dies. But when it comes to our own death, Heidegger says, we are "fugitives" from the truth: we run from facing it.[8]

And yet death, for Heidegger, is exactly what I need to face in order to achieve authenticity—not to be constantly thinking about death (morbidly "brooding over it," as Heidegger says) or trying to imagine this possibility "become real" for me (which is impossible); rather, to "face up" to death is to anticipate death as "the possibility of the impossibility of any existence at all"—it is being-towards my *not* being, not as a vague certainty but as something I "understand" in such a way that it *focuses* my life. To face this, Heidegger says, is disclosive: it's revealing, unveiling; it lays bare who I am, what matters to me. "They" can't answer for me. To face up to death in this way is to face up to what I'm doing with my *life*. That, says Heidegger, is authenticity.

How to die is really a question of how to live. This insight of Hannah Arendt, who was Heidegger's student, emerges from her own direct encounter with St. Augustine. "The trouble with human happiness," she points out, "is that it is constantly beset by fear."[9] If love is a kind of craving, and "to love is indeed nothing else than to crave something for its own sake," as an end in itself, then the possibility of losing what I love hangs over my happiness like the sword of Damocles. Craving is haunted by losing. Hence "fearlessness is what love seeks."[10] What love hopes to find is a beloved who could never be lost.

Which is precisely why the fear that death spawns has to somehow be lived with. As she later formulates it: "It is no longer so much a question of coming to terms with death but life."[11] Arendt then cites Augustine: "For there are those who die with equanimity; but perfect are those who *live* with equanimity."[12] How to die is a question of how to live, but how to live is a matter of knowing how to *love*: how to find a love that isn't haunted by fear, a love that is stronger than death—figuring out how to love rightly and live lightly with all the mortal beauties of creation without despising or resenting their mortality either. To love and live in a way that faces up to our death, and the mortality that hangs over our finitude, without simply becoming what Kierkegaard calls "knights of resignation," caught in the false dichotomy of God *or* the world, who can only manage to live with death by hating this life.

Pretending you never wanted life anyway is decidedly not the Augustinian solution. Augustine affirms the *conatus essendi*, our desire-to-be. "The more you love to be," the early Augustine remarked, "the more you will desire eternal life."[13] The hope of eternal life does not efface the desire to live—it is the fulfillment of the desire to live, to live in a way that we can never lose what we love. Much later in his life, in a sermon praising the heroism of martyrs, he would affirm our love of life while also noting the trick of knowing *how* to love and live. "They really loved this life," he says of the martyrs. Their death wasn't some sort of sanctified suicide, an eagerness to get out.

They really loved this life; yet they weighed it up. They thought of how much they should love the things eternal; if they were capable of so much love for things that pass away. . . . *I know you want to keep on living.* You do not want to die. And you want to pass from this life to another in such a way that you will not rise again, as a dead man, but fully alive and transformed. This is what you desire. This is the deepest human feeling: mysteriously, the soul itself wishes and instinctively desires it.[14]

The desire to live forever is a desire to *live*, to know love, to be happy. It is the realization of our most human cravings and longings, not their evisceration. How to die is a question of how to live, how to love, how to hope.

How to die, though, is also a question of how to lose in the meantime. In this vale of tears, how to live is synonymous with the question of how to grieve. Augustine is most honest about the fear of death when he talks about the horror of grief—even if his self-criticism on this score might puzzle us.

Augustine gives us a glimpse into two gut-wrenching experiences of loss in his life. The first is early in the *Confessions*, when he recounts the sudden, unexpected death of an unnamed friend in his hometown of Thagaste. He and Augustine had become friends when Augustine returned to teach, though part of their camaraderie stemmed from their mutual disdain of the Christian faith of their parents. When his friend fell ill with a fever and was unconscious, his devout parents, fearing the worst, had him baptized without his knowing. When he later recovered, Augustine laughingly derided the parents' benighted efforts, expecting his friend to share in his enlightened dismissal of such superstition. But in fact his friend was aghast at Augustine's impudence. He received this gift of unexpected recovery as an opportunity to live into this baptism and curtly told Augustine that if that was going to be his attitude, they could no longer be friends. Augustine, "dumbfounded and perturbed," reeled at this response and waited for his friend to come back to his senses. But in the days of his waiting, his friend died, and he was never able to restore their friendship.

The bottom fell out of Augustine's world. "Everything on which I set my gaze was death," he confesses. "My home town became a torture to me."[15] What was familiar became *Unheimlich*, uncanny, not-at-home. He was swimming in a sea of despair; nothing could hold him; nothing seemed solid anymore; his world melted away in grief; everything familiar became a sea of sadness. "I found myself heavily weighed down by a sense of being tired of living and scared of dying. I suppose that the more I loved him, the more hatred and fear I felt for the death which had taken him from me, as if it were my most ferocious enemy. I thought that since death had consumed him, it was suddenly going to engulf all humanity."[16]

When Augustine reconsiders this episode in retrospect, his analysis is incisive, if somewhat off-putting at first. By the time he's writing the *Confessions*, he is trying to get a handle on why his world dissolved at this loss. He suggests it's because he hadn't yet learned *how* to love, and hence hadn't yet learned how to live amid mortals. He resented those still alive, and wanted to die himself, because "he whom I had loved *as if he would never die* was dead."[17] The problem wasn't that he loved his friend, or that he loved something mortal, or even that he grieved. The problem was *how* he loved him and hence *how* he lost him. He had loved him as if he wouldn't die, grasping onto him as if he were immortal. "What madness not to understand how to love human beings with awareness of the human condition!"[18] This is not some gnostic diminution of earthly goods, nor a pie-in-the-sky resignation that talks itself into imagining happiness as trying to live like angels without bodies or friends. It is once again a realist spirituality that is trying to understand how to love what is mortal, how to live amid the ephemeral, how to deal with the crooked timber of our hearts and our penchant to deny all of this and cling to the mortal as if it were immortal.

"The reason why that grief had penetrated me so easily and deeply," he concludes, "was that I had poured out my soul on to the sand by loving a person sure to die as if he would never die." Notice, the problem isn't *that* he loved his friend; the problem is *how*. "I loved what I loved as a substitute for you."[19] If Augustine invokes idolatry here, that is not a harsh dismissal of our grief but a diagnostic account of what's going on in our grief in order to help us imagine grieving otherwise. Indeed, Augustine is honest enough to admit that he made an idolatry of his grieving: "I was so wretched that I felt a greater attachment to my life of misery than to my dead friend."[20] Such is the curvature of the crooked human heart: it is always prone to bend back upon itself, such that I make even grief about me.

How we grieve tells us something about how we have loved, and it can sometimes disclose the twisted logic of our loves: "For wherever the human soul turns itself, other than to you, it is fixed in sorrows, even if it is fixed upon beautiful things."[21] Even the most beautiful things and faithful friends share something in common: they are made, created, finite, temporal, and therefore mortal. To love them as ultimate, to cling to them as what gives meaning, is to stake one's happiness on realities that are fugitive and fleeting—or as Augustine already hinted: it is to build one's house on the sand.

But what if we leaned on the rock instead of the sand? What if there was someone who gathered up all that is lost? What if there was a beloved who could never die, who loved you first, whose love called everything into existence and is therefore stronger than death? It is this radical alternative that makes possible a very different *how*. "'Happy is the person who loves you,'" Augustine says (citing Tobit 13:18), "and his friend in you, and his enemy because of you." Happiness is loving everyone and everything *in* God, the immortal one who holds all mortal creatures in his hand. When one loves in this way—in this "order," so to speak—then, "though left alone, he loses none dear to him; for all are dear in the one who cannot be lost."[22] The solution to loving mortals isn't to withhold our love in a protective hedge against loss; rather, we can love long and hard, trusting in the God who is all in all, who gathers up our losses in a time beyond time. Even our grieving is suffused with hope because all our loves are caught up in the immortal Beloved who loves us first. All is not lost.

This is the difference between the death of Augustine's unnamed friend and the loss of his cherished mother, Monica. It's certainly not the case that Augustine no longer grieves. In fact, you can still detect a hint of embarrassment in the middle-aged man at how much his mother's passing undid him. Like Mersault swimming after the death of mama in Camus's *The Stranger*, Augustine went to the baths with some cathartic hope, but it didn't work. His inner Stoic refuses to cry. But then the breakthrough: "I felt like crying in your sight, about her and for her, about myself and for myself. I let go the tears I'd held in, letting them run out as freely as they wanted, and out of them I made a bed for my heart. And it rested on those tears, since there only you could hear."[23]

By this point the way he grieved his friend has become unimaginable to him, because he can't imagine how anyone could survive such loss without the comfort of God's mercy and the consolation of eternity. Even his loss is now tethered to kingdom come. The resurrection casts a long shadow over his grief, a shadow that is its own sort of light. Augustine never made it "back home" with his mother; but now his loss is released into the hope of seeing her in the home country of the city of God, where God will wipe away every tear.

THERE IS A tender letter that Augustine wrote to a grieving young woman, Sapida, whose brother Timothy had recently died. Sapida had woven a tunic for her brother, who served as a deacon, but Timothy died before he was ever able to wear it. So Sapida gave it to the bishop, Augustine. The first words of Augustine's letter paint a moving picture for the grieving young woman: he's wearing Timothy's tunic for her. "I have accepted the tunic you sent, and, when I wrote this, I had already begun to wear it." All is not lost of your labors, Augustine assures her. He meets Sapida in her mourning. "It is of course reason for tears that you no longer see, as you once did, your loving brother, a deacon of the church of Carthage, coming and going, busy with the work of his ministry in the Church. . . . And you do not hear from him the words of respect that he paid to the holiness of his sister with indulgent, pious, and dutiful affection. When one thinks of these things, one must do violence to one's feelings, one's heart is pierced, and the tears of one's own heart flow like blood."[24]

But then he offers consolation on a higher register: "Let your heart be lifted up"—the passive here seems especially tender—"and your eyes will be dry. For the love by which Timothy loved *and loves* Sapida has not perished because those things, which you mourn as having been removed from you, have passed away over time. That love remains, preserved in its repository, and *is hidden with Christ in the Lord*"—the Lord who "was willing to die for us so that we might live, even though we have died, so that human beings would not fear death as if it were going to destroy them, and so that none of the dead for whom life itself died would grieve as if they had lost life."[25] The hope of enduring love, a love stronger than death, is not some natural immortality; it is a life bought by the death of God, the resurrection of the Crucified, which now yields hope as a spoil of victory over the grave. So the hope Augustine commends isn't simply "rational," like a Platonic conclusion to immortality, or the achievement of some kind of Buddhist detachment from loss. It is a hope that is bought by the One "who can restore what has been lost, bring to life what has died, repair what has been corrupted, and keep thereafter without end what has come to an end." So take consolation, Sapida, that I am clothed with the tunic you wove for Timothy, Augustine says; but see it as a sign, an icon of our greater hope. For "how much more amply and certainly ought you to be consoled because he for whom it was prepared will then need no incorruptible garb but will be clothed with incorruptibility and immortality."[26]

We have another snippet from Augustine of what we might call "self-consolation," in which he mourns the loss of a friend and tries to address his own sense of loss with the assurance of hope. Augustine's dear friend from Africa, Nebridius, had been a constant companion from their time in Carthage, even leaving Africa to join Augustine in Milan, and eventually joining Augustine in the journey to Christian faith back in Africa. But Nebridius died prematurely and when, in the *Confessions*, Augustine recalls his friend, he also hopes that he is remembered *by* his friend. Recalling so many animated conversations, humbled that Nebridius was always interested in what Augustine thought, Augustine imagines his friend in heaven: "He no longer pricks up his ears when I speak," Augustine admits. He's not around to put up with me the way he did, constantly asking questions and hungry for conversation. Instead, he is hidden with Christ in God where he "puts his spiritual mouth to your fountain and avidly drinks as much as he can of wisdom, happy without end." Then Augustine allows himself a happy, consoling thought: "I do not think him so intoxicated by that as to forget me, since you, Lord, whom he drinks, are mindful of us."[27] I miss our conversations, Augustine says, and I take comfort in the thought that Nebridius remembers them too, and is eager to pick up where we left off.

DEANNA AND I spent several weeks retracing Augustine's steps in Italy, from Ostia to Milan. It was like retracing his long Italian detour that turned out to be the road to himself, disembarking at the port in Ostia with Manichean dreams and imperial aspirations, only to end up in Milan, entranced by a bishop who would become his spiritual father.

After Augustine buried Monica in Ostia, he set sail home to Africa—to the vocation that was before him and to a legacy he could never imagine. He would never set foot in Italy again.

But Deanna pointed out that Augustine's bones had made a posthumous journey back to Italy, his relics now interred in Pavia in the San Pietro in Ciel d'Oro basilica, just twenty-five miles south of the cathedral where he was baptized. Our journey there was, in many ways, the culmination of a pilgrimage we'd been making, on the road with St. Augustine.

I recall the day vividly: I'm exhausted and, to be honest, have been a jerk all day. The fatigue of travel has finally coalesced, compounded by the guilt of the privileged guest (who am I to complain?). I'm baffled by the regional train system, and my frustration bubbles over into a curt anger that is the iceberg tip of my anxiety and exhaustion. I'm buying tickets to visit the remains of St. Augustine, one of the few philosophical psychologists of the West who could honestly identify the pains of affluenza, the unique temptations and burdens and idolatries that come with success and privilege. Having alienated Deanna with my anger, we board the train in tense silence.

The train courses through dense suburbs of high-rises on the south side of Milan, which quickly give way to flat wheat fields and the ruins of family farms. In the tension, forty-five kilometers feels like forever. As is always the case, upon arrival, Deanna forgives me yet again (I have a treasured picture of her postmercy smirk at a café on a narrow cobbled street). We wend our way to the basilica. It is out of the way, a humble red brick church that seems to be crumbling at its edges. It feels like we walk in through the back door, a small entrée into a space that then explodes open. What looks almost abandoned from the outside has a quiet hum of activity inside, where we witness an active parish. People are praying in the chapels and pews. Fittingly, we are greeted by an African priest who is warm and friendly.

As my eyes acclimate to the light, what I'm looking at comes into focus: just behind the altar is a stunning, mammoth "ark" that towers above the relics of St. Augustine, who, like his mother, was indifferent to the location of his body since he knew his homeland was a city not built by human hands. A memorial obelisk includes a small map illustrating the early medieval journey of Augustine's remains, from Africa, through Sardinia, ultimately settling in this small town under the care of Augustinian hermits. Around the altar are other memorials of pilgrimages made by Pope John Paul II and Benedict XVI. A notebook includes handwritten petitions in Italian, English, Thai, and other languages. People from different corners of the globe have traveled long roads to revere this saint.

The ark itself is Augustine's story in stone, like a gothic cathedral in miniature. Its size, I begin to realize, is just to make room for all the people who crowd around it in admiration and gratitude. The ark is its own communion of the saints, with ninety-five statues and fifty bas-reliefs that include kings and popes, Monica and Simplicianus, as well as an array of ordinary folk—mothers and children, laborers and masons—who have been caught up in Augustine's story. Ambrose is preaching from a pulpit. Around the top are scenes from Augustine's life, a marbled echo of Gozzoli's frescoes not far away. This cycle includes a touching portrayal of Ambrose helping Augustine into his baptismal gown with Adeodatus kneeling beside him, waiting to receive the sacrament with his father. And then a tender portrayal of Augustine, the bishop, baptizing a crowd of children in Hippo. A beautiful irony is performed in sculpture: this tomb bustles with life. That irony is what Christians call hope.

High above our heads, a life-sized Augustine is veiled from us. Lying in repose, he is surrounded by attendants who lift the edges of a shroud round about him. We catch only a glimpse of his face and mitre. The sculpture reiterates the posture of the *Confessions* themselves: "This isn't about me."

Not even my Protestant heart can resist the frisson of proximity here. I seem to have the space to myself, though Deanna, my Alypius, is nearby, just like Augustine in the garden. A silence descends on everything. I'm standing before the urn that holds Augustine's mortal remains, and for the first moment I think: "I can't believe I'm this close to him." But that geographical inclination gives way, and I realize that the sacred charge that enchants this place for me is an odd sense of arrival, the convergence of two journeys. I've been on the road with this saint for what feels like a lifetime, and here we finally cross paths and all I can think to say is, "Thank you."

AUGUSTINE TRAVELED FREQUENTLY, often on the back of a mule, in harsh weather, to visit the members of his diocese. In 418, at the age of sixty-five, he journeyed more than 1,000 kilometers to Mauretania Caesarea. In fact he traveled over 2,200 kilometers that year.[28] In one of his earliest letters, Augustine the seasoned traveler wrote, "The ultimate voyage—death—is the only one that should occupy your thoughts."[29] And at the end of his life, in some of his final letters, death occupies his thoughts. Corresponding with a deacon in Carthage, Augustine closes with a request: "Also, if you have perchance heard of the passing of any holy bishops, let me know about it. God keep you."[30] Without the obituary pages to study, the aging Augustine is looking for news about the passing of his friends.

In the final year of his life, Augustine corresponded with Count Darius, an official of the imperial court in Ravenna who had recently visited North Africa to try to make peace with Boniface, a Roman general who'd gone rogue. Darius had hoped to meet Augustine, but Augustine's age and illness prevented it. Because his fellow bishops sang the praises of Darius's virtue, Augustine reached out with a letter. He apologizes that "the double chill . . . of winter and old age" prevented their meeting in person. But he feels that he has already seen "the form of your heart" through the testimony of others. He blesses Darius the peacemaker, noting that "a mark of greater glory" is not to slay human beings with the sword but "to slay wars themselves by the word," encouraging Darius in his diplomatic peace mission.[31] Augustine is tickled to find out that not only has Darius heard of him, but he has *read* him. And so Augustine praises and exhorts Darius in his work and character, then eagerly entreats him to send a letter in return. There's something beautifully human in this: the rock-star bishop and influential author, who's already admitted he's a sucker for praise and admiration, is asking a government official what he thinks about Augustine's books.

Darius writes a long letter of fanboy enthusiasm in reply. It gushes in exactly the way you'd expect, just as I'm sure I would have done. But at the heart of it is a wise plea to the aging St. Augustine: "I pray to the sovereign God on your behalf," Darius tells Augustine, "and I ask for your intercession, my holy father, so that, though I am aware that I have not merited such high praise, I may at some point turn out to be such a man."[32] Pray to the Father, St. Augustine, that I might become the person you've made me want to be.

HOMECOMING

"That last thing is what you can't get," Sal Paradise reminds his fellow wanderers in *On the Road*. "Nobody can get to that last thing. We keep on living in hopes of catching it once for all."[1] This is the counsel of someone who has decided "the road is life." The road is long enough to tempt you to believe this. It seems like there is no end in sight—that we can't get the last thing, can't even glimpse its end, can't imagine rest. Despair is natural.

Running faster won't help. Crumpling into the middle of the road and giving up doesn't really solve anything either. And telling yourself "the road is life" over and over and over again starts to ring as a hollow consolation.

You can't get there from here. But what if someone came to get you? You can't get to that last thing, but what if it came to you? And what if that thing turned out to be a someone? And what if that someone not only knows where the end of the road is but promises to accompany you the rest of the way, to never leave you or forsake you until you arrive?

This is the God who runs down the road to meet prodigals. Grace isn't high-speed transport all the way to the end but the gift of his presence the rest of the way. And it is the remarkable promise of his Son, who meets us in this distance: "My Father's house has many rooms" (John 14:2). There is room for you in the Father's house. His home is your end. He is with you every step of the way there.

IN THE DUOMO in Milan, built on the site of the cathedral Augustine visited so often, sitting now atop the baptistry where he was raised to new life, there is a quiet section of the church where you will see a curious sign. Marking off an "Area Reserved to Worshipers," this sign instructs: "Please, no tourists. Do not go beyond this point except for confession."

You reach a point on the road with Augustine where mere tourism comes to an end. You're faced with a choice: Do you want to step in there? The next step isn't arrival. It's not the end of the road. To make that step won't solve all your problems or quell every anxiety. But it is the first step of giving yourself away, arriving at the end of yourself and giving yourself over to One who gave his life for you. It is the first step of belonging to a pilgrim people who will walk alongside you, listen, and share their stories of the God who doesn't just send a raft but climbs onto the cross that brings us back.

ACKNOWLEDGMENTS

I feel like I've been writing this book for half my life, so I will undoubtedly forget to thank some of those who've nourished me along the way. But that failure is worth the risk of expressing my gratitude.

I have to begin with a word of thanks to the community I found at Villanova University. While I was warmly greeted and supported by my doctoral advisor in philosophy, John Caputo, this book reflects the impact of those I didn't know I was going there to meet, particularly a cadre of Augustinian priests and patristics scholars who welcomed a curious Protestant into the conversation (I always used to tease them by reminding them about Martin Luther, OSA). I'm especially grateful to Fr. Robert Dodaro and Fr. Thomas Martin (*of blessed memory*) for their exemplary scholarship and warm teaching that introduced me to the "whole" Augustine—not just the author of treatises, but the pastor, bishop, and advocate who preached sermons and wrote letters. I can't imagine this book without that lesson.

There is also a community of Augustine scholars beneath much of this, even if they don't show up in the notes. Who isn't still indebted to the magisterial biography by Peter Brown, for example? But closer to me is the work of friends like Eric Gregory, Gregory Lee, Joseph Clair, and others from whom I'm still learning.

Undergirding this book is a three-week journey in the footsteps of Augustine in Italy in March 2017 (terror threats in the border region of Algeria and Tunisia frustrated our plans to visit his African homeland). The trip was a series of epiphanies for me, made possible by a grant from the Calvin Alumni Association, which is itself a beautiful testimony to the way the wider constituency of Calvin University remains invested in scholarship. A Calvin Research Fellowship also bought me some time, early on, to draft a couple of early chapters. And a grant from the Theology of Joy project of the Yale Center for Faith and Culture, funded by a grant from the Templeton Foundation, underwrote a trip to southern France to revisit some of Camus's haunts in Provence and consider the émigré community of Marseille. I'm grateful for all these tangible modes of patronage.

I was able to present early drafts of some of these chapters as part of two lecture series: the 2018 Parchman Lectures at Truett Seminary of Baylor University and the 2018 Bailey Lectures, hosted by the Front Porch ministry of All Saints' Episcopal Church in Austin, Texas. Both communities provided a warm welcome, thoughtful engagement, and incredibly helpful feedback.

As always, I remain thankful for the team at Brazos and Baker Publishing Group, particularly Bob Hosack, my longtime editor, and Jeremy Wells, marketing director, both of whom have championed my work and given me a long leash, dreaming with me about what this book might be.

I'd also like to acknowledge the significant role of Tim Hibma, my counselor during a critical season of my life, who helped me live into the story of a gracious heavenly Father who found me and loves me and will never leave me. This book is in many ways the fruit of soul work we did together—and it's a veiled way of trying to share that same story with others.

A significant portion of the first draft of this book was written in the enchanted space of David and Susan Hoekema's home on the shore of Lake Michigan. At just the right time, in ways I couldn't have realized, they offered Deanna and me a respite and retreat that turned out to be both restorative *and* productive, a combination that is sure to make any Calvinist's heart glad. Thank you.

Finally, the most inadequate thank you of all. As I mentioned, in many ways this book is fueled by an extraordinary journey that Deanna and I took in the footsteps of St. Augustine. What began as a research itinerary (with, sure, a fair bit of Tuscan wine-tasting built in) turned into a spiritual adventure that was both a microcosm and a blossoming of our twenty-nine years together. Like Augustine with Alypius, I started on the Way with Deanna by my side from the beginning. We've grown up together, kids raising kids. But we've also grown in the faith together—we've walked valleys of doubt together, mourned losses together, been humbled by parenting together, and been surprised by God in ways we wouldn't have known to dream. The vignettes in this book won't adequately capture what we learned about ourselves and God's grace on the way. But for us, the Via Agostino has become a road we share. We will treasure memories of our children alongside us in Milan and Cassiciacum. And we'll never forget the bright sun on our shoulders while walking the ancient stones of Ostia, the cool hush of Monica's tomb in Rome, or an unforgettable lunch at the café in San Gimignano that was like its own foretaste of a heavenly banquet. If I've entrusted myself to the One who will never leave me or forsake me, it's because he was gracious enough to give me this partner who is the embodiment of that on the way home.

READERS HAVE COME to expect a soundtrack for my books, and I don't want to disappoint. The background music for this project is an eclectic mix, from Simon & Garfunkel's "Homeward Bound" to "February Seven" by the Avett Brothers, Tunde Olaniran's remarkable album *Stranger,* Jason's Isbell's "Cover Me Up" (a favorite of Deanna's), Jeff Tweedy's "Via Chicago," Moby's *Play: The B Sides,* and more. Watch for a Spotify playlist online.

NOTES

As Augustine's works were later compiled into standard editions, they were "versified," in a way, like the Scriptures: organized into chapters and subsections. I follow the standard practice of citation for each work so readers can locate a passage across different translations.

Introduction

1. Leslie Jamison, *The Recovering: Intoxication and Its Aftermath* (New York: Little, Brown, 2018), 361.

2. Augustine, *Confessions* 2.18, trans. Sarah Ruden (New York: Modern Library, 2017), 50.

3. Sally Mann, *Hold Still* (New York: Little, Brown, 2015), 361.

Heart on the Run

1. Jack Kerouac, *On the Road* (New York: Penguin, 1999), 200.

2. Kerouac, *On the Road*, 1.

3. Kerouac, *On the Road*, 23.

4. Kerouac, *On the Road*, 31.

5. When, on "the saddest night," the women that Dean and Sal use and abuse finally resist, to denounce Dean's scoundrelness, then look "at Dean the way a mother looks at the dearest and most errant child," Sal's response is to distract them with geographical redirection: "We're going to Italy." Kerouac, *On the Road*, 184.

6. Kerouac, *On the Road*, 79.

7. Kerouac, *On the Road*, 115.

8. Kerouac, *On the Road*, 197.

9. Kerouac, *On the Road*, 18.

10. Augustine, *Confessions* 5.8.15, trans. Henry Chadwick (Oxford: Oxford University Press, 1991), 82.

11. John Foot, *Milan since the Miracle: City, Culture and Identity* (Oxford: Berg, 2001), 4.

12. Cf. Patty Griffin's song "Mary": "Jesus said, 'Mother, I couldn't stay another day longer.'"

13. In the next scene, the arrival in Milan, we see a servant removing Augustine's riding clothes, almost as if Milan will become his home. Of course, Augustine finds home elsewhere.

14. Augustine, *Confessions* 4.22, trans. Sarah Ruden (New York: Modern Library, 2017), 96.

15. *Confessions* 1.18.28 (trans. Chadwick, 20).

16. *Confessions* 2.2 (trans. Ruden, 35).

17. *Confessions* 5.2, 2.18 (trans. Ruden, 107, 50).

18. Augustine, *Teaching Christianity* 1.35.39, in *Teaching Christianity*, trans. Edmund Hill, OP, ed. John E. Rotelle, OSA, The Works of Saint Augustine I/11 (Hyde Park, NY: New City, 1996), 123.

19. Augustine, *Homilies on the Gospel of John* 2.2, in *Homilies on the Gospel of John 1–40*, trans. Edmund Hill, OP, ed. Allan D. Fitzgerald, OSA, The Works of Saint Augustine III/12 (Hyde Park, NY: New City, 2009), 56.

20. *Homilies on the Gospel of John* 2.2 (trans. Hill, 56).

21. *Confessions* 4.19 (trans. Ruden, 93).

22. *Confessions* 6.26 (trans. Ruden, 166).

23. Augustine, *On the Free Choice of the Will* 2.16.41, in *On the Free Choice of the Will, On Grace and Free*

Choice, and Other Writings, ed. and trans. Peter King (Cambridge: Cambridge University Press, 2010), 62.

24. Peter Brown, *Augustine of Hippo: A Biography* (Berkeley: University of California Press, 1967), 152.

25. This is exactly why Osteenism is such a lie: Christianity never promises "your best life *now*"!

26. Peter Brown describes a similar dynamic as a sign of Augustine's "romanticism": "If to be a 'Romantic' means to be a man acutely aware of being caught in an existence that denies him the fullness for which he craves, to feel that he is defined by his tension towards something else, by his capacity for faith, for hope, for longing, to think of himself as a wanderer seeking a country that is always distant, but made ever-present to him by the quality of the love that 'groans' for it, then Augustine has imperceptibly become a 'Romantic.'" *Augustine of Hippo*, 156.

27. Augustine, *Exposition of the Psalms* 72.5, in *Expositions of the Psalms 51–72*, trans. Maria Boulding, OSB, ed. John E. Rotelle, OSA, The Works of Saint Augustine III/17 (Hyde Park, NY: New City, 2001), 474–75.

28. *Confessions* 10.31.47 (trans. Chadwick, 207). Oscar Wilde shared this admiration: "Humanity will always love Rousseau for having confessed his sins, not to a priest, but to the world, and the couchant nymphs that Cellini wrought in bronze for the castle of King Francis, the green and gold Perseus, even, that in the open Loggia at Florence shows the moon the dead terror that once turned life to stone, have not given it more pleasure than has that autobiography in which the supreme scoundrel of the Renaissance relates the story of his splendor and his shame. The opinions, the character, the achievements of the man, matter very little. He may be a sceptic like the gentle Sieur de Montaigne, or a saint like the bitter son of Monica, but when he tells us his own secrets he can always charm our ears to listening and our lips to silence. The mode of thought that Cardinal Newman represented—if that can be called a mode of thought which seeks to solve intellectual problems by a denial of the supremacy of the intellect—may not, cannot, I think, survive. But the world will never weary of watching that troubled soul in its progress from darkness to darkness." Wilde, "The Critic as Artist" (1891), in *The Portable Oscar Wilde* (London: Penguin, 1981), 52.

29. Jay-Z, *Decoded* (New York: Spiegel & Grau, 2010), 239–40, cited in Wyatt Mason, "A Comprehensive Look Back at the Brilliance That Is Shawn Carter," *Esquire*, June 7, 2017, https://www.esquire.com/entertainment/music/a55372/a-to-jay-z.

30. Jean-Luc Marion, *In the Self's Place: The Approach of Augustine*, trans. Jeffrey L. Kosky (Stanford, CA: Stanford University Press, 2012), 146.

31. *Confessions* 10.28.39 (trans. Chadwick, 202).

32. Marion, *In the Self's Place*, 154.

33. Augustine, *Exposition of the Psalms* 59:9, in *Expositions of the Psalms*, trans. Maria Boulding, OSB, ed. John E. Rotelle, OSA, 6 vols., The Works of Saint Augustine III/15–20 (Hyde Park, NY: New City, 2000–2004), 3:186.

Augustine Our Contemporary

1. Sarah Bakewell, *At the Existentialist Café: Freedom, Being, and Apricot Cocktails* (New York: Other Press, 2016), 33.

2. Augustine makes one cameo appearance in Bakewell's *At the Existentialist Café*, on the very first page, along with Pascal and Job, as historical antecedents of existentialism: "anyone, in short, who has ever felt disgruntled, rebellious, or alienated about anything" (1).

3. One legend has it that Spanish Franciscans named the place Santa Monica because the flow of the local springs reminded them of Monica's tears over her wayward son.

4. Unlike, e.g., Botticelli's famous portrait of Augustine in his studio, hand on heart, his visage reflecting his North African heritage.

5. See Stephen Menn's masterful study, *Descartes and Augustine* (Cambridge: Cambridge University Press, 1998); and Michael Hanby's more polemical account, *Augustine and Modernity* (London: Routledge, 2003).

6. Jean-François Lyotard, *The Postmodern Condition* (Minneapolis: University of Minnesota Press, 1984), 13.

7. John D. Caputo, *Radical Hermeneutics: Repetition, Deconstruction, and the Hermeneutic Project* (Bloomington: Indiana University Press, 1988).

8. The later translators of this book into English (in 2004) were both members of my doctoral cohort at Villanova University. We graduated together in 1999.

9. Bakewell, *At the Existentialist Café*, 79.

10. See Adam Gopnik's engaging profile of philosophically inclined winemaker Randall Graham, which opens with a paragraph about Heidegger: "Bottled Dreams," *New Yorker*, May 21, 2018, 66–73.

11. Bakewell, *At the Existentialist Café*, 317.

12. My notes in my copy show that I read Arendt in June 1997, likely just after, or even concurrent with, my first reading of Heidegger's *Phenomenology of Religious Life*.

13. Hannah Arendt, *Love and Saint Augustine*, ed. Joanna Vecchiarelli Scott and Judith Chelius Stark (Chicago: University of Chicago Press, 1996), 4.

14. This may have been something she saw modeled in Heidegger's engagement with Augustine. As Heidegger exhorted his students when reading

book 10 of the *Confessions*: don't reduce Augustine's observations to the "mere hair-splitting reflections of a pedantic 'moralizer.'" Martin Heidegger, *Phenomenology of Religious Life*, trans. Matthias Fritsch and Jennifer Anna Gosetti-Ferencei (Bloomington: Indiana University Press, 2004), 155.

15. Albert Camus, *Christian Metaphysics and Neo-platonism*, trans. Ronald D. Srigley (South Bend, IN: St. Augustine's Press, 2015). Camus's dissertation was passed with a grade of 28/40. But because of his health (he suffered from tuberculosis his whole life), Camus was unable to sit for the *agrégation* exam that would have allowed him to become a teacher. This perhaps confirmed what one of the dissertation examiners noted: "More a writer than a philosopher." For the situation around the writing of this text, see Srigley, "Translator's Introduction," in Camus, *Christian Metaphysics*, 1–7.

16. Sartre would describe Camus as having "a classic temperament, a man of the Mediterranean." Jean-Paul Sartre, "Camus' *The Outsider*," in *Literary and Philosophical Essays*, trans. Annette Michelson (New York: Collier, 1962), 28, available at http://www.auto didactproject.org/quote/sartre_camus02.html.

17. In Camus, *Resistance, Rebellion, and Death*, trans. Justin O'Brien (1960; repr., New York: Vintage, 1974), 69–71.

18. Olivier Todd, *Albert Camus: A Life* (New York: Knopf, 1997), 296.

19. Sartre, "Camus' *The Outsider*," 29.

20. David Bellos, introduction to *The Plague, The Fall, Exile and Kingdom, and Selected Essays*, by Albert Camus, ed. David Bellos (New York: Everyman's Library, 2004), xv.

21. Conor Cruise O'Brien, *Camus* (Glasgow: Fontana, 1970), 81. O'Brien points to Camus's confirmation of this reading: "When in a review in *The Spectator* of the English version of *The Fall*, I stressed its Christian tendency, Camus wrote to his English publishers . . . confirming that this approach to the novel was sound" (81).

22. Geoffrey Bennington and Jacques Derrida, *Jacques Derrida* (Chicago: University of Chicago Press, 1999), 155.

23. See Jean-François Lyotard, *The Confession of Augustine*, trans. Richard Beardsworth (Stanford, CA: Stanford University Press, 2000); and Jean-Luc Marion, *In the Self's Place: The Approach of Augustine*, trans. Jeffrey L. Kosky (Stanford, CA: Stanford University Press, 2012).

24. Mark Lilla, review of *Augustine* by Robin Lane Fox, *New York Times*, November 20, 2015, https://www .nytimes.com/2015/11/22/books/review/augustine -conversions-to-confessions-by-robin-lane-fox.html.

A Refugee Spirituality

1. Albert Camus, *The Stranger*, trans. Matthew Ward (New York: Everyman's Library, 1993), 19.

2. Camus, *The Stranger*, 73.

3. Camus, *The Stranger*, 100.

4. Camus, *The Stranger*, 116–17.

5. Sarah Bakewell, *At the Existentialist Café: Freedom, Being, and Apricot Cocktails* (New York: Other Press, 2016), 147–48.

6. Captured in a more recent translation: Camus, *The Outsider*, trans. Sandra Smith (London: Penguin, 2013).

7. Cf. Daniel Mendelsohn, *An Odyssey: A Father, A Son, and an Epic* (New York: Knopf, 2017).

8. Albert Camus, *The Myth of Sisyphus*, in *The Plague, The Fall, Exile and Kingdom, and Selected Essays*, ed. David Bellos (New York: Everyman's Library, 2004), 497.

9. Camus, *Myth of Sisyphus*, 506.

10. Camus, *Myth of Sisyphus*, 504.

11. Camus, *Myth of Sisyphus*, 509. For Camus, the absurd does not "inhere" in the world, so to speak. It is forged in the space between us and the world; it is inherently relational: "What is absurd is the confrontation of this irrational and the wild longing for clarity whose call echoes in the human heart. The absurd depends as much on man as on the world" (509). Later: "The Absurd is not in man (if such a metaphor could have a meaning) nor in the world, but in their presence together" (517). I can't help but think of Martin Heidegger's *Being and Time*, trans. John Macquarrie and Edward Robinson (New York: Harper & Row, 1962), §44: There is no truth apart from Dasein. (And only Dasein can be lonely.)

12. Camus, *Myth of Sisyphus*, 535.

13. Camus, *Myth of Sisyphus*, 534.

14. Camus, *Myth of Sisyphus*, 592.

15. Camus, *Myth of Sisyphus*, 593.

16. See Martin Heidegger, *Phenomenology of Religious Life*, trans. Matthias Fritsch and Jennifer Anna Gosetti-Ferencei (Bloomington: Indiana University Press, 2004), 157–84, where we see that what will be analyzed as "fallenness" in *Being and Time* first emerges here as "ruination," his account of temptation in Augustine's *Confessions*.

17. In his notes for the Augustine course, Heidegger sees "the Appeal" as the alternative to "temptation" that pulls us into worldly everydayness (*Phenomenology of Religious Life*, 202).

18. Bakewell, *At the Existentialist Café*, 47.

19. Stefan Zweig, *The World of Yesterday*, trans. Anthea Bell (Lincoln: University of Nebraska Press, 2013), 438–39.

20. Zweig, *World of Yesterday*, 184.

21. Zweig, *World of Yesterday*, 378.

22. Zweig, *World of Yesterday*, 378.

23. Peter Brown, *Augustine of Hippo: A Biography* (Berkeley: University of California Press, 1967), 22.

24. Even later in his career as a bishop and polemicist, Julian (the Pelagian) basically made racial slurs against Augustine, ad hominem disparagements of "the African" and the "hard-headed Numidian," the "Punic polemicist." He also claimed Augustine was still a Manichean (François Decret, *Early Christianity in North Africa*, trans. Edward Smither [Cambridge: James Clark, 2011], 179–80). Much later, Barack Obama, an American of African descent, might recognize these sorts of tactics.

25. Zweig, *World of Yesterday*, 299.

26. Justo L. González, *The Mestizo Augustine: A Theologian between Two Cultures* (Downers Grove, IL: IVP Academic, 2016), 15.

27. González, *Mestizo Augustine*, 9.

28. Letter 91.1–2, in Augustine, *Political Writings*, ed. E. M. Atkins and R. J. Dodaro (Cambridge: Cambridge University Press, 2001), 2–3.

29. Cf. Jacques Derrida, *Monolingualism of the Other*, trans. Patrick Mensah (Stanford, CA: Stanford University Press, 1998): "I only have one language, yet it is not mine" (2). But "when I said that the only language I speak is *not mine*, I did not say it was foreign to me" (5).

30. Augustine, *Confessions* 10.22.32, trans. Henry Chadwick (Oxford: Oxford University Press, 1991), 198.

31. *Confessions* 1.1.1 (trans. Chadwick, 3).

32. *Confessions* 13.35.50 (trans. Chadwick, 304).

33. *Confessions* 13.9.10 (trans. Chadwick, 278).

34. This is the core thesis of Henri de Lubac, *The Mystery of the Supernatural* (New York: Herder & Herder, 1998).

35. *Confessions* 5.13.23.

36. M. A. Claussen points out that Augustine stops associating *peregrinatio* with *reditus* (the Neoplatonic concept of the soul's "return") just about the time he started writing *City of God* when he realized "one could not, in any meaningful sense, peregrinate to a place where one had already been." Claussen, "'Peregrinatio' and 'Peregrini' in Augustine's 'City of God,'" *Traditio* 46 (1991): 72–73. In terms of the prodigal structure noted above, Augustine would say that now, after the Fall, we are born already exiled, in a distant country, born on the run (original sin).

37. Letter 92A, in *Letters*, trans. Roland Teske, SJ, ed. Boniface Ramsey, 4 vols., The Works of Saint Augustine II/1–4 (Hyde Park, NY: New City, 2001–2005), 1:375 (modified slightly).

38. Claussen, "'Peregrinatio' and 'Peregrini,'" 48.

39. My thinking on these matters was significantly catalyzed by a presentation by Dr. Sean Hannan of MacEwan University entitled "*Tempus Refugit*: Reimagining Pilgrimage as Migrancy in Augustine's *City of God*," at the American Academy of Religion annual meeting, Boston, Massachusetts, November 2017. My thanks to Dr. Hannan for sharing a copy of his talk with me.

40. Hannan, "*Tempus Refugit*," 8.

41. Claussen, "'Peregrinatio' and 'Peregrini,'" 63.

42. Zweig, *World of Yesterday*, 435.

43. González, *Mestizo Augustine*, 166.

44. Augustine, *Sermon Guelfer* 25, cited in Decret, *Early Christianity in North Africa*, 168.

45. Michael Jackson, *Lifeworlds: Essays in Existential Anthropology* (Chicago: University of Chicago Press, 2013), 263.

46. Jackson, *Lifeworlds*, 263, 262.

Freedom

1. Augustine, *Confessions* 3.1.1, trans. Henry Chadwick (Oxford: Oxford University Press, 1991), 35.

2. *Confessions* 3.2.2–4.

3. Planned Parenthood v. Casey, 505 U.S. 833 (1992).

4. Martin Heidegger, *Being and Time*, trans. John Macquarrie and Edward Robinson (New York: Harper & Row, 1962), §50: "Being-towards-death, as anticipation of possibility," he summarizes, "is what first *makes* this possibility *possible*, and sets it free as possibility."

5. Heidegger, *Being and Time*, §§56–58.

6. "Anticipation turns out to be the possibility of understanding one's *ownmost* and uttermost potentiality-for-Being—that is to say, the possibility of *authentic existence*." Heidegger, *Being and Time*, 307.

7. Augustine, *Confessions* 2.2, trans. Sarah Ruden (New York: Modern Library, 2017), 35.

8. Jonathan Franzen, *Freedom* (New York: Farrar, Straus and Giroux, 2010), 181.

9. *Confessions* 3.3.5 (trans. Chadwick, 38).

10. *Confessions* 3.1 (trans. Ruden, 52).

11. *Confessions* 8.5.10 (trans. Chadwick, 140).

12. *Confessions* 8.5.10 (trans. Chadwick, 140).

13. *Confessions* 8.5.10; 8.5.11 (trans. Chadwick, 140).

14. *Confessions* 8.5.12 (trans. Chadwick, 141).

15. See Isaiah Berlin's classic discussion in "Two Concepts of Liberty," in *Liberty*, ed. Henry Hardy (Oxford: Oxford University Press, 2002), 166–217.

16. Leslie Jamison, *The Recovering: Intoxication and Its Aftermath* (New York: Little, Brown, 2018), 9.

17. Jamison, *The Recovering*, 112.

18. Jamison, *The Recovering*, 328.

19. Jamison, *The Recovering*, 304.

20. Augustine, *On Reprimand and Grace* 1.2, in *On the Free Choice of the Will, On Grace and Free Choice, and Other Writings*, ed. and trans. Peter King (Cambridge: Cambridge University Press, 2010), 186.

21. *Confessions* 2.2.3–4 (trans. Chadwick, 25).

22. Listen, e.g., to Declan McKenna's "The Kids Don't Wanna Come Home."

23. *Confessions* 2.6 (trans. Ruden, 38–39).

24. *On Reprimand and Grace* 11.31 (trans. King, 212).

25. *Confessions* 8.8.19 (trans. Chadwick, 147).

26. *Confessions* 4.1.1 (trans. Chadwick, 52).

27. *Confessions* 8.10.22 (trans. Chadwick, 148).

28. Augustine, *On the Free Choice of the Will* 1.14.30, in *On the Free Choice of the Will, On Grace and Free Choice, and Other Writings*, ed. and trans. Peter King (Cambridge: Cambridge University Press, 2010), 25.

29. *Confessions* 8.10.24; 8.11.26 (trans. Chadwick, 150, 151). See also 8.10.24–8.11.27, 8.8.20.

30. For more on this dialectic and dance, see James H. Olthuis, "Be(com)ing: Humankind as Gift and Call," *Philosophia Reformata* 58 (1993): 153–72.

31. *Confessions* 8.12.29 (trans. Chadwick, 152–53, emphasis added).

32. *Confessions* 8.12.29 (trans. Chadwick, 153).

33. *On Reprimand and Grace* 8.17 (trans. King, 200).

34. *On Reprimand and Grace* 11.32 (trans. King, 213).

35. *On Reprimand and Grace* 12.33 (trans. King, 214).

36. "God did not want Adam, whom He left to his free choice, to be without His grace," so God gives an original "assistance" that humanity abandons. Nonetheless, "this is the first grace which was given to the First Adam" (*On Reprimand and Grace* 11.31 [trans. King, 212]). Don't let the language of Adam distract you too much here. For an account that weaves this into our evolutionary understanding of human origins, see James K. A. Smith, "What Stands on the Fall? A Philosophical Exploration," in *Evolution and the Fall*, ed. William Cavanaugh and James K. A. Smith (Grand Rapids: Eerdmans, 2017): 48–65.

37. *On Reprimand and Grace* 11.31 (trans. King, 212).

38. This hope for "second grace" is found in Nick Drake's "Fly," which is the plaintive soundtrack for Richie Tenenbaum's postsuicidal bus ride home in Wes Anderson's film *The Royal Tenenbaums*. We'll revisit the film in the "Fathers" chapter.

39. *On Reprimand and Grace* 12.35 (trans. King, 215).

40. *On Reprimand and Grace* 12.35 (trans. King, 215).

41. Augustine, *On the Gift of Perseverance* 8.19, in *On the Free Choice of the Will, On Grace and Free Choice, and Other Writings*, ed. and trans. Peter King (Cambridge: Cambridge University Press, 2010), 231, citing Ambrose, *The Escape from the World* 1.2.

42. *On the Gift of Perseverance* 13.33 (trans. King, 244), citing Ambrose, *Escape from the World* 1.2.

43. *On the Gift of Perseverance* 13.33 (trans. King, 245).

44. For a more extended discussion, see James K. A. Smith, *You Are What You Love: The Spiritual Power of Habit* (Grand Rapids: Brazos, 2016).

45. Jamison, *The Recovering*, 196–97.

46. Jamison, *The Recovering*, 301.

47. Jamison, *The Recovering*, 302–3, quoting David Foster Wallace.

48. *Confessions* 5.2.2 (trans. Chadwick, 73).

49. Cited (without reference) by Gabriel Marcel in *Homo Viator: Introduction to the Metaphysics of Hope*, trans. Emma Crawford and Paul Seaton (South Bend, IN: St. Augustine's Press, 2010), 22.

Ambition

1. Walker, "Troy, Betty Crocker, and Mother Mary: Reflections on Gender and Ambition," in Luci Shaw and Jeanne Murray Walker, eds., *Ambition* (Eugene, OR: Cascade, 2015), 72, 74, 77; Scott Cairns, introduction to *Ambition*, edited by Shaw and Walker, xi.

2. The preceding essays and quotations appear in Shaw and Walker, *Ambition*. Eugene Peterson, "Ambition: Lilies That Fester," 56; Erin McGraw, "What's a Heaven For?," 2; Luci Shaw, "What I Learned in Lent," 22; and Emilie Griffin, "The Lure of Fame: The Yearning, the Drive, the Question Mark," 31.

3. Augustine, *Confessions* 1.12.19, trans. Henry Chadwick (Oxford: Oxford University Press, 1991), 14–15.

4. *Confessions* 2.2.4 (trans. Chadwick, 26).

5. *Confessions* 2.3.5 (trans. Chadwick, 26).

6. Justo L. González, *The Mestizo Augustine: A Theologian between Two Cultures* (Downers Grove, IL: IVP Academic, 2016), 31.

7. Wallace Stegner, *Crossing to Safety* (New York: Penguin, 1987), 263.

8. Stegner, *Crossing to Safety*, 187.

9. *Confessions* 3.4.7 (trans. Chadwick, 38).

10. *Confessions* 4.1.1 (trans. Chadwick, 52).

11. Augustine, *Teaching Christianity* 1.4.4.

12. Ben Wofford, "Up in the Air," *Rolling Stone*, July 20, 2015, https://www.rollingstone.com/culture/culture-news/up-in-the-air-meet-the-man-who-flies-around-the-world-for-free-43961. Quotes in this section come from this article.

13. John Foot, *Milan since the Miracle: City, Culture and Identity* (Oxford: Berg, 2001), 1.

14. *Confessions* 6.6.9 (trans. Chadwick, 97).

15. *Confessions* 6.6.9 (trans. Chadwick, 97).

16. Augustine, *Confessions* 6.19, trans. Sarah Ruden (New York: Modern Library, 2017), 158.

17. *Confessions* 6.19 (trans. Ruden, 159).

18. Ponticianus was working in the branch of the emperor's government that managed the *cursus publicus*, the imperial communication system and its routes, the means of transport Augustine enjoyed from Rome to Milan, given his imperial appointment.

19. *Confessions* 8.6.15 (trans. Chadwick, 143).

20. On "the father's lap," see *Homilies on the Gospel of John* 3.17, in *Homilies on the Gospel of John 1–40*,

trans. Edmund Hill, OP, ed. Allan D. Fitzgerald, OSA, *The Works of Saint Augustine* III/12 (Hyde Park, NY: New City, 2009), 80.

21. Andre Agassi, *Open: An Autobiography* (New York: Knopf, 2009), 375.

22. Blaise Pascal, *Pensées and Other Writings*, trans. Honor Levi (Oxford: Oxford University Press, 1995), §520, p. 124.

23. See, e.g., *Confessions* 10.3.3.

24. *Confessions* 10.36.59 (trans. Chadwick, 213–14).

25. *Confessions* 10.36.59–10.37.60 (trans. Chadwick, 214–15).

Sex

1. Augustine, *Confessions* 10.30.41–42.

2. *Confessions* 2.2.2, trans. Henry Chadwick (Oxford: Oxford University Press, 1991), 24.

3. When Kofman asks Derrida, "Do you think you would want people to ask you such a question?" he is more reticent: "I never said I'd respond to such a question." But as he goes on to point out, it's not like his books don't include such divulgences. Indeed, he divulges a lot in "Circumfession" (in Geoffrey Bennington and Jacques Derrida, *Jacques Derrida* [Chicago: University of Chicago Press, 1999]), the same work in which he tracks Augustine.

4. For an eyes-wide-open consideration of these sorts of critiques and caricatures of Augustine, see *Feminist Interpretations of Augustine*, ed. Judith Chelius Stark (University Park: Pennsylvania State University Press, 2007).

5. *Confessions* 8.12.29.

6. Often best attested in poetry, e.g., Michael Donaghy, "Pentecost," and Heather McHugh, "Coming," both in *Joy: 100 Poems*, ed. Christian Wiman (New Haven: Yale University Press, 2017).

7. *Confessions* 2.2.2 (trans. Chadwick, 24).

8. *Confessions* 2.4, trans. Sarah Ruden (New York: Modern Library, 2017), 37.

9. *Confessions* 3.1.1 (trans. Chadwick, 35).

10. "Joe Rogan Experience #1021—Russell Brand," YouTube, October 5, 2017, https://youtu.be/iZPH6r_ZDvM. Quotes in this section come from this podcast.

11. Emily Chang, "'Oh My God, This Is So F——ed Up': Inside Silicon Valley's Secretive, Orgiastic Dark Side," *Vanity Fair*, February 2018, https://www.vanityfair.com/news/2018/01/brotopia-silicon-valley-secretive-orgiastic-inner-sanctum. This article is an adaptation from Emily Chang, *Brotopia: Breaking Up the Boys' Club of Silicon Valley* (New York: Portfolio, 2018).

12. Recall Augustine's silent scream: "If only someone could have imposed restraint on my disorder!" *Confessions* 2.2.3 (trans. Chadwick, 25).

13. *Confessions* 2.2.4 (trans. Chadwick, 25).

14. Brand's own "confessions" repay reading, however. See Russell Brand, *Recovery: Freedom from Our Addictions* (New York: Henry Holt, 2017).

15. *Confessions* 8.11.27 (trans. Chadwick, 151).

16. *Confessions* 8.11.27 (trans. Chadwick, 151).

17. On the Reformation as an Augustinian renewal movement within the church catholic, see James K. A. Smith, *Letters to a Young Calvinist* (Grand Rapids: Brazos, 2010), 38–41. See also Charles Taylor, *A Secular Age* (Cambridge, MA: Harvard University Press, 2007), 62–66, on two-tiered Christianity.

18. Kyle Harper, *From Shame to Sin: The Christian Transformation of Sexual Morality in Late Antiquity* (Cambridge, MA: Harvard University Press, 2013), 137. See also Peter Brown, *The Body and Society: Men, Women and Sexual Renunciation in Early Christianity*, 2nd ed. (New York: Columbia University Press, 2008).

19. Augustine, *City of God* 14.22–23.

20. Augustine, *Against Julian* 14.28, cited in Peter Brown, *Augustine of Hippo: A Biography* (Berkeley: University of California Press, 1967), 393.

21. Cf. Jenell Williams Paris, *The End of Sexual Identity: Why Sex Is Too Important to Define Who We Are* (Downers Grove, IL: InterVarsity, 2011).

22. Cf. *Confessions* 6.11.20.

23. Cf. Kyle Harper's discussion of "pastoral Christianity" as a gracious accommodation to the realities in which Christians found themselves (*From Shame to Sin*, 177–90).

24. Augustine, *On the Good of Marriage* 6, in *A Select Library of Nicene and Post-Nicene Fathers of the Christian Church*, 1st series, ed. Philip Schaff and Henry Wace, 14 vols. (1890–1900; repr., Peabody, MA: Hendrickson, 1994), 3:401.

25. Joseph Clair, *Discerning the Good in the Letters and Sermons of Augustine* (Oxford: Oxford University Press, 2016), 67.

26. *On the Good of Marriage* 5.

27. Cf. Caitlin Flanagan's tongue-in-check comment in one article: "Take it a step further. What if we asked for a lifetime commitment, a binding legal document and the presence of witnesses at the vow taking? Could work." Flanagan, "Getting 'Consent' for Sex Is Too Low a Bar," *New York Times*, July 18, 2018, https://www.nytimes.com/2018/07/18/well/getting-consent-for-sex-is-too-low-a-bar.html.

28. See Robin Lane Fox, *Augustine: Conversions to Confessions* (New York: Basic Books, 2015), 77.

29. For a creative, novelistic insight into this relationship, between Augustine and his concubine, but also between his concubine and Monica, see Suzanne Wolfe, *The Confessions of X* (Nashville: Thomas Nelson, 2016).

30. *Confessions* 4.2.2 (trans. Chadwick, 53). A lot has been made of the fact that this woman is unnamed by Augustine. I follow Peter Brown (*Augustine of Hippo: A Biography* [Berkeley: University of California Press, 1967]) in seeing this as actually a sign of respect, a way of guarding her from what would be the late ancient paparazzi who would be looking to find a bishop's old flame. (There is some evidence that she lived in a convent not far from Hippo.) Interestingly, in *On the Good of Marriage* when Augustine disparages exactly what he himself had done—taking to himself someone for a time, "until he find another worthy either of his honors or his means"—he also embeds a kind of backhanded praise of the woman in such an arrangement: "there are many matrons to whom she is to be preferred" (5).

31. *Confessions* 6.15.25 (trans. Chadwick, 109). Augustine immediately takes another concubine, which might also explain why he was so tired of having to "take care of" his sexual desire by book 8.

32. *True Religion* 1.16.30, in *On Christian Belief*, trans. Edmund Hill, OP, ed. Boniface Ramsey, The Works of Saint Augustine I/8 (Hyde Park, NY: New City, 2005), 48.

Mothers

1. Jonathan Franzen, *The Corrections* (New York: Farrar, Straus and Giroux, 2001), 75–76.

2. Recounted in Olivier Todd, *Albert Camus: A Life* (New York: Knopf, 1997), 305–6, 359. Perhaps Camus's point about a "Mediterranean" account of freedom, at the end of *Rebel*, hints at why freedom isn't synonymous with independence, and why a mother's love doesn't rob a person of identity, but grants it.

3. Todd, *Albert Camus*, 378. A journalist later said that what Camus meant was, "If that [terrorism] is your 'justice,' I prefer my mother to justice" (379).

4. Derrida, "Circumfession," in Geoffrey Bennington and Jacques Derrida, *Jacques Derrida* (Chicago: University of Chicago Press, 1999), 19.

5. Derrida, "Circumfession," 22.

6. Derrida, "Circumfession," 23, 25.

7. An important plotline in Suzanne Wolfe's fictionalization of the relationship in her novel *The Confessions of X* (Nashville: Thomas Nelson, 2016).

8. Augustine, *Confessions* 5.8.15, trans. Henry Chadwick (Oxford: Oxford University Press, 1991), 82.

9. *Confessions* 6.1.1 (trans. Chadwick, 90).

10. Justo L. González, *The Mestizo Augustine: A Theologian between Two Cultures* (Downers Grove, IL: IVP Academic, 2016), 18.

11. The term "the Brights" comes from a famous op-ed by philosopher Daniel Dennett, "The Bright Stuff," *New York Times*, July 12, 2003, https://www .nytimes.com/2003/07/12/opinion/the-bright-stuff .html. We'll return to this in the "Enlightenment" chapter.

12. *Confessions* 6.2.2 (trans. Chadwick, 92).

13. González remarks about Augustine, "Throughout most of his life, it would seem that the Roman in him had become dominant; but when, after the Roman disaster of 410, he tried to read what had happened from a Christian perspective, he was quite critical of the entire Roman culture and civilization, and this criticism was partly grounded on principles learned long before from his Berber mother." *Mestizo Augustine*, 18–19.

14. Augustine, *Confessions* 9.22, trans. Sarah Ruden (New York: Modern Library, 2017), 262.

15. Rob Doyle, *This Is the Ritual* (London: Bloomsbury, 2017), 18.

16. Doyle, *This Is the Ritual*, 29, 30.

17. Doyle, *This Is the Ritual*, 31.

18. Karr, "The Burning Girl," in *Tropic of Squalor: Poems* (New York: HarperCollins, 2018), 6–7. Copyright © 2018 by Mary Karr. Reprinted by permission of HarperCollins Publishers.

19. Augustine, *On the Free Choice of the Will* 3.23.67, in *On the Free Choice of the Will, On Grace and Free Choice, and Other Writings*, ed. and trans. Peter King (Cambridge: Cambridge University Press, 2010), 119.

20. *Exposition of the Psalms* 58(1):10, in *Expositions of the Psalms*, trans. Maria Boulding, OSB, ed. John E. Rotelle, OSA, 6 vols., The Works of Saint Augustine III/15–20 (Hyde Park, NY: New City, 2000–2004), 3:156.

21. *Confessions* 9.26 (trans. Ruden, 266).

22. *Confessions* 9.27, 9.28 (trans. Ruden, 267, 268). She didn't "care about a tomb in her homeland" (9.36, trans. Ruden, 274).

23. *Confessions* 9.30 (trans. Ruden, 269).

Friendship

1. Heidegger's term "Dasein" is a technical term he uses instead of the usual philosophical notion of "the subject," "the ego," etc., trying to give a more existential, embedded picture of what it means to be "me." Dasein means "being there," being here and now, *existing* in a world. Heidegger's English translators almost universally leave the term untranslated, such that "Dasein" is now almost like a Germanic philosophical character.

2. Martin Heidegger, *Being and Time*, trans. John Macquarrie and Edward Robinson (New York: Harper & Row, 1962), 154.

3. Heidegger, *Being and Time*, 163–64.

4. Heidegger, *Being and Time*, 164.

5. Heidegger, *Being and Time*, 163.

6. Heidegger, *Being and Time*, 164.

7. Heidegger, *Being and Time*, 165–66.

8. Heidegger, *Being and Time*, 317.

9. Heidegger, *Being and Time*, 372–73.

10. Heidegger, *Being and Time*, 354.

11. Jean-Paul Sartre, *Being and Nothingness*, trans. Hazel Barnes (London: Routledge, 2003), 463.

12. See discussion in Sarah Bakewell, *At the Existentialist Café: Freedom, Being, and Apricot Cocktails* (New York: Other Press, 2016), 213–14. She cites Iris Murdoch's droll remark that Sartre turns love into "a battle between two hypnotists in a closed room" (214).

13. Gabriel Marcel, *The Philosophy of Existentialism*, trans. Manya Harari (New York: Citadel, 1956), 82.

14. As we'll see below, this will be an interesting point vis-à-vis Heidegger.

15. Marcel, *Philosophy of Existentialism*, 79.

16. Marcel, *Philosophy of Existentialism*, 76.

17. Martin Heidegger, *Phenomenology of Religious Life*, trans. Matthias Fritsch and Jennifer Anna Gosetti-Ferencei (Bloomington: Indiana University Press, 2004), 170.

18. Heidegger, *Phenomenology of Religious Life*, 171, 176.

19. Augustine, *Confessions* 2.4.9, trans. Henry Chadwick (Oxford: Oxford University Press, 1991), 29.

20. *Confessions* 2.8.16–2.9.17 (trans. Chadwick, 33–34).

21. "This Place Is a Prison," track 8 on the Postal Service, *Give Up*, SubPop, 2003.

22. *Confessions* 2.8.16–2.9.17 (trans. Chadwick, 33–34). Augustine admits he himself played this role of frenemy to a friend who died (4.4.7–8).

23. *Confessions* 6.8.13 (trans. Chadwick, 100).

24. *Confessions* 6.8.13 (trans. Chadwick, 100–101).

25. Augustine, *Confessions* 6.13, trans. Sarah Ruden (New York: Modern Library, 2017), 152.

26. Kipling D. Williams, "Ostracism: A Temporal Need-Threat Model," in *Advances in Experimental Social Psychology*, vol. 41, ed. Mark P. Zanna (London: Academic Press, 2009), 279–314.

27. See Edward Davies, "Loneliness Is a Modern Scourge, but It Doesn't Have to Be," Centre for Social Justice, accessed December 18, 2018, http://thecentreforsocialjustice.cmail20.com/t/ViewEmail/y/7CB805AF716F58B3/FC687629C2073D80907C5D7C792C0FF8.

28. Franz Wright, *Walking to Martha's Vineyard* (New York: Knopf, 2003), 17.

29. Clay Routledge, "The Curse of Modern Loneliness," *National Review*, January 16, 2018, https://www.nationalreview.com/2018/01/digital-age-loneliness-public-health-political-problem.

30. Heidegger, *Being and Time*, 156–57.

31. Marina Keegan, "The Opposite of Loneliness," *Yale Daily News*, May 27, 2012, https://yaledailynews.com/blog/2012/05/27/keegan-the-opposite-of-loneliness.

32. *Confessions* 6.26 (trans. Ruden, 166).

33. *Confessions* 2.2.2 (trans. Chadwick, 24).

34. *Confessions* 8.1.1 (trans. Chadwick, 133).

35. *Confessions* 8.5.10 (trans. Chadwick, 139).

36. *Confessions* 8.6.15 (trans. Chadwick, 144).

37. *Confessions* 8.7.16 (trans. Chadwick, 144).

38. Heidegger, *Being and Time*, 158.

39. Heidegger, *Being and Time*, 158–59.

40. *Confessions* 8.8.19 (trans. Chadwick, 146).

41. *Confessions* 8.11.27 (trans. Chadwick, 152).

42. Leslie Jamison, *The Recovering: Intoxication and Its Aftermath* (New York: Little, Brown, 2018), 192.

43. Jamison, *The Recovering*, 193.

44. Lena Dunham, "The All-American Menstrual Hut," *Lenny*, January 31, 2017, https://www.lennyletter.com/story/the-all-american-menstrual-hut.

45. *Confessions* 8.12.30 (trans. Chadwick, 153).

46. Augustine, *Soliloquies* 1.2.7, in *Earlier Writings*, ed. J. H. S. Burleigh (Philadelphia: Westminster, 1953), 26.

47. *Soliloquies* 1.3.8 (Burleigh, 28).

48. Letter 10*.1, in *Letters*, trans. Roland Teske, SJ, ed. Boniface Ramsey, 4 vols., The Works of Saint Augustine II/1–4 (Hyde Park, NY: New City, 2001–2005), 4:262.

49. The text of the *Rule of Augustine* can be found at https://www.midwestaugustinians.org/roots-of-augustinian-spirituality.

Enlightenment

1. Augustine, *Confessions* 3.3.6, trans. Henry Chadwick (Oxford: Oxford University Press, 1991), 38.

2. *Confessions* 3.4.7 (trans. Chadwick, 39).

3. See Charles Taylor, *A Secular Age* (Cambridge, MA: Harvard University Press, 2007), 300–304. For discussion, see James K. A. Smith, *How (Not) to Be Secular: Reading Charles Taylor* (Grand Rapids: Eerdmans, 2014), 62–65.

4. Hence he connects this with the "buzz of distraction" (*Confessions* 10.35.56).

5. Augustine, *Confessions* 6.9, trans. Sarah Ruden (New York: Modern Library, 2017), 147.

6. *Confessions* 10.23.34 (trans. Chadwick, 199–200).

7. Martin Heidegger, *Phenomenology of Religious Life*, trans. Matthias Fritsch and Jennifer Anna Gosetti-Ferencei (Bloomington: Indiana University Press, 2004), 147.

8. Heidegger, *Phenomenology of Religious Life*, 148.

9. Heidegger, *Phenomenology of Religious Life*, 147. See the *Atlantic*'s conversation with William Deresiewicz: Lauren Cassani Davis, "The Ivy League,

Mental Health, and the Meaning of Life," *Atlantic*, August 19, 2014, https://www.theatlantic.com/education/archive/2014/08/qa-the-miseducation-of-our-college-elite/377524.

10. Cf. Augustine, *The Happy Life* 1.4.

11. Robin Lane Fox, *Augustine: Conversions to Confessions* (New York: Basic Books, 2015), 105–11, quote on 105.

12. For an introduction to the cult of the Brights, see Daniel Dennett, "The Bright Stuff," *New York Times*, July 12, 2003, https://www.nytimes.com/2003/07/12/opinion/the-bright-stuff.html.

13. Augustine, *The Advantage of Believing* 1.1, in *On Christian Belief*, trans. Ray Kearney, ed. Boniface Ramsey, The Works of Saint Augustine I/8 (Hyde Park, NY: New City, 2005), 116.

14. *Advantage of Believing* 1.2 (trans. Kearney, 117).

15. *Confessions* 5.6.10–5.7.13.

16. *Advantage of Believing* 9.21 (trans. Kearney, 133).

17. *Advantage of Believing* 10.24.

18. *Advantage of Believing* 10.23 (trans. Kearney, 134).

19. *Advantage of Believing* 14.30 (trans. Kearney, 141).

20. *Advantage of Believing* 15.33 (trans. Kearney, 144).

21. Sermon 182.4–5, cited in Justo L. González, *The Mestizo Augustine: A Theologian between Two Cultures* (Downers Grove, IL: IVP Academic, 2016), 93.

22. See Augustine's early dialogue, *Contra academicos*, in *Against the Academicians and the Teacher*, trans. Peter King (Indianapolis: Hackett, 1995).

23. *Confessions* 5.23 (trans. Ruden, 131).

24. *Confessions* 5.23 (trans. Ruden, 131).

25. *Confessions* 6.5 (trans. Ruden, 141).

26. Augustine, *Soliloquies* 1.6.12, in *Earlier Writings*, ed. J. H. S. Burleigh (Philadelphia: Westminster, 1953), 30.

27. *Soliloquies* 1.6.12 (Burleigh, 31, emphasis added).

28. *Confessions* 7.1.1.

29. *Confessions* 7.5.7 (trans. Chadwick, 115).

30. Augustine, *Of True Religion* 3.3–4.7.

31. *Confessions* 7.9.13 (trans. Chadwick, 121).

32. *Confessions* 7.9.14 (trans. Chadwick, 121–22).

33. *Confessions* 8.9.19 (trans. Chadwick, 146).

34. *Confessions* 7.9.14 (trans. Chadwick, 122).

35. *Confessions* 7.14 (trans. Ruden, 186–87).

36. Albert Camus, *Christian Metaphysics and Neoplatonism*, trans. Ronald D. Srigley (South Bend, IN: St. Augustine's Press, 2015), 53.

37. Camus, *Christian Metaphysics*, 67, 69 (emphasis added).

38. Camus, *Christian Metaphysics*, 93.

39. Camus, *Christian Metaphysics*, 108.

40. Camus, *Christian Metaphysics*, 116, 117.

41. Camus, *Christian Metaphysics*, 46.

42. *On Reprimand and Grace* 8.17, in *On the Free Choice of the Will, On Grace and Free Choice, and Other Writings*, ed. and trans. Peter King (Cambridge: Cambridge University Press, 2010), 199.

43. Augustine, *The Retractations*, trans. Sister Mary Inez Bogan, RSM (Washington, DC: Catholic University of America Press, 1968), prologue, 1.

44. Augustine, *True Religion* 39.73, in *On Christian Belief*, trans. Ray Kearney, ed. Boniface Ramsey, The Works of Saint Augustine I/8 (Hyde Park, NY: New City, 2005), 78.

Story

1. Leslie Jamison, *The Recovering: Intoxication and Its Aftermath* (New York: Little, Brown, 2018), 9.

2. Jamison, *The Recovering*, 9.

3. Jamison, *The Recovering*, 310.

4. Jamison, *The Recovering*, 205. This function of "witness authority" is precisely why Simplicianus told Augustine the story of Victorinus—because he knew that at the end of such a story, Augustine could realize: "That's me." Or: "That *could be* me."

5. *Confessions* 10.3, trans. Sarah Ruden (New York: Modern Library, 2017), 278.

6. *Confessions* 10.4 (trans. Ruden, 279).

7. Jean-Luc Marion, *In the Self's Place: The Approach of Saint Augustine*, trans. Jeffrey L. Kosky (Stanford, CA: Stanford University Press, 2012), 41–42.

8. Marion, *In the Self's Place*, 44.

9. "The majority of modern readers (even the most knowledgeable or the most devout) remain essentially curious. But they must be granted an excuse: the most notable retrievals of the Augustinian project, Montaigne and Rousseau, have deformed the model and, willing or not it matters little, missed the point." Marion, *In the Self's Place*, 51.

10. Marion, *In the Self's Place*, 45 (translation modified).

11. Jonathan Franzen, *Freedom* (New York: Farrar, Straus and Giroux, 2010), 318–19.

12. Thomas Wright, *Built of Books: How Reading Defined the Life of Oscar Wilde* (New York: Henry Holt, 2008), 1–3.

13. Wright, *Built of Books*, 5.

14. Wright, *Built of Books*, 6.

15. Wright, *Built of Books*, 7.

16. Augustine, *The Retractations* 2.93, trans. Sister Mary Inez Bogan, RSM (Washington, DC: Catholic University of America Press, 1968), xvi.

17. Brian Stock, *Augustine the Reader: Meditation, Self-Knowledge, and the Ethics of Interpretation* (Cambridge, MA: Harvard University Press, 1996), 273.

18. Jacques Derrida, *Monolingualism of the Other*, trans. Patrick Mensah (Stanford, CA: Stanford University Press, 1998), 5.

19. Cf. Marion, *In the Self's Place*, 45: "I find myself cited *to* God by citing the word of God."

20. *Confessions* 10.3.3, trans. Henry Chadwick (Oxford: Oxford University Press, 1991), 180.

21. *Confessions* 8.29 (trans. Ruden, 236–37).

22. *Confessions* 10.6 (trans. Ruden, 281).

23. *Confessions* 9.8 (trans. Ruden, 246).

24. *Confessions* 9.13 (trans. Ruden, 252).

25. Cardinal Joseph Ratzinger, "Funeral Homily for Msgr. Luigi Giussani," *Communio: International Catholic Review* 31, no. 4 (Winter 2004): 685, available at https://www.communio-icr.com/files/ratzinger31-4.pdf.

26. *Confessions* 10.3.4 (trans. Chadwick, 180).

27. *Confessions* 10.3.3 (trans. Chadwick, 180).

28. *Confessions* 10.36.59.

29. *Confessions* 10.3.4 (trans. Chadwick, 180).

30. *Confessions* 8.5.10; 8.8.19.

31. Augustine, *City of God* 11.2, in *City of God*, trans. Henry Bettenson (London: Penguin, 1984), 430–31.

32. *City of God* 11.3 (trans. Bettenson, 431).

33. See Michael Clarke, *The Concise Oxford Dictionary of Art Terms*, 2nd ed. (Oxford: Oxford University Press, 2010), s.v. "swagger portrait" (p. 240).

Justice

1. Ta-Nehisi Coates, *We Were Eight Years in Power: An American Tragedy* (New York: One World, 2017), 109.

2. Coates, *Eight Years in Power*, 110.

3. Camus's 1948 remarks at the Dominican Monastery of Latour-Maubourg are included as "The Unbeliever and Christians," in Albert Camus, *Resistance, Rebellion, and Death*, trans. Justin O'Brien (New York: Vintage, 1960), 71.

4. Camus, *Resistance, Rebellion, and Death*, 69–70.

5. Camus, *Resistance, Rebellion, and Death*, 71.

6. Camus, *Resistance, Rebellion, and Death*, 73. Camus is alluding to *Confessions* 7.5.7.

7. Olivier Todd, *Albert Camus: A Life* (New York: Knopf, 1997), 230.

8. Albert Camus, *The Stranger*, trans. Matthew Ward (New York: Everyman's Library, 1993), 116–17.

9. You can listen to these lines sampled at the beginning of Explosions in the Sky's song, "Have You Passed through This Night?" where the soundtrack evolves into a discordant score of defiance.

10. Augustine, *Confessions* 7.5.7, trans. Henry Chadwick (Oxford: Oxford University Press, 1991), 115.

11. *Confessions* 2.4.9 (trans. Chadwick, 29).

12. Augustine, *On the Free Choice of the Will* 1.1.1, in *On the Free Choice of the Will, On Grace and Free Choice, and Other Writings*, ed. and trans. Peter King (Cambridge: Cambridge University Press, 2010), 3.

13. "Whereof one cannot speak, thereof one must remain silent." Ludwig Wittgenstein, *Tractatus*, proposition 7.

14. *On the Free Choice of the Will* 3.1.1.

15. *On the Free Choice of the Will* 3.1.2.

16. *On the Free Choice of the Will* 3.17.48 (trans. King, 107).

17. *On the Free Choice of the Will* 3.17.48–49 (trans. King, 107).

18. Augustine, *City of God* 12.6, in *City of God*, trans. Henry Bettenson (London: Penguin, 1984), 477.

19. *City of God* 12.7 (trans. Bettenson, 479–80).

20. *City of God* 11.15 (trans. Bettenson, 446).

21. Google the scene "Who Lit This Flame in Us" to appreciate the visuals and soundtrack.

22. In *City of God* 12.6, Augustine explicates the evil will as a perverse choosing of lower over higher goods but emphasizes that this doesn't mean these "lower" goods (temporal things) are to blame. "It is not the inferior thing which causes the evil choice; it is the will itself, *because it is created*, that desires the inferior thing in a perverted and inordinate manner" (trans. Bettenson, 478, emphasis added). Now, I think Augustine is saying created wills are susceptible to this because they are not divine; but it leaves open the door that finitude qua finitude is a problem.

23. *City of God* 11.22. The danger here is that the darkness of evil can become an "apparent" evil that we see *as* evil only because we can't see the whole. In this case, Augustine is trying to defend God's goodness by assuring us that everything has a "purpose."

24. *Confessions* 9.6.14 (trans. Chadwick, 164).

25. Peter Brown, *Augustine of Hippo: A Biography* (Berkeley: University of California Press, 1967), 135.

26. Sermon 159B.9, in *Sermons*, trans. Edmund Hill, OP, ed. John E. Rotelle, 11 vols., The Works of Saint Augustine III/1–11 (Hyde Park, NY: New City, 1997), 5:155.

27. Sermon 159B.4 (trans. Hill, 5:149).

28. Sermon 159B.9 (trans. Hill, 5:155).

29. Lyrics used with permission.

30. This is the title of John Owen's 1647 treatise *The Death of Death in the Death of Christ*.

31. Letter 153.3, in *Letters*, trans. Roland Teske, SJ, ed. Boniface Ramsey, 4 vols., The Works of Saint Augustine II/1–4 (Hyde Park, NY: New City, 2001–2005), 2:392. For a compelling account of what an Augustinian criminal justice might look like, particularly in an age of mass incarceration, see Gregory W. Lee, "Mercy and Mass Incarceration: Augustinian Reflections on 'The New Jim Crow,'" *Journal of Religion* 98, no. 2 (April 2018): 192–223.

32. Robert Dodaro, "Between the Two Cities: Political Action in Augustine of Hippo," in *Augustine and Politics*, ed. John Doody, Kevin L. Hughes, and Kim Paffenroth (Lanham, MD: Lexington, 2005), 104.

33. Dodaro, "Between the Two Cities," 106–7.

34. Coates, *Eight Years in Power*, 110–11.

35. Coates, *Eight Years in Power*, 214.

36. Reinhold Niebuhr, *The Irony of American History*, in *Major Works on Religion and Politics*, ed. Elisabeth Sifton (New York: Library of America, 2015), 480. Niebuhr notes that though such "innocence" suffuses much of modern liberalism, American political institutions are more Augustinian than we might realize, containing "many of the safeguards against the selfish abuse of power which our Calvinist fathers insisted upon" (481).

Fathers

1. As Daniel Mendelsohn remarks in his moving book, *An Odyssey: A Father, A Son, and an Epic* (New York: Knopf, 2017), the four opening books of the *Odyssey*, the "Telemachy" of the son, Telemachus, is "that mini-bildungsroman in which the character of Odysseus' young son comes to be molded, *educated*, in the course of the search for his father" (118).

2. Thomas Wolfe, *Look Homeward, Angel* (New York: Scribner's Sons, 1952), 451.

3. David Remnick, "We Are Alive: Bruce Springsteen at Sixty-Two," *New Yorker*, July 30, 2012, https://www.newyorker.com/magazine/2012/07/30/we-are-alive.

4. Paul Auster, *The Invention of Solitude*, in *Collected Prose* (London: Faber & Faber, 2014), 15.

5. Auster, *Invention of Solitude*, 17.

6. Jack Kerouac, *On the Road* (New York: Penguin, 1999), 293.

7. Thomas Wolfe, *The Story of a Novel* (New York: Scribner's Sons, 1936), 39.

8. Margo Maine, *Father Hunger: Fathers, Daughters, and Food* (Carlsbad, CA: Gurze, 1991).

9. See Andrew Root on the *ontological* effects of divorce in *Children of Divorce: The Loss of Family as the Loss of Being* (Grand Rapids: Baker Academic, 2007).

10. Augustine, *Confessions* 2.3.6, trans. Henry Chadwick (Oxford: Oxford University Press, 1991), 27.

11. *Confessions* 9.9.19–21.

12. *Confessions* 9.9.22 (trans. Chadwick, 170).

13. Augustine leaves laudatory testimony about his son, who died young, in *Confessions* 9.6.14.

14. Auster, *Invention of Solitude*, 54.

15. Augustine, *Questions on the Gospels*, bk. 2, q. 33 (Patrologia Latina 35:1344–48).

16. Everclear, "Father of Mine."

17. Augustine, *Confessions* 5.23, trans. Sarah Ruden (New York: Modern Library, 2017), 131.

18. Kelly Clarkson, "Piece by Piece." Again, do yourself a favor and Google "Piece by Piece American Idol" to listen to Clarkson's tearful rendition of this. Watch Keith Urban's face.

19. Leslie Jamison, *The Recovering: Intoxication and Its Aftermath* (New York: Little, Brown, 2018), 414.

20. Cited in Jamison, *The Recovering*, 415.

21. *Confessions* 9.14 (trans. Ruden, 253, emphasis added).

Death

1. For two different slants on this, see Evelyn Waugh, *The Loved One*, and Jessica Mitford's still-relevant classic, *The American Way of Death Revisited* (New York: Vintage, 2000).

2. Raymond Barfield, "When Self-Help Means Less Help," in *Comment*, October 11, 2018, available at https://www.cardus.ca/comment/article/when-self-help-means-less-help, reviewing Barbara Ehrenreich, *Natural Causes: An Epidemic of Wellness, the Certainty of Dying, and Killing Ourselves to Live Longer* (New York: Twelve, 2018).

3. Gary Shteyngart, *Super Sad True Love Story* (New York: Random House, 2010), 57.

4. Shteyngart, *Super Sad True Love Story*, 126.

5. Augustine mentions the martyrs and Ambrose's discovery of their relics in *Confessions* 9.7.16.

6. Jeremy Bentham's "auto-icon" notwithstanding.

7. George Weigel, *Letters to a Young Catholic* (New York: Basic Books, 2015), 209.

8. Martin Heidegger, *Being and Time*, trans. John Macquarrie and Edward Robinson (New York: Harper & Row, 1962), 303 (§52).

9. Hannah Arendt, *Love and Saint Augustine*, ed. Joanna Vecchiarelli Scott and Judith Chelius Stark (Chicago: University of Chicago Press, 1996), 10.

10. Arendt, *Love and Saint Augustine*, 11.

11. Arendt, *Love and Saint Augustine*, 35.

12. Augustine, *Homilies on First John* 9.2, cited by Arendt, *Love and Saint Augustine*, 35 (emphasis added).

13. Augustine, *On the Free Choice of the Will* 3.7.21, in *On the Free Choice of the Will, On Grace and Free Choice, and Other Writings*, ed. and trans. Peter King (Cambridge: Cambridge University Press, 2010), 88.

14. Sermon 344.4, cited in Peter Brown, *Augustine of Hippo: A Biography* (Berkeley: University of California Press, 1967), 431 (emphasis added).

15. *Confessions* 4.4.9, trans. Henry Chadwick (Oxford: Oxford University Press, 1991), 57.

16. *Confessions* 4.6.11 (trans. Chadwick, 59).

17. *Confessions* 4.6.11 (trans. Chadwick, 59, emphasis added).

18. *Confessions* 4.7.12 (trans. Chadwick, 59).

19. *Confessions* 4.8.13 (trans. Chadwick, 60).

20. *Confessions* 4.6.11 (trans. Chadwick, 58).

21. *Confessions* 4.10.15 (trans. Chadwick, 61).

22. *Confessions* 4.9.14 (trans. Chadwick, 61).

23. *Confessions* 9.33, trans. Sarah Ruden (New York: Modern Library, 2017), 272.

24. Letter 263.1–2, in *Letters*, trans. Roland Teske, SJ, ed. Boniface Ramsey, 4 vols., The Works of Saint Augustine II/1–4 (Hyde Park, NY: New City, 2001–2005), 4:209.

25. Letter 263.2 (trans. Teske, 4:209–10, first emphasis added).

26. Letter 263.4 (trans. Teske, 4:211).

27. *Confessions* 9.3.6 (trans. Chadwick, 159).

28. François Decret, *Early Christianity in North Africa*, trans. Edward Smither (Cambridge: James Clark, 2011), 167.

29. Letter 10.2, in Decret, *Early Christianity in North Africa*, 189.

30. Letter 222.3 (trans. Teske, 4:82).

31. Letter 229.1–2 (trans. Teske, 4:113).

32. Letter 230.2 (trans. Teske, 4:116).

Homecoming

1. Jack Kerouac, *On the Road* (New York: Penguin, 1999), 43.

INDEX

INDEX